The **Business**

INTERMEDIATE Student's Book

John Allison with Paul Emmerson

D0863377

MACMILLAN

The Business

INTERMEDIATE

To the student

The objective of *The* Business is to help you learn two things: how to do business in English and the language you need to do it. The new language and structures are presented in the Student's Book whilst the DVD-ROM provides language practice and extension.

Here is a summary of what you will find in each.

Student's Book

The modules

The Student's Book contains 48 modules in eight units. Each unit deals with a key sector of activity in the business world. There are six different types of module:

1 About business

These modules contain information and language for the topic area of each unit. The focus is on understanding the topic and the general sense of the texts – don't worry too much about details such as new vocabulary.

2 Vocabulary

These modules build on the important words and phrases introduced in the previous module and provide thorough practice.

3 Grammar

The first part of these modules – Test yourself – tests your knowledge of important grammatical structures. Do this before and / or after the practice activities in the second part. If necessary, refer to the Grammar and practice section at the back of the book for help.

4 Speaking

These modules develop understanding and speaking skills in typical business situations. Good and bad examples are given for comparison, and the speaking activities allow you to practise key phrases and skills in realistic situations with other people.

5 Writing

These modules provide practice for the most important types of document you will need to write at work. Model texts are examined and used as a basis to write your own.

6 Case study

The case studies provide an opportunity to apply all the language, skills and ideas you have worked on in the unit. They present authentic problem-solving situations similar those you will meet in business.

Internet research

Every module includes an Internet research task. The Internet provides almost unlimited resources for improving your English and learning more about business. These tasks direct you to interesting background and details on topics related to each module. The tasks can be done before or after working on the module.

Other features

In addition to the eight main units, the Student's Book contains the following:

Reviews
These units can be used in three ways: to consolidate your work on the units, to catch up quickly if you have missed a lesson, and to revise before tests or exams.

Additional material
This section contains all the extra materials you need to do pair or group work activities.

Grammar and practice
This section gives a very useful summary of rules with clear examples, but also provides further practice of the essential grammar points in this level of the course.

Recordings
Full scripts of all the audio recordings are given, allowing you to study the audio dialogues in detail. However, try not to rely on reading them to understand the listenings – very often, you don't need to understand every word, just the main ideas.

Wordlist
In the modules, words which you may not know are in grey; you will find definitions in the wordlist, often with examples. Words in red are high-frequency items, which you should try to learn and use. The others, in black, are words you just need to understand.

The DVD-ROM

The DVD-ROM is designed to help you continue improving your English on your own, away from the classroom. It includes an interactive workbook which, like the Review units in the Student's Book, can be used in three ways: to improve your listening, grammar, vocabulary and pronunciation; to catch up on lessons you have missed; to revise for tests and exams.

Interactive workbook

This includes everything you would normally find in a workbook, and more; activities for vocabulary, grammar, pronunciation, writing and listening practice.

Video

Each unit includes an episode of a mini-drama illustrating the communication and people skills practised in each unit, with exercises to practise the functional language used in the video.

Business dilemmas

There are four problem-solving games to allow you to review and practise functional language from the Student's Book. Try doing these with a partner to practise discussing problems and solutions.

Tests

Four tests, one for every two units, allow you to check your progress through the DVD-ROM. If you do well on a test, you get 'promoted'; if you do well on all four tests, you become CEO!

Business documents

There is a model document for each unit, including letters, invoices, CVs, etc. Each document includes annotations explaining the structure and key phrases, and a follow-up activity tests understanding of this.

Grammar reference

You can refer to this section any time for helpful grammar rules and examples.

Class audio

This section of the DVD-ROM contains all the audio recordings from the Student's Book, together with scrollable scripts.

Downloadables

The DVD-ROM includes a set of downloadable files for use outside the DVD-ROM or away from your computer. There is a downloadable and printable PDF of the answers to the Student's Book exercises; a Word file containing the text of each Business document; and MP3 files of all the Student's Book audio that you can transfer to your MP3 player or iPod for listening on the move.

We sincerely hope you will enjoy working with *The* Business.
Good luck!

John Allison
Paul Emmerson

Contents

The *Wordlist* is a module-by-module glossary of all the words in grey in this coursebook.

1 | Corporate culture

Discussion

1 You've just started working for a new company. Do you:
- a) wear your best clothes or b) wear jeans and a T-shirt like all the other employees? Why?
- a) stop work at five o'clock like everyone else or b) stay longer to finish your work? Why?
- a) share your ideas and opinions at staff meetings immediately or b) say nothing like most of your colleagues? Why?

Internet research

Search for the keywords "work fun". Find out how companies are trying to create a fun atmosphere at work.

Scan reading

2 Scan the article opposite to find:

1 what the monkey experiment demonstrated.
2 seven examples of unwritten rules.
3 what new staff learn about work culture and how they learn it.

The words in grey are explained in the *Wordlist* on page 148.

Discussion

3 In small groups, discuss the questions.

1 What do you think organizations and companies can do to avoid negative unwritten rules?
2 What unwritten rules do you imagine you might encounter in your country as an intern in:
 - a government department?
 - a small public relations firm?
 - a manufacturing company?
 Think about:
 - office etiquette, e.g. dress code, punctuality, personal calls, coffee and lunch breaks.
 - relationships with colleagues, management and clients / business partners.
 - autonomy and initiative.
3 Which work culture above would you prefer to work in? Which would be the most difficult to adapt to? Why?

Listening for gist

4 🔊 1:01, 1:02 Listen to Alessandra, an Italian business student, and David, a British civil service manager, talking about problems they experienced with work placements, and answer the questions.

1 What problems did Alessandra and David have?
2 What were the misunderstandings that caused these problems?

Listening for detail

5 Listen again. What mistakes did the students and the supervisors make in each case?

Brainstorming and presentation

6 In small groups, hold a brainstorming meeting to decide how companies can help interns to adapt to their work culture. Design a set of guidelines for supervisors of interns. Then present your guidelines to another group, and give feedback on the other group's ideas.

GUIDELINES FOR SUPERVISORS

Thank you for agreeing to supervise a student work placement. The following guidelines are designed to help you ensure your intern adapts quickly to the work culture of the organization.

- If possible, give advice about office etiquette by telephone before the beginning of the placement.
- Give the student a copy of the company rules on the first day.
-
-
-

Monkey business?

Scientists put a group of five monkeys in a cage. At the top of a ladder, they hung a banana. As soon as a monkey climbed the ladder, he was showered with cold water; the group soon gave up trying to reach the banana.

"... the others pulled him down and gave him a good beating."

5 Next, the scientists disconnected the cold water and replaced one of the five monkeys. When the new monkey tried to climb the ladder, the others immediately pulled him down and gave him a good beating. The new monkey learned quickly, and enthusiastically joined 10 in beating the next new recruit. One by one, the five original monkeys were replaced. Although none of the new group knew why, no monkey was ever allowed to climb the ladder.

Like the monkeys in the experiment, every culture 15 and organization has its unwritten rules. These rules are probably the single most influential factor on the work environment and employee happiness. Though many work cultures embrace positive values, such as loyalty, solidarity, efficiency, quality, personal development and 20 customer service, all too often they reinforce negative attitudes.

In many businesses, an unwritten rule states that working long hours is more important than achieving results. In one medium-sized company, the boss never 25 leaves the office until it is dark. Outside in the car park, he checks to see who is still working and whose office windows are dark. Staff who risk leaving earlier now leave their office lights on all night.

Other common unwritten rules state that the boss is 30 always right, even when he's wrong; if you're not at your desk, you're not working; nobody complains, because nothing ever changes; women, ethnic minorities and the over 50s are not promoted; the customer is king, but don't tell anyone, because management are more 35 interested in profitability.

Often nobody really knows where these unwritten rules came from, but like the new monkeys, new recruits pick them up very quickly, despite the best intentions of induction and orientation programmes. 40 The way staff speak to management, to customers and to each other gives subtle but strategic clues to an organization's culture, as do the differences between what is said, decided or promised, and what actually gets done. New staff quickly learn when their ideas 45 and opinions are listened to and valued, and when it's better to keep them to themselves. They learn which assignments and aspects of their performance will be checked and evaluated, and whose objectives and instructions they can safely ignore. Monkeys may be 50 more direct, but work culture is every bit as effective at enforcing unwritten rules as a good beating.

1 | Corporate culture

Discussion

1 With a partner, rank the words in each group according to importance or size.

1 line manager   director   project leader   supervisor   foreman
2 department   division   unit   branch   office   subsidiary   section   company
3 job   task   assignment   project

Listening for detail

2 🎵 1:03 Listen to a supervisor describing a company's structure to a new intern and complete the organigram.

> Warndar TECHNOLOGIES

| Merilyn Warner |
| CEO |

| David Darren |
| _____ |

Administration	_____	_____	_____	_____
Monica Overstreet	Bertram Newman	Douglas Pearson	Herb Monroe	Roxane Pawle
_____ Manager	_____ Manager	R&D Manager	Program Manager	_____

| Two _____ | One art director; one _____ officer; two salesmen | Seven _____ | Two software engineers; one _____ | One _____; two _____ |

3 Listen again and answer the questions.

1 Why is the organization simple for the moment?
2 Why does Bertram say it's going to change?
3 Why does the Office Manager also take care of personnel matters?
4 What is the difference between the roles of the CEO and the COO at Warndar?
5 Who are Irysis? What happened about two years ago?
6 What happened to Roxane Pawle's predecessor?
7 Which three departments are involved in development programmes?
8 How are development programmes coordinated?

4 Match the parts of these sentences from the listening to complete ways of describing responsibilities.

1 You're going to report
2 She also looks
3 She has two accountants working
4 David runs the business
5 Merilyn deals
6 Our Office Manager
7 He's responsible
8 Roxane is in charge
9 My role is
10 He liaises

a) on a day-to-day basis.
b) with strategy.
c) directly to me.
d) under her.
e) after finance.
f) to manage Marketing & Sales.
g) with me in Marketing.
h) for building our product package.
i) takes care of personnel.
j) of IT and Technical Support.

Internet research

CEO, COO, CFO ...
Search for the keywords *Chief Officer* to find more C...Os. Make a list, dividing them into two categories, serious and humorous.

Prepositions

5 Complete the electronic newsletter by using each preposition once.

on   in   alongside   as   under   at

This month *Warndar News* is delighted to welcome Sam Shenton, our new intern. Sam, who hails from Boston, will be working (1) _____ Jake and Saidah in Marketing. Let's give her a real Texas welcome!

Andy Highlands has moved from R&D. He is now working (2) _____ IT Manager Roxane Pawle in IT and Technical Support, a department which is scheduled to grow rapidly in the coming months. Good move, Andy!

News of Jackson Tyler, our former IT Manager: after a short stay in Washington, working (3) _____ Head of IT (4) _____ Sterns & Lowe, a large consultancy, Jackson is now back in San Antonio, working (5) _____ the leisure industry. He hopes this is only a temporary position as he is also working (6) _____ a book about his experiences. We wish him the best of luck!

Discussion and presentation

6 Work in groups of three. You want to open a private music school that offers music lessons to people of all ages. Decide:

- who is responsible for the areas in the box below.
- how many extra staff members you will need.
- who everyone reports to.

Draw an organigram of the company structure.

purchasing   recruiting teachers   advertising   registrations   legal questions
organizing concerts   CD and music library   planning timetables   discipline
cleaning and maintenance   accounts   public relations   educational policy   sound systems
quality and complaints   instrument repairs   salaries   transport and logistics   insurance
reception and office

7 Work with a partner from a different group. Present your music school's organization using relevant phrases and vocabulary from the previous exercises.

Defining words

8 With a partner, practise defining words relating to work organization.

Student A: turn to page 110.
Student B: turn to page 114.

1 | Corporate culture

Past simple
He told them.
completed actions

Past continuous
He was telling them.
background situations

Past perfect
He had already *told them.*
one past event before another

▶ Grammar reference page 118

Advice structures

▶ Grammar reference page 119

1.3 Grammar Past tenses and advice structures

Test yourself: Past tenses

1 Complete the anecdote by choosing the best tense in each case: past continuous (*was / were doing*), past simple (*did*) or past perfect (*had done*).

A large corporation had just hired a new CEO. As the old CEO was leaving, he discreetly presented his successor with three envelopes numbered one, two and three. 'If you have a problem you can't solve, open the first of these,' he (1) _____ (tell) the new CEO.

Well, at first things went smoothly, but after six months sales (2) _____ (fall) by 10% and the shareholders were getting very impatient. The CEO (3) _____ (begin) to despair, when he remembered the envelopes the old CEO (4) _____ (give) him.

He went to his office, closed the door and opened the first envelope. The message read, 'Try blaming your predecessor.' The new CEO (5) _____ (call) a press conference and tactfully blamed the previous CEO for the company's problems. The shareholders and the press were satisfied with his explanations, and a few weeks later the CEO was relieved to see that sales (6) _____ (improve) by 12%.

About a year later, the company was having serious production problems. The CEO (7) _____ (learn) from his previous experience: as soon as he (8) _____ (close) his office door, he opened the second envelope. The message read, 'You ought to reorganize.' He immediately reorganized production, and the company quickly recovered.

A year or two after that, costs (9) _____ (rise) day by day and the company was in trouble again. The CEO went to his office, (10) _____ (close) the door and opened the third envelope. The message read, 'You might want to prepare three envelopes.'

Test yourself: Advice structures

2 An intern needs help understanding a company's work culture. Complete the advice structures using *ask*, *asking* or *to ask*.

1 You should _____ your supervisor.
2 Have you considered _____ your supervisor?
3 How about _____ your supervisor?
4 It's a good idea _____ your supervisor.
5 Have you thought of _____ your supervisor?
6 You could _____ your supervisor.
7 It's wise _____ your supervisor.
8 Why don't you _____ your supervisor?
9 You ought _____ your supervisor.
10 You might want _____ your supervisor.
11 Have you tried _____ your supervisor?
12 It's important _____ your supervisor.

Which five phrases are examples of strong recommendations?

Which seven phrases are examples of careful or friendly suggestions?

Internet research

Search for the keywords *"business jokes"*. Which other tenses do business jokes use? Tell a joke in your own words, without using notes.

Listening for detail

3 🔊 1:04   Listen to an after-dinner story. In each pair of events below, <u>underline</u> the event that happened first.

1 The CEO did very well for himself. The CEO gave a party.
2 The CEO challenged his team. He showed the executives the pool.
3 There was a loud splash. Everyone followed the CEO to the barbecue.
4 The CFO swam for his life. Everyone arrived back at the pool.
5 The CFO reached the edge. The crocodiles tried to catch him.
6 A crocodile tried to bite the CFO. The CFO climbed out of the pool.

4 Complete the sentences from the story. Then listen again and check your answers.

1 The boss _____ very well for himself, so he _____ the executives around his luxurious country house.
2 At the back of the house, he _____ the largest swimming pool any of them had ever seen.
3 They _____ to follow the CEO towards the barbecue when suddenly there _____ a loud splash.
4 Everyone _____ and _____ to the pool where the Chief Financial Officer _____ for his life.
5 The crocodiles _____ him when he _____ the edge of the pool.
6 He _____ to climb out of the pool when he _____ the mouth of the biggest crocodile close shut – snap – behind him.

Telling a story

5 With a partner, tell a story in your own words using appropriate past tenses.

Student A: turn to page 110.
Student B: turn to page 114.

Giving advice

6 Match the parts of these sentences to give advice to new employees.

1 You should   a) expect to finish on time every day.
2 It's unwise   b) learn to set goals.
3 It's a good idea   c) dress appropriately.
4 You should   d) to make too many personal phone calls.
5 You shouldn't   e) to learn proper meeting behaviour.

6 It's a good idea to   f) accept responsibility for mistakes.
7 It's important   g) learn who does what and how things get done.
8 You shouldn't   h) not to neglect forming effective relationships at work.
9 You should   i) to reduce stress by balancing your life.
10 You ought   j) expect that you will like every task.

7 With a partner, take turns asking for and giving advice.

Student A: turn to page 110.
Student B: turn to page 114.

1.4 Speaking   Meetings – one-to-one

Discussion

1 Do the questionnaire from a business magazine. Mark the statements *T* (true), *F* (false) or *D* (it depends). Then compare and justify your answers. Talk about how different cultural and business contexts affect your answers.

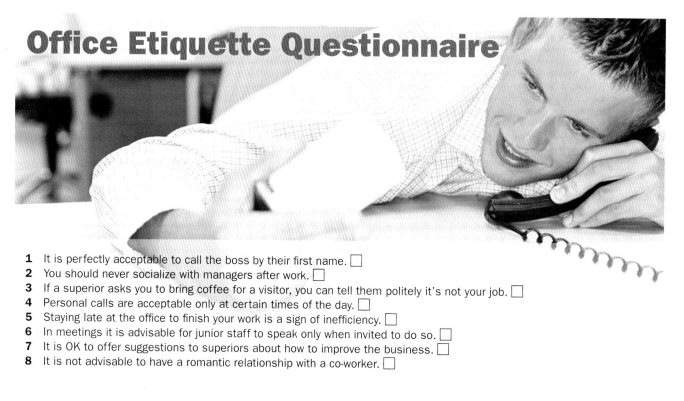

Office Etiquette Questionnaire

1 It is perfectly acceptable to call the boss by their first name. ☐
2 You should never socialize with managers after work. ☐
3 If a superior asks you to bring coffee for a visitor, you can tell them politely it's not your job. ☐
4 Personal calls are acceptable only at certain times of the day. ☐
5 Staying late at the office to finish your work is a sign of inefficiency. ☐
6 In meetings it is advisable for junior staff to speak only when invited to do so. ☐
7 It is OK to offer suggestions to superiors about how to improve the business. ☐
8 It is not advisable to have a romantic relationship with a co-worker. ☐

Listening for detail

2 🔊 1:05, 1:06 Listen to two versions of a conversation between Tifany, an intern, and Simon, her supervisor. Underline the words that describe Simon's behaviour. Then compare your answers with a partner.

Version 1 – Simon is:	**Version 2 –** Simon is:
objective impatient a good listener dogmatic diplomatic friendly firm understanding insincere authoritarian threatening weak frank	objective impatient a good listener dogmatic diplomatic friendly firm understanding insincere authoritarian threatening weak frank

3 With a partner, discuss how Simon's language is different in each version.

4 Listen again and complete the sentences.

Version 1
1 You _____ talk about your colleagues like that.
2 Yes, _____ to refuse.
3 You _____ from people like Maureen if you're rude.
4 You _____ there'll be trouble.

Version 2
1 I think _____ more careful about how you talk about your colleagues.
2 You _____ why she couldn't help you.
3 _____ get better results from people like Maureen by being a little more diplomatic?
4 _____ ask Maureen to have a coffee with you, and just clear the air?

Diplomatic advice

5 In Version 2, Simon uses modal verbs, introductory phrases and negative questions to make his advice more diplomatic. Add these phrases to the correct category in the table below. Some phrases are used in more than one category.

It seems to me that ... Wouldn't you agree that ...? Actually, I think ...	
You could maybe ... Wouldn't it be better to ...? You'd do better to ...	
Why don't you ... ?	

Modals *would, could* and *might*	You might want to ...
Introductory phrases	I think perhaps ...
Negative questions	Don't you think ... ?

6 Make these comments more diplomatic.

1   You shouldn't disturb your co-workers.
2   You won't meet deadlines if you don't prioritize.
3   Delegate, or you'll never finish the job.
4   You shouldn't eat at your desk.
5   Don't make personal calls at work.
6   If you ignore your colleagues, don't expect them to help.
7   You'll make yourself ill if you don't take care of your life-work balance.

Pronunciation

7 In each sentence below, two words are more important than the others. These two keywords carry the stress. <u>Underline</u> the two keywords (or syllables) that are stressed in each sentence.

1   I hear you had a problem.
2   Perhaps you should be more careful.
3   You ought to do the same.
4   I appreciate that you work hard.
5   I didn't mean to be rude.
6   It can happen to anyone.

8 🔊 1:07 Listen and check your answers. Then practise saying the sentences with the stress on the keywords (or syllables).

9 The stresses have a regular rhythm. To allow this, the words between the stresses have to be very short and sound as if they are joined together, e.g. *youhada, youshouldbemore*. This is one of the main reasons why listening to English can be difficult. Listen to the sentences again. Then practise saying them with a regular rhythm.

Internet research

Search for the keywords *"learn English"*. What are the best e-learning resources for English available on the Web?

Roleplay

10 With a partner, hold informal problem-solving meetings. Use diplomatic language to help you agree, unless you feel a more directive approach is necessary.

Student A: turn to page 110.
Student B: turn to page 116.

1 | Corporate culture

Discussion

1 Henry has just finished his placement at Cambro Corp. in Littlehampton and has to write a report on his experiences. Discuss what you think this report will contain and what style it will be written in.

Skim reading

2 Read the extracts from Henry's report and number the section headings one to five.

☐ Observations about the company
☐ Appendix
☐ Introduction
☐ Professional achievements
☐ Experience during work placement

1 … a six-month placement with Cambro Corp. in Littlehampton from February to July, under the supervision of Mr Geoffrey Thomson, Marketing Manager. The objective of the internship was to design, conduct and analyse the results of a market study to identify customer needs for a new range of electronic gearboxes for industrial conveyor belts.

Cambro Corp. is a subsidiary of the HDE group based in New Jersey. The company has 450 employees in its Littlehampton plant, and designs, produces and markets gearboxes for the North American market. Founded in 1954, the firm …

2 … and this experience was extremely valuable. I had not expected such a poor response rate to the first mailshot. When customers were contacted by telephone, it became clear that many of them had not answered the questionnaire simply because they had not understood the first question. The order of the items was therefore modified and the response rate increased by 200% …

3 … a long history of involvement in the local community. Cambro's reputation as a company which looks after its employees and which sponsors local sports and cultural events is one of its greatest strengths. To obtain a similar result through media campaigns would cost millions. This aspect of the company's marketing and PR policy was most impressive …

4 … communication skills in particular. Developing and performing a market study in less than six months was a major challenge. Fortunately, I was able to apply the knowledge I had acquired in marketing in year two of my degree, and the results of my study were extremely well received. In future, I think it would be very helpful if …

5 … including the following documents:
A Daily journal   B Thank you letter to Mr Thomson   C Evaluation letter from Mr Thomson   D Résumé
E Cambro brochure and sales literature

Reading for detail

3 Decide which section in 2 above these topics should be in.

☐ Conclusions
☐ Analysis of successes and failures
☐ Objectives of the internship
☐ Details of your responsibilities
☐ Analysis of what you learned
☐ Evaluation of the company as a potential employer
☐ Suggestions for the future
☐ Description of the company and how it is organized
☐ Practical details about the placement
☐ Observations on the company's culture and policies

Internet research

How and where can you find an internship? Search for the keywords *find internships* to learn more.

4 Match these informal diary entries with formal phrases used to talk about the same things in the extracts in 2. Underline the phrases.

1 My boss is a guy called Geoff.

2 Today I called lots of customers.

3 I finally understood what the problem was!

4 So, I changed the questions around.

5 This is worth a fortune! Much better than paying for advertising.

6 ... was cool!

7 It was really difficult and exhausting.

8 Thank goodness I'd learnt how to do a market survey!

9 Geoff was really happy with what I did.

Listening and note-taking

5 1:08 Listen to a conversation between Jason, who has recently completed a placement at Diftco, and his friend Alex. Take notes about Jason's placement in preparation for writing his placement report.

Ordering and writing

6 With a partner, organize your notes from 5 and Jason's notes below into the five placement report sections listed in 2. Then write Jason's placement report. Remember to use more formal language.

- good rapport with export staff, warehouse staff more difficult
- equipment assembled and packed in warehouse
- double-check information – very important lesson!
- waste problem in warehouse – don't recycle enough
- remember to attach daily journal – journal.doc
- one of most profitable firms in region
- learnt bar code system – interesting
- too much routine paperwork – very boring!
- copies of letters to and from Ms Witten, supervisor
- most of time in Export Office, also checking containers in warehouse
- very tiring – need a holiday now!

1.6 Case study Counselling

Discussion

1 What kind of personal problems can interns or employees experience when working abroad? With a partner, brainstorm a list.

Listening for detail

2 🔊 1:09 Listen to an extract from a lecture on counselling skills and complete the handout.

COUNSELLING

Counselling = helping someone _manage_ a personal problem using their own _resources_

COUNSELLING SKILLS

☑ listening   ☑ helping   ☑ assisting   ☐ solving (for them)
☐ manipulating   ☐ persuading   ☑ exploring problems
☑ talking   ☐ telling   ☐ reassuring

THE THREE PHASES OF COUNSELLING

Phase one = _Talk_   Phase two = _Think_   Phase three = _Act_

---

3 With a partner, describe a situation when you helped someone with a problem, or when someone helped you. Did your experience correspond to what you heard in the lecture?

Counselling language

4 Match each phrase in the box to a counselling skill on the second handout below.

> How did you feel?   Why not start by –ing … ?   What's your first priority?
> You were _surprised_?   What would happen if (+ _past tense_)?   Right.
> So, to sum up, …   So you're saying that … ?   What are the options?

COUNSELLING SKILLS CHECKLIST

Counselling skill	Description of skill	Useful phrases or body language
1 Asking open questions	Ask who, why, what, where, how, etc. to get them talking about the issues.	
2 Paraphrasing	Clarify your understanding by rephrasing what they said, and feed it back to them.	
3 Paying attention	Use positive body language to show that you are really listening.	look person in the eye, smile, nod head
4 Encouraging	Show you're interested by nodding and saying Uh-huh, Mmm, Yeah, I see, etc.	
5 Echoing	Encourage them to tell you more about a topic by repeating a key phrase or word.	
6 Summarizing	Show you have understood all they said by pulling it all together in two sentences.	
7 Establishing options	Get ideas from them on possible alternatives to resolve the problem.	
8 Asking hypothetical questions	Encourage the problem holder to think through the implications of their suggestions.	
9 Prioritizing	Establish which of the possible options the problem holder chooses to tackle first.	
10 Action-planning	Suggest a clear first step they can take to help them manage their problem.	

5 Add one more phrase of your own to each counselling skill in the handout in 4.

Internet research

Find out more about living and working in either Japan, the UK or the USA.

Roleplay

6 Work in groups of three. Take turns being the problem holder, the counsellor and the observer.

Problem holder
Problem holder A: turn to page 110.
Problem holder B: turn to page 114.
Problem holder C: turn to page 116.
Use the information given to respond to the counsellor.

Counsellor
Guide the problem holder through the three phases of counselling in 2. Use the counselling skills in the checklist in 4 to help the problem holder find solutions to their problems.

Observer
Observe the counselling session and take notes. Use the checklist in 4 to note which counselling skills the counsellor uses and how well they use them. At the end of the session, give the counsellor feedback to help them improve their skills.

Writing

7 Work with a partner. You are on a placement in a foreign country.

1 Write an email to your partner explaining the problems you are having.
2 Exchange emails with your partner. Write a reply, giving your advice. Use some of the expressions in the box to show that you understand your partner's problems and to encourage them to think positively.

I can see exactly what you mean about ...   It can't be easy to ... when / if you ...
You must be feeling very ...   I know just how you feel.   It's perfectly normal to feel that way.
You have to keep things in perspective.   I'm confident you'll be able to find a solution.
I'm sure you'll bounce back.

2 | Customer support

2.1 About business Call centres

Discussion

1 With a partner, think of four reasons why someone would or would not want to work in a call centre.

Summarizing

2 Read paragraphs A to E of the article opposite. The words in grey are explained in the *Wordlist* on page 149. Find the correct heading for each paragraph.

☐ Call of the East   ☐ Unions strike back   ☐ More Britons concerned
Ⓐ Smarter Indians   ☐ UK jobs leak

3 Now read paragraphs F to H. Write a sentence summarizing each paragraph.

4 Choose the sentence that is the best summary of the whole article.
1 Trade unions are worried about poor working conditions and exploitation of workers in India in a growing industry where jobs are highly desirable.
2 Trade unions are worried about companies moving to India where working conditions are poor and work is highly stressful.
3 Trade unions are worried about job losses, poor working conditions and exploitation of workers worldwide in a growing industry where work is stressful.
4 Trade unions are worried about job losses, poor working conditions and exploitation of workers in Britain in a growing industry where workloads are unreasonable.

Discussion

5 Do you share the trade unions' concerns? Discuss your reactions with your partner.

Predicting and listening

6 🎵 1:10 You are going to hear a radio discussion between Lavanya Fernandes, a Customer Relationship Management expert, and Tashar Mahendra, a Centre Manager, about working in call centres. With a partner, try to predict what the speakers will say about each of the following five topics. Then listen and check your predictions.

Why India?   Changes to call centres   Perks of the job
Employee profile and training   Promotion prospects

Listening for detail

7 Listen again and use the key words and phrases in the table to write notes that summarize the discussion.

Why India?	Changes to call centres	Perks of the job	Employee profile and training	Promotion prospects
1 … one million English-speaking college graduates enter … 2 Low labour costs for …	1 New technology: 2 The operator's job has become … 3 Centres are trying hard to …	1 Transport: 2 Good working conditions with …	1 Good communication skills: 2 Technical skills: 3 Special training:	1 Can become a supervisor after … 2 Experience in a contact centre is …

Debate

8 Divide into two groups, *for* and *against* outsourcing call centres from industrialized countries to the developing world.

For: turn to page 110.
Against: turn to page 114.

At the end of the line

Next time you phone a call centre, your customer service adviser could be talking to you from India. Helen Taylor looks at how companies are increasingly farming out their operations abroad, all in the name of cost cutting.

A The chief executive of HSBC bank, Sir Keith Whitson, caused uproar recently when he said he would rather use call centre workers in India than those in Britain. He claimed that workers in Asia are smartly dressed, enthusiastic, more efficient and are often graduates. Of course, he may also have been persuaded by the fact that wages in India are about £4 a day, which is more like the hourly rate over here.

B The bank already has 3,100 call centre staff in Asia answering calls from British customers, and it expects to increase that to 4,500 by the end of the year. With wages so low, the additional cost of redirecting phone calls to India is easily met. And HSBC isn't the only company to be looking East. British Airways, Zurich Insurance, GE and others have all sent their call centre services overseas.

C The public service workers' union, UNISON, is concerned by Thames Water's recent decision to export its call centre services, probably to India, in an attempt to reduce its overall costs. The company plans to cut 150 jobs initially, adding that a possible 1,000 staff could be affected in some way in the future. 'The proposal to transfer these jobs out of the UK is very worrying indeed,' said UNISON regional officer, Ron Harley. 'This is a slap in the face for our members who have worked tirelessly to improve services to customers over many years.'

D Reality, a part of the GUS retail chain, also came into conflict with British staff over plans to move some of its operations to India. More than 80% of USDAW members at the company voted in September for strike action, after saying they'd been betrayed by the company's secret deal with India.

E But in spite of job losses in the industry, with BT alone axing more than two thousand posts earlier this year, call centres remain a major employer in Britain. One job in 50 in Britain is currently in a call centre, which is expected to rise to one in 30 in the next five or six years. And that is in spite of serious concerns about working conditions in the industry, with complaints about stress, bullying and unreasonable workloads.

F In India, however, call centre work is seen as highly desirable. With school teachers earning just £50 a month, call centre wages of double that are seen as attractive. This means that the industry attracts the young, well-educated, middle classes who are eager to work in a clean and modern environment. A recent BBC Radio 4 programme, *India Calling, How*

> **'... the finer points of British culture, such as which Spice Girl married David Beckham ...'**

May I Help?, described the great lengths that would-be employees in India have to go to in order to work in a British call centre. Many pay a massive £200 for a three-week training course on the finer points of British culture, such as which Spice Girl married David Beckham and the plot of *East Enders*. They are also taught how to 'neutralize' their accents to suit a British audience and some adopt English names.

G Callers from Dundee to Dover need never know that the young woman on the other end of the line is in Delhi not Durham. Nor do they need to know that the goods or services they are buying are beyond the wildest dreams of the cheery telephone operator. Workers quoted in the Radio 4 programme talked of how it felt to handle customers spending £50 on a T-shirt – the equivalent of two weeks' wages for those taking the calls. Yet they were also well aware that the only reason the jobs had come to India in the first place was because they earned a tenth of the wages their British counterparts could command. It is estimated that 100,000 people work in the call centre industry in India and some think that could grow tenfold over the coming years.

H Workers around the world are becoming more and more likely to spend their working day in a call centre. Their experiences may differ, depending on the conditions in their workplace and the society in which they live, but their lives are no longer worlds apart. The jobs of staff in Britain need to be defended and working conditions improved. But workers in India, too, should be protected from exploitation as a result of the demands of an increasingly globalized market, which is motivated by profit. Wherever it is located, call centre work is potentially stressful and monotonous and call centre staff need adequate remuneration and respect in recognition of this fact.

Adjectives

1 With a partner, decide whether these adjectives are most likely to be used to describe customers, helpline operators or both. Write *C*, *H* or *B* next to each.

abusive C annoyed B appreciative C cheerful H competent H difficult C frustrated B
grateful C helpful H irritated B knowledgeable H patient H persuasive H pleasant H
reassuring H rude C satisfied C sympathetic H understanding H upset C

2 Which nine adjectives do *not* have the stress on their first syllable?
Of those nine, which three adjectives have the stress on their third syllable?

Listening for attitude

3 🔊 1:11–1:20 Listen to ten extracts from helpline conversations and choose appropriate adjectives from 1 to describe the speakers.

Describing problems

4 Decide which device each of the sentences can refer to and tick the appropriate columns.

	car	fax	photocopier	PC	mobile phone
1 When I switch it on, nothing happens.		✓	✓	✓	✓
2 It broke down on the way to work.					
3 It keeps crashing.					
4 There's something stuck inside.					
5 I can't switch it off.					
6 It's not working properly.					
7 It won't start.					
8 It's out of order.					
9 I think it's a complete write-off.					
10 The battery's dead.					

Collocations

5 Choose the best verb from the box to complete each collocation. Use each verb once only.

identify   talk   arrange   give   sort out   escalate   exchange   diagnose

1 _____ the symptoms
2 _____ the fault
3 _____ a problem
4 _____ the customer through the process
5 _____ the problem to a supervisor
6 _____ a visit from our technician
7 _____ the product
8 _____ a full refund

Antonyms

6 Match each verb with its opposite.

1	connect	a)	disconnect
2	insert	b)	fasten
3	lift out	c)	push in (to)
4	release	d)	remove
5	replace	e)	remove
6	screw in	f)	switch off
7	turn on	g)	unscrew

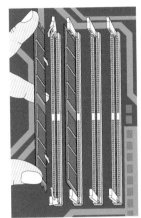

7 Complete the instructions for upgrading a PC memory module using 12 of the verbs in 6.

First, (1) _____ the PC. Do not (2) _____ the power cable, so that the PC remains earthed. Then (3) _____ and (4) _____ the side panel. Next, (5) _____ the retaining clips at each end of the old memory module. (6) _____ the old memory module. Carefully (7) _____ the new memory module and (8) _____ it firmly _____ the slot. (9) _____ the clips at each end. (10) _____ and (11) _____ the side panel. Finally, (12) _____ the PC and check that the new memory is recognized.

Phrasal verbs

8 Complete the sentences using the verbs in the box. Then match them to the correct 'translation'.

hang	speak	call	get	hold	get	take	put	ring

Call centre telephone code	'Translation'
1 Could you _____ on a moment, please?	a) Maybe. If I have nothing else to do!
2 We tried to contact you, but we couldn't _____ through.	b) I'm in the middle of an interesting conversation.
3 I'm going to _____ you through to my supervisor.	c) We lost your phone number.
4 Could you _____ up, and I'll _____ you back?	d) Heh, heh, let's see how *she* likes your ridiculous questions.
5 I'll just _____ down your details.	e) We don't know what you're talking about!
6 I can't hear you very well. Could you _____ up, please?	f) I'll pretend to do something useful.
7 We'll _____ back to you as soon as we solve the problem.	g) They're playing my favourite song on the radio.
8 The engineer is out at the moment. Please _____ back later.	h) We might ring next week if we remember.

Listening for detail

9 🔊 1:21 Listen to an interview for a customer satisfaction survey. Which one of these ten words and expressions is *not* used?

annoyed   call you back   it doesn't work   escalate   hold on   competent
get your problems sorted out   knowledgeable   pleasant   provide a solution

Internet research

Search for the keywords "golden rules of customer service". Compare your findings with your own 'golden rules' from 10.

Discussion

10 In small groups, brainstorm ten 'golden rules' of customer service. Then present your 'golden rules' to another group.

Refresh your memory

Yes / no questions
auxiliary verb + subject
+ main verb

Wh- questions
question word +
auxiliary verb + subject
+ main verb
<u>except if</u> *who, what* or
which is the subject: no
auxiliary is needed

▶ **Grammar reference** page 120

2.3 Grammar Asking questions and giving instructions

Test yourself: Asking questions and giving instructions

1 Complete the conversation between a customer support adviser (A) and a customer (C).
More than one answer may be possible in each case.

A: Good afternoon. Alistair speaking. How (1) _can___ help you?

C: Oh, hi. I'm having problems installing my Wi-Fi router. I can't get the Internet to work.

A: I see. What about the Wi-Fi network? (2) _____ working?

C: Yes, that's fine. It's just the Internet that's the problem.

A: OK. I'm sure we can sort that out. (3) _____ mind giving me the reference of the router?

C: No problem. Er, where (4) _____ find it?

A: It's on the front of the box, in the bottom left corner.

C: Oh, OK. It's WWJ108G–GB.

A: Ah yes, the all-in-one modem / router / Wi-Fi access point. (5) _____ have a broadband modem on your PC before installing the router?

C: Yes.

A: And (6) _____ working properly?

C: Yes, it was fine.

A: OK. (7) _____ tried uninstalling the old modem?

C: No, not yet. (8) _____ have to?

A: Well, no, (9) _____ have to, but it makes it easier to configure the new set-up. All right, on the desktop, (10) _____ just double-click on the 'My Computer' icon? …

A: … so I'm afraid there does seem to be a problem with the modem.

C: OK. (11) _____ have a technician call round?

A: No. Just take it back to the shop, with the receipt, and they'll exchange it.

C: Right. (12) _____ to reinstall the software?

A: No. (13) _____. But (14) _____ to configure the modem with your ISP details. If you have any problems, call me back.

C: OK, I'll do that. Thanks a lot.

A: You're welcome. Goodbye.

Listening

2 🔊 1:22 Listen to a radio game of *Guess the Product*. At the beep, guess what the mystery product is. Then continue listening to check your answer.

3 Listen again and complete the questions for the given answers.

1 _____ on TV? No, it isn't.
2 _____ for work? Yes, you do.
3 _____ in every office? Yes, you would.
4 _____ in your pocket? Yes, you can.
5 _____ ten years ago? No, it didn't.

6 _____ electricity? Yes, it does.
7 _____ speak to people? No, you don't.
8 _____ with computers? Yes, there is.
9 _____ more than $30? No, it doesn't.
10 _____ the floppy disk? Yes it has.

4 In small groups, take turns choosing a mystery product and play *Guess the Product*.

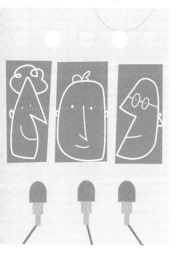

Internet research

What's the best way to learn English? How long will it take? Do I have to learn grammar? How can I learn more vocabulary? Search for the keywords *FAQ learning English* to find the most frequently asked questions and some of the answers.

Making requests

5 Complete these requests with *fax* or *faxing* then put them in order from the most direct to the most polite.

☐ Can you _____ me the details?
☐ Would you mind _____ me the details?
☐ Do you think you could possibly _____ me the details, please?
☐ _____ me the details, will you?
☐ Could you _____ me the details, please?
☐ I was wondering if you would have any objection to _____ me the details?

6 Which *one* of these responses is *not* appropriate for *all* the requests in 5, and why?

a) I'm afraid my fax is out of order.
b) I'll do it straight away.
c) I'm sorry, but I'm not in the office.
d) I'm a bit short of time, actually.
e) No, no problem.

Roleplay

7 With a partner, take turns beginning these telephone roleplays and responding. Choose suitable forms for your requests, according to the answer expected, and give appropriate answers. Ask your:

- colleague to send you an email to test your new address.
- boss to give you an advance on next month's salary.
- supplier to postpone a delivery by one week.
- supervisor to write a reference for your job application.
- friend to lend you their laptop for the weekend.
- customer to call back later when the sales manager comes back from lunch.
- bank manager to lend you a million dollars.
- supplier to upgrade the office coffee machine, at no charge.

Giving instructions

8 Complete Steve's side of the telephone conversation using *don't, might have to, 'll have to, 'll need to, don't have to* or *needn't*.

Steve: OK, Pete. First of all, you open the printer. No, wait a minute, (1) _____ just open it. Select 'change cartridge' from the menu.
Pete: _____
Steve: Er, yes, of course you (2) _____ switch it on, otherwise you can't use the menu!
Pete: _____
Steve: No, that's all right, you (3) _____ switch the PC on, just the printer.
Pete: _____
Steve: So now you gently remove the old cartridge. (4) _____ force it. If it's difficult, you (5) _____ pull it back first, then upwards.
Pete: _____
Steve: OK. So now you can install the new cartridge. You (6) _____ remove the adhesive tape first, but be careful you (7) _____ touch the printed circuits – they're very fragile.
Pete: _____
Steve: Right. It'll ask you if you want to align the new cartridge, but you (8) _____ bother. Usually it's fine as it is.
Pete: _____
Steve: Oh no, (9) _____ throw the old cartridge away. You can recycle them.
Pete: _____
Steve: No, that's all right, Pete. You (10) _____ worry. Just buy me a beer some time!

9 🔊 1:23 Write Pete's side of the conversation. Then listen and compare your version with the recording.

10 Choose something you don't know how to do from the list below.

- change the oil in your car
- upgrade the processor in your PC
- organize a press conference
- publish your website
- (your own idea)

Find someone who knows how to do it and ask them to explain what to do. Ask questions and / or reformulate their answers to check that you understand.

2 | Customer support

Giving instructions

1 With a partner, practise giving instructions by describing a symbol so that your partner can draw it. Do not look at each other's pages during the exercise.

Student A: turn to page 111.
Student B: turn to page 115.

Listening

2 1:24 Listen to a software helpline conversation and answer the questions.

1 What is the customer's problem?
2 What help does the operator give?

3 Listen again and find expressions that mean the same as:

1   I'm just putting you on hold for a moment.
2   This is Dean.
3   What can I do for you?
4   Could you explain the problem you're having?
5   The line's bad.
6   Can you talk a bit louder?

7   I'll connect you to …
8   The line's engaged.
9   Can I get her to call you back?
10   So, your number is …
11   What's your name please?
12   You're welcome.

Improving a conversation

4 With a partner, read this conversation aloud.

Helpline: Superword helpline, wait a minute …Yeah? What's your problem?
Customer: I'm having trouble with PDF files. I can't print them.
Helpline: What? I can't hear you.
Customer: I said I can't print PDF files.
Helpline: Oh. I don't do PDFs.
Customer: Well, could you connect me to someone who does?
Helpline: Can't. The PDF expert's gone out for lunch. Give me your name and we'll call you later.
Customer: Oh, all right. It's Gearhirt. Jamila Gearhirt.
Helpline: Er, come again?
Customer: That's G-E-A-R-H-I-R-T.
Helpline: OK.
Customer: All right. Well, I'd appreciate it if you could call me as soon as possible. Goodbye.
Helpline: Yeah, right.

1   Decide how the conversation could be improved.
2   Practise your improved version.
3   Now change roles, turn to page 110 and do the same with a similar conversation.

Handling problems

5 1:25 Listen to another helpline conversation, which is based on a true story, and answer the questions.

1   What is the customer's problem?
2   What is the operator's solution?

6 Listen again and complete the expressions.

A Explaining the problem
I'm having _____ with WordPerfect.
It doesn't _____.
_____ accept anything when I type.
Nothing _____.
_____ type anything.

B Diagnosing the causes
Was it _____ before that?
What does your screen _____ now?
Have you _____ 'Escape'?
_____ quit WordPerfect?
_____ move the cursor around?
_____ a power indicator?

C Giving instructions
_____ on the back of the monitor?
Now _____ follow the cord to the plug.
_____ look back there again.
_____ go and get them.
Then _____ take it back to the store.

D Promising help
_____ the electricity company.

7 Decide in which category in 6 (A, B, C or D) the following expressions belong.

- [ ] Have you installed any new software?
- [ ] I'll get our technical expert to help you.
- [ ] I'm having difficulty connecting to the Internet.
- [ ] It keeps crashing.
- [ ] You'll have to adjust the settings in the control panel.
- [ ] We'll get back to you in a couple of hours.
- [ ] What happens if you press 'Control' – 'Alt' – 'Delete'?
- [ ] I'll have a technician call as soon as possible.

Pronunciation

8 🔊 1:26 Listen to these questions from 5.

1 Note whether the intonation goes up (↗) or down (↘) at the end of the question.

   a) What does your screen look like now?
   b) What's a toolbar?
   c) Did you quit WordPerfect?
   d) Does your monitor have a power indicator?
   e) Can you see the toolbar on the screen?
   f) What do I tell them?

2 With a partner, practise reading questions a)–f) above with appropriate intonation.

Roleplay

9 With a partner, use the chart to roleplay helping a colleague with the technical problems below. Take turns being Student A and Student B.

- You can't print your report.
- Your mobile phone doesn't work.
- The video projector doesn't work.
- There are no lights in your office.

- Your car won't start.
- Your laptop is frozen.
- (your own problem)

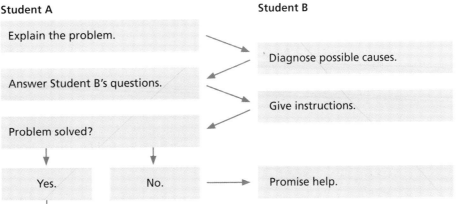

DOGBERT'S TECH SUPPORT

YOU HAVE A BAD CASE OF COMPUTER ROT.

YOUR COMPUTER IS DESIGNED TO BECOME SLOWER AND MORE UNRELIABLE OVER TIME SO YOU HAVE TO UPGRADE.

BUT IF YOU'D LIKE SOME FALSE HOPE, I CAN TELL YOU HOW TO DEFRAGMENT YOUR DISK DRIVE.

Cartoon from Dilbert.com 28/5/05

2.5 Writing   Formal and informal correspondence

Discussion

1 With a partner, discuss what differences you would find in your own language between formal correspondence, e.g. a letter to your bank manager, and informal messages, e.g. an email to a friend.

Skim reading

2 Read the four emails below and answer the questions.

1   Which email is from:

☐ a customer service department?   ☐ a junior colleague?
☐ a senior colleague?   ☐ a customer?

1

Dear Ms Reckett,

I am writing with regard to a computer problem. You may remember we met at the office Christmas party, and I believe you mentioned having a similar problem with your laptop. Unfortunately I have dropped mine and the screen is cracked. I was wondering if you could give me any advice on getting it repaired? I would very much appreciate any help you might be able to give me.

Yours sincerely,

James Blair

2

Dear Sir or Madam,

I am writing to enquire about having a television repaired. The set is a Goodson TV750 which we bought 18 months ago and therefore is unfortunately no longer under guarantee. Currently we have a picture but no sound.

I would be very grateful if you could give me the address of an authorized repair centre in the Greater Manchester area. Thank you for your help.

Yours faithfully,

J. Roebotham (Miss)

3

Hi James,

Thanks for your mail. Bad luck about the laptop. Mine was a write-off – had to get a new one! Why don't you try Harrowson's in Oldham? They're usually good. Hope this helps.

Cheers,

Margaret

P.S. Of course I remember you. Give me a ring next time you're in town and we'll go for a drink!

4

Dear Miss Roebotham,

Re your email of 10 September: your TV is in fact covered by a two-year manufacturer's guarantee. Can you just send the set back in its original packaging and we will repair or exchange it asap. Don't hesitate to get back to me if you need any more information.

Regards,

Max Hurst

P.S. Are you by any chance the Jenny Roebotham I knew at Manchester Business School in 98 / 99?

---

2   Which two emails are formal? Which two are neutral / informal?

Internet research

The advantages of email are obvious – but what risks must companies consider? Search for the keywords *"email risk policy"* to find out.

Reading for detail

3 Find expressions in the four emails in 2 to complete the table.

	Formal	Neutral / Informal
Greeting	Dear / Dear	Hi
Opening		
Requests		
Closing		
Salutation		

Skim reading

4 Read the next four emails the people in 2 sent.

1 Which two writers have changed style? Why?
2 Find and correct the two inconsistencies of style in each email.

---

5 Dear Mr Hurst,

Thanks for your email of 12 September. I am afraid you have mistaken me for my cousin, who attended Manchester Business School in 1998. I am very pleased to learn that the TV set is still under guarantee. Unfortunately, I no longer have the original packaging, so I think it would be preferable if I deliver the TV directly to your repair centre after work. Could you possibly let me know the opening hours?
Cheers,
Jane Roebotham

---

7 Dear Miss Roebotham,

I am writing with reference to the repair of your Goodson TV750. Our Manchester repair centre is open from 9am to 6pm from Monday to Saturday. I've attached a leaflet with the details and a map. Hope this helps.
Yours sincerely,
Max Hurst.
P.S. Please accept my apologies for confusing you with your cousin.

---

6 Hi Margaret,

Thanks for your email. I wasn't sure if you'd remember me – it was quite a party, wasn't it? Funnily enough, I will be in town next Thursday so perhaps we could have that drink? I would be very grateful if you could let me know if you are free around 6.30? Looking forward to seeing you.
James
P.S. I would like to express my gratitude for your help with the computer. I'm getting it fixed tomorrow.

---

8 James,

Re next Thursday. It will be lovely to see you. Actually, my husband will be in Indonesia that week, so I need to be at home to look after the cats. I was wondering if you would mind coming over to our place? I've attached a map – get back to me if it's not clear.
Yours sincerely,
Margaret

Writing

5 Work in groups of three to write and reply to business emails using appropriate styles.

Student A: look at page 111.
Student B: look at page 112.
Student C: look at page 115.

2.6 Case study · Cybertartan Software

Discussion

1 What annoys you most as a customer?

> waiting for service   products that don't do what they claim   high prices   hidden costs
> planned obsolescence   deadlines not respected   incompetent service
> poorly translated instructions   being put on hold   other?

With a partner, discuss what you as a customer can do about these problems.

Scan reading

2 Read the email from Hamish Hamilton, CEO of Cybertartan Software and answer the questions.

1 What are his four problems?
2 How are the problems linked?

really pleased with the solutions you recommended.

For your next project, I need you to take a look at our Kirkcaldy contact centre. Our Q4 customer satisfaction survey is disastrous (see charts and report extract attached) and this represents a major risk to our corporate image and future sales. We have serious recruitment problems and a high staff turnover. These two problems are obviously linked. I suggest you talk to Laurie McAllister, our HR Manager there. I'd like you to come up with some proposals but without significantly increasing costs, which are another problem. Currently we estimate that on average a customer call costs us £4.50. We cover this from the call charge (currently £0.50 per minute), which is why we keep customers on hold for around six minutes. They spend about the same time with an adviser, although if possible we need to reduce this because at the moment we can't take enough calls. Obviously, we can't afford to increase salaries. I'm counting on you to come up with some creative ideas: get back to me as soon as you can.

Best regards,

Hamish

Customer satisfaction Q1

very satisfied	26%
satisfied	44%
dissatisfied	21%
very dissatisfied	9%

TOP FIVE REASONS FOR CUSTOMER DISSATISFACTION	
1 Difficult to get through to customer adviser	76%
2 Time spent on hold	65%
3 Several calls needed to solve problem	53%
4 Cost of calls	49%
5 Can't get help by email	32%

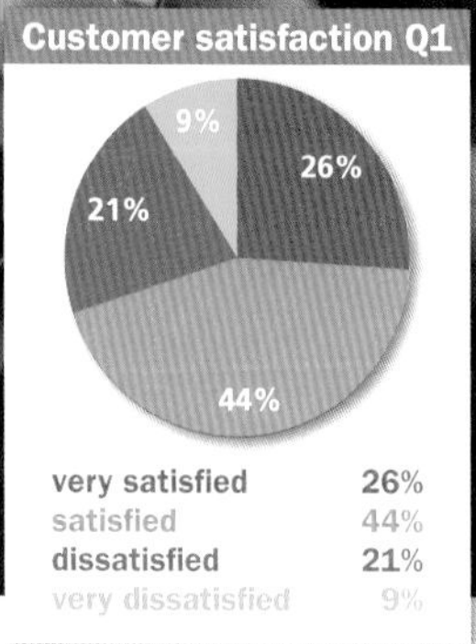

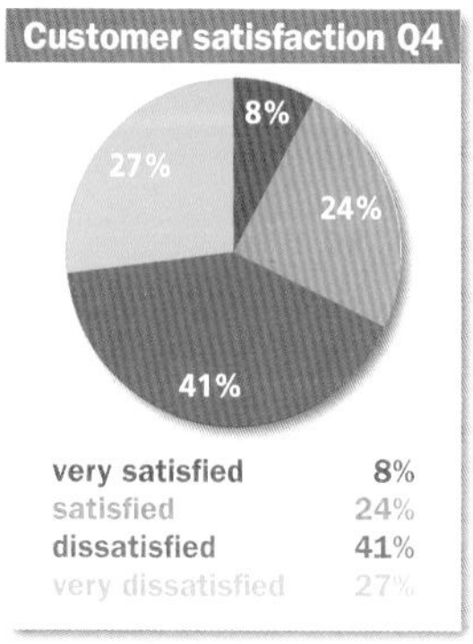

Customer satisfaction Q4

very satisfied	8%
satisfied	24%
dissatisfied	41%
very dissatisfied	27%

Reading for detail

3 Mark these statements *T* (true), *F* (false) or *D* (it depends).

1 Hamish Hamilton is probably writing to an external consulting group. ☐
2 The Kirkcaldy contact centre has satisfied employees and dissatisfied customers. ☐
3 The contact centre is losing money at the moment. ☐
4 If the centre employs more advisers, its income will increase. ☐
5 More than two thirds of customers were satisfied or very satisfied in Q1. ☐
6 The number of both dissatisfied and very dissatisfied customers tripled in Q4. ☐
7 About half of their customers would be prepared to pay for support if their problems were solved quickly. ☐

Internet research

What is the FLSA? What are employees' rights on bathroom and meal breaks in the USA? Are they similar to those in your country? Search for the keywords *"meal rest breaks"* to find out.

Listening for detail

4 🔊 1:27 Listen to part of an interview with Laurie McAllister, HR Manager at the Kirkcaldy contact centre. In her opinion, what is the biggest problem for advisers?

5 Listen again. What are the effects on the contact centre of the following?

1 Employees have poor working conditions and low job satisfaction.
2 The workload is heavier than before.
3 The bus service is inadequate.
4 Desks are shared with colleagues on other shifts.
5 Software products have become very complex.
6 Advisers don't get enough training.
7 The shift system is inflexible.

Solving problems

6 Work in small groups. You are the consultants that Hamish Hamilton wrote to in 2. Hold a meeting to discuss the agenda below.

Kirkcaldy Contact Centre

AGENDA FOR CONSULTANTS' MEETING

The situation
Isolate the problems and prioritize them as:
a) important and urgent
b) important but not urgent
c) not important.

Solutions
Brainstorm solutions to the problems prioritized as a) and b) above.
• Review company policy on customer services?
• Review company policy on working conditions for advisers?

Recommendations
Define recommendations for short- and long-term policy.

Writing presentation slides

7 Prepare slides to present to Cybertartan Software summarizing your recommendations. For each problem, make recommendations, give reasons for these and outline the expected results.

Presentations

8 In your groups, present your recommendations and take questions from the class.

Review 1

Corporate culture

1 Make expressions about internships by matching each verb to a phrase a–f below.

1 Incorporate ... ☐
2 Enhance ... ☐
3 Relate ... ☐
4 Be assessed ... ☐
5 Be supervised ... ☐
6 Offer ... ☐

a) ... your academic study to the workplace.
b) ... work experience into a university degree.
c) ... by your institution through reports, appraisals, etc.
d) ... closely by someone from the workplace and a university staff member.
e) ... your career prospects by doing an internship.
f) ... permanent employment to a student after graduation.

2 Match each word in the box to its definition below. Then translate the words into your language.

appraisal	commitment	deadline	etiquette
insight	outcome	overview	predecessor
threaten	workload		

1 A date by which you have to do something: _____
2 An ability to understand something clearly: _____
3 An opinion about how successful someone is: _____
4 The amount of work that a person has to do: _____
5 Enthusiasm, determination and loyalty: _____
6 A set of rules for behaving correctly: _____
7 A description of the main features of something:
_____
8 The person who had a job before someone else: _____
9 The final result of a process, meeting, etc.: _____
10 To tell someone you might cause them harm: _____

3 Underline the correct preposition (in **bold**) in each expression.

1 Be in charge **to / of / from** a department or project.
2 Be involved **on / in / for** doing something.
3 Be responsible **to / for / with** an area of work.
4 Deal **with / on / for** an area of work.
5 Have somebody working **of / under / on** you.
6 Liaise **for / to / with** someone about an area of the business.
7 Look **through / with / after** an area of work.
8 Report directly **to / for / under** somebody.
9 Run the business **from / with / on** a day-to-day basis.
10 Take care **with / of / for** an area of work.

4 The sentences below all have the same meaning. Complete them using expressions from 3.

Maria	1 is __ _____ __	the marketing side of the business.
	2 is _____ __	
	3 _____ _____	
	4 _____ _____	
	5 _____ _____ __	

5 Mark these statements about work organization *T* (true) or *F* (false).

1 A task is bigger than an assignment. ☐
2 A line manager has a higher position than a project leader. ☐
3 A branch is bigger than a division. ☐
4 COO stands for Chief Organization Officer. ☐
5 The Public Relations officer will often work in the Marketing Department. ☐
6 Personnel is one of the functions of Human Resources. ☐
7 R&D stands for Resources and Deployment. ☐
8 A parent company owns several smaller companies called *subsidies*. ☐
9 *Purchasing* is a more formal way of saying *buying*. ☐
10 Company structure can be shown visually using an 'organichart'. ☐

6 In each sentence, put one verb in the past simple (*did*), one in the past continuous (*was / were doing*) and one in the past perfect (*had done*).

1 While I _____ (work) in my father's business I _____ (start) to understand the importance of marketing – I _____ (never / think) about it before.
2 I _____ (already / be) in the job for two months when I first _____ (speak) to the big boss, the CEO: I nearly hit his car as I _____ (park) mine!

7 Complete the expressions for giving diplomatic advice (in **bold**) by filling in the missing letters.

1 **A_____, I think** there's a better way to do this.
2 **It s____ to me that** there has been a misunderstanding.
3 **You m____ want to** ask Sue for her opinion.
4 **You c____ maybe** try a different approach.
5 **D__'_ you think that** making personal calls at work creates an unprofessional atmosphere?
6 **W_____'_ you agree that** it's important to meet all our deadlines?

8 Match these words relating to report writing to their definitions below.

| description | observation | evaluation |
| suggestion | analysis | |

1 Examining something in order to understand it:
_____
2 A statement about what something is like: _____
3 Considering something in order to discover how good or bad it is: _____
4 A comment about something you have seen, heard or felt: _____
5 An idea or plan that you offer for someone to consider:
_____

Review 2

Customer support

1 In each set of four below, match an adjective on the left with a noun on the right to make collocations about working conditions.

1	clean	customer
2	satisfied	environment
3	high	meals
4	subsidized	staff turnover
5	heavy	rate
6	hourly	staff
7	competent	job
8	dead-end	workload

2 Make adjectives from these nouns.

1	annoyance	_____	6	knowledge	_____
2	competence	_____	7	persuasion	_____
3	frustration	_____	8	reassurance	_____
4	gratitude	_____	9	satisfaction	_____
5	help	_____	10	rudeness	_____

3 The collocations below are useful in customer support. Cross out the one verb in each group (in **bold**) that does *not* collocate with the noun.

1 **Deal with / look into / push in / sort out** a problem.
2 **Describe / identify / replace / treat** the symptoms.
3 **Diagnose / locate / offer / repair** the fault.
4 **Escalate / exchange / launch / replace** the product.
5 **Ask for / call / give / offer** a full refund.
6 **Escalate / fax / refer / replace** the problem to a supervisor.

4 In this customer support dialogue the verbs in **bold** are all in the wrong places. Put them in the correct places.

Helpline operator:	Before I can **locate** the problem, I first need to **escalate** exactly where the fault is.
Customer:	OK, no problem, we can do that. But if it's still not working properly, can you **sort out** the product, or at least **replace** me a refund?
Helpline operator:	Yes, that's possible, but I'm not authorized to do it. I would first have to **give** the problem to my supervisor.

5 Complete this useful phrase for after sales service using the letters in brackets.

'I'll ____ into it, ____ it out, and ___ back to you tomorrow.' (gklrstteooo)

6 Complete the sentences typical of customer support telephone calls 1–10 using the prepositions in the box.

down	down	in	into	on	on
up	through	through	up	

1 We tried to contact you, but we couldn't get _____.
2 The machine broke _____ after only a few days.
3 Replace and screw _____ the side panel.
4 When I switch it _____, nothing happens.
5 I'm going to put you _____ to my supervisor.
6 I'll just take _____ your details.

7 Push the new module _____ the slot.
8 Please hold _____ a moment while I find your records on our database.
9 The line is bad. Please hang _____ and I'll call you back.
10 The line is bad. Could you speak _____, please?

7 Read the definitions and complete the words by filling in the missing letters.

1 Computer screen: m_____r
2 A row of icons on a computer screen: too___r
3 Something you hope your computer doesn't do: c___h
4 Make a computer more powerful: u____de
5 Something that goes in a printer: ca____dge
6 Connect to the electricity supply: p__g in
7 Send a document with an email: a___ch
8 Someone who a business sells to: c_____r
9 Someone who a business buys from: s_____r
10 A written promise that a company will repair something you buy from them: g_____e

8 Complete the email using the words in the box.

appreciate	attached	could	further
get back to	grateful	hesitate	regard
urgently	would		

Dear Mr White

I am writing with (1) _____ to my order placed online last week. It still hasn't arrived. I (2) _____ be (3) _____ if you (4) _____ ship the order immediately. For your reference, I have (5) _____ a copy of the confirmation you sent me. Do not (6) _____ to (7) _____ me if you need any (8) _____ information. I would (9) _____ a quick response as these items are needed (10) _____.

Best regards

J Garcia

9 The extracts below come from an email between colleagues at a customer contact centre. Use one word to fill each gap. The clues in brackets will help you.

1 I _____ you to take a look at our Metz contact centre. (**Clue**: not *want*, but a similar single word more often used in a business context)
2 Our _____ customer satisfaction survey is disastrous. (**Clue**: how business people often write *fourth quarter*)
3 This represents a major _____ to our corporate image. (**Clue**: it means *the possibility that something bad may happen*!)
4 These two problems are obviously _____. (**Clue**: not *connected*, although the meaning is the same)
5 I _____ you talk to Marie Pinon. (**Clue**: the meaning is close to *recommend*, although less definite)
6 I'm _____ on you to come up with some ideas. (**Clue**: not *relying*, although the meaning is the same)

3 | Products and packaging

Discussion

1 With a partner, think of three examples of products which are packaged well or badly, and say why. Think about protection, identification, transport, storage, display and security.

Listening for gist

2 🔊 1:28 Listen to an interview with Charlie Wang, President of New China Packaging, a design consultancy based in Taipei, and answer the questions.

1 Why does he think packaging is so important?
2 What is special about New China Packaging's approach?

Listening for detail

3 Listen again and mark these statements *T* (true) or *F* (false).

1 Branding is not enough to differentiate almost identical products. ☐
2 American business guru Jack Trout thinks that companies overcommunicate their difference. ☐
3 Most customers decide which product to buy before going to the store. ☐
4 Wal-Mart believe that a product must communicate its difference from 15 feet away. ☐
5 In the past, design teams were isolated from financial and manufacturing problems so that they would be as creative as possible. ☐
6 Creative ideas are often simplified and adapted because consumers in focus groups don't like them. ☐
7 New China Packaging task forces can't leave their hotel until every stakeholder is enthusiastic about the new packaging concept. ☐
8 Consumers are not always conscious of what they need. ☐
9 New China Packaging's task forces need months or years to deliver a consumer-validated package. ☐
10 New China Packaging helps its customers to react quickly to new trends in the market. ☐

Internet research

Search for the keywords *"universal design"* packaging to find out about Universal Design and its impact on packaging.

Discussion

4 Read comments a) and b) below on cross-functional task forces and answer the questions.

a) 'It is very helpful to involve everybody who will interface with the new employee in the selection process. We can never know candidates' future jobs and the qualities required, or the people they will work with.'

b) 'In our department they're probably less useful than in Marketing. The customer is unlikely to enjoy having several different contacts.'

1 Decide which department from the box made each comment and whether they are for or against cross-functional task forces.

Sales	R&D	Training	IT	HR

2 Discuss what people in the other three departments might say about cross-functional task forces.

Scan reading

5 Read the article and answer the questions. The words in grey are explained in the *Wordlist* on page 151.

1   What is wrap rage?
2   Who suffers from it?
3   What triggers it?
4   What are the underlying causes?

Paraphrasing

6 Reformulate these phrases from the article in your own words.

1   to reduce in-shop shrinkage due to pilfering (line 10)
2   the most common triggers of wrap rage (line 19)
3   even wrestling to remove price tags … can raise blood pressure (line 22)
4   a red rag to the ecologically-minded bull (line 24)
5   there's light at the end of the tunnel (line 26)
6   The bottom line is that if they don't react, they risk losing sales … (line 29)

Discussion

7 You have invented a new children's toy – MP-Bunny, an electronic rabbit which dances, talks and plays children's favourite songs. In small groups, discuss how you will package it. Think about the questions below.

1   What different materials could you use? What are their advantages and disadvantages?
2   What design elements will you incorporate? Think about shape, colour, photos, logos and text.
3   How will your packaging make your product look different from other electronic toys?

Present your packaging solution to another group.

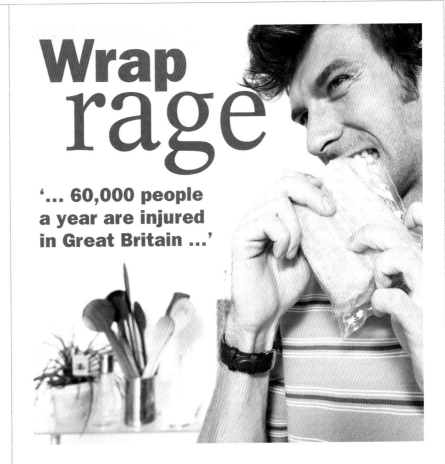

Wrap rage

'... 60,000 people a year are injured in Great Britain ...'

SURVEYS show that intense frustration and even injury caused by modern packaging is on the increase, especially amongst seniors. Seventy per cent of over 50s admit to suffering cuts, sprains and bruises to fingers, hands and shoulders as a result of 'wrap rage',
5   a new term used to describe the irritation and loss of self-control experienced when struggling to open wrapping.

In recent years manufacturers have been under increasing pressure to keep food items sterile, to provide child-proof packaging for dangerous or toxic household cleaning products, to protect
10   products during transport and to reduce in-shop shrinkage due to pilfering. At the same time, they are forced to keep costs to a minimum. As a result, packaging has become ever more resistant to fingers, nails and even teeth. In their frustration with blister packs and welded plastic, which defeat all attempts to be pulled, torn or
15   even cut open with scissors, consumers resort to stabbing with screwdrivers, twisting with pliers or slashing with knives. At best, the product inside the packaging is at risk; at worst, it is hardly surprising that 60,000 people a year are injured in Great Britain alone.

Some of the most common triggers of wrap rage are processed
20   cheese packages, tightly wrapped CDs, child-proof tops on medicine bottles, and milk and juice cartons. Ring-pull cans are particularly problematic for arthritic fingers and delicate skin. Even wrestling to remove price tags from items bought as gifts can raise blood pressure, and unnecessary overpackaging is a red rag to the
25   ecologically-minded bull.

However it seems there's light at the end of the tunnel. Manufacturers are listening to customers' complaints, and some have begun to research and invest in more consumer-friendly packaging. The bottom line is that if they don't react, they risk losing
30   sales if customers simply stop buying products with packaging that offers too much resistance.

Products and packaging

Discussion

1 Put these stages of product development into the most likely chronological order.

☐ Beta test the product by users in typical situations.
☐ Conduct market studies to test the concept.
☐ Launch the product.
☐ Draw sketches and build mockups.
☐ Go into production.
☐ Draw up specifications for the product.
☐ 1 Generate new ideas in focus groups and brainstorming meetings.
☐ Screen out unfeasible or unprofitable ideas.

Reading for detail

2 Read the information on the FedEx Box and FedEx Tube and complete the product specification summaries below.

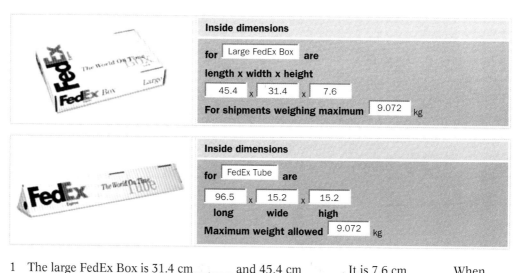

Inside dimensions

for Large FedEx Box **are**

length x width x height

| 45.4 | x | 31.4 | x | 7.6 |

For shipments weighing maximum 9.072 kg

Inside dimensions

for FedEx Tube **are**

| 96.5 | x | 15.2 | x | 15.2 |
| long | wide | high |

Maximum weight allowed 9.072 kg

1 The large FedEx Box is 31.4 cm _____ and 45.4 cm _____. It is 7.6 cm _____. When empty, the box _____ 400 g; it can be used to ship small parts or computer printouts up to 9 kg in _____.

2 The FedEx Tube is 96.5 cm in _____ and 15.2 cm in _____ and _____. With a _____ of 450 g when empty, it can be used to ship plans, posters, blueprints, etc. _____ up to 9 kg.

Describing products

3 Describe the dimensions of objects in your pockets or your bag. Your partner should try to guess what they are.

Collocations

4 Match the nouns in the box with the compound adjectives they usually collocate with.

materials   packaging   ~~devices~~   design   personal stereos   technology

1 energy-saving	devices	4 child-resistant
labour-saving		tamper-resistant
2 fire-retardant		5 future-proof
water-resistant		foolproof
3 waterproof		6 eye-catching
shockproof		attention-grabbing

Internet research

What are the best ways of recording and learning vocabulary? Search for the keywords *recording vocabulary* and make a list of possible techniques. Rank the techniques on your list from the most to the least useful for you personally.

Listening for gist

5 🔊 1:29–1:34 Listen to six conversations. Use collocations from 4 to describe what is being discussed.

6 🔊 1:35 Listen to a presentation of the Maptech i3. What are its three main features?

Listening for detail

7 Listen again and complete these expressions for structuring a product presentation using the correct preposition from the box.

| about | to | with | up | back | by | of | on |

1 I'm here today to tell you _____ (the Maptech i3 ...)
2 Let's start _____ (Touch Screen Command).
3 Let me show you an example _____ (what I mean).
4 Moving _____ to (what's below the water ...)
5 Can I just turn _____ (communications)?
6 I'll just sum _____ (the Maptech i3's three main features ...)
7 Let's just go _____ to (our midnight fishing trip).
8 I'd like to finish _____ (inviting you to ...)

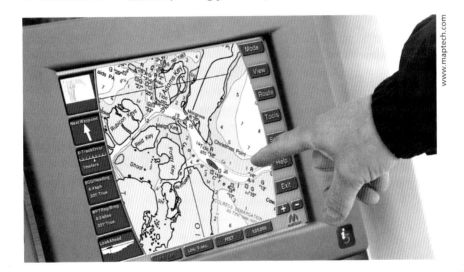

www.maptech.com

8 Match the expressions in 7 with their function in the presentation a)–e).

a) Beginning the presentation
b) Moving to a new point
c) Developing an idea
d) Returning to a point made earlier
e) Ending the presentation

Presentation

9 Work in small groups. Use the vocabulary and expressions in the previous exercises to present the specifications and features of an electronic device of your choice.

Refresh your memory

Articles

a/an: non-specific or not previously mentioned
the: specific, unique or previously mentioned
no article: generalizations

▶ Grammar reference page 122

Relative clauses

who: people
which: things
that: people or things, but not after a comma

▶ Grammar reference page 122

Noun combinations

The main noun comes at the end. Any others describe it.

▶ Grammar reference page 123

3.3 Grammar   Articles, relative clauses and noun combinations

Test yourself: Articles

1 Insert the missing articles *a(n)* or *the* in the text below.

> Did you know …
> - … that some popular products took 100 years or more to get to **the** marketplace? In 1485, Leonardo da Vinci made detailed sketches of parachutes. He also sketched studies for helicopter, tank and retractable landing gear. First helicopter that could carry person was flown by Paul Cornu at beginning of twentieth century. During First World War, tanks were first used in France in 1917. Airplane with retractable landing gear was built in United States in 1933.
> - Bar codes were invented by Silver and Woodland in 1948. They used light to read set of concentric circles, but it was two decades before advent of computers and lasers made system practical. However, bar code system in use today is Universal Product Code, introduced by IBM in 1973. First bar-coded items sold were packs of chewing gum in 1974.
> - Computer was launched in 1943, more than 100 years after Charles Babbage designed first programmable device. In 1998, Science Museum in London built working replica of Babbage machine, using materials and work methods available in Babbage's time. It worked just as Babbage had intended.

Test yourself: Relative clauses

2 Complete the relative clauses by choosing the correct pronoun or group of pronouns from the box.

> who   which   that / which   that / which / no pronoun

> 1   The fax process, _which_ was first patented in 1843 by Alexander Bain, did not go into commercial service until 1964.
> 2   Penicillin, the antibiotic compound _____ was discovered by Alexander Fleming in 1928, only went into production in 1942.
> 3   The steam engine _____ George Stephenson famously demonstrated in 1815 was actually discovered in 50 BC by Heron of Greece.
> 4   Kevin Tuohy, _who_ invented the soft plastic lens in 1948, was not the first person to suggest contact lenses: Adolph Fick had the idea in 1888.
> 5   Orville Wright is the man _who_ is usually credited with the first powered flight in 1903, but Gustave Whitehead and Richard Pearse were also experimenting with flying machines at the same time.
> 6   Several other people claim to be the inventors of the machine _____ John Logie Baird demonstrated in 1926 and called a 'televisor'.

Test yourself: Noun combinations

3 Put the words in the noun combinations (in **bold**) in the correct order.

> As new technologies arrive on an increasingly globalized market, companies are facing (1) **development product cycles ever-shorter**. What's more, as products become more sophisticated, manufacturers are having to work with (2) **support increasingly requirements complex technical**. One of the new tools available to help cope with such difficulties are (3) **programs web-based feedback customer**, which enable firms to work with (4) **real-world product pre-market feedback**. Another time-saving innovation is the (5) **product cross-functional team development**, which can make dramatic cuts in development lead-times.

Expanding notes

4 1:36 When writing notes in English, pronouns, articles and common verbs like *be* and *have* are often omitted. Listen to a product review and write the words you hear which the customer omitted in the notes below.

> *s is   the   It's the   the   I have already it*
> Easily best phone so far. Perfect phone for basic user. Already bumped and dropped it
> few times but still going strong. Battery life incredible. Overall real workhorse
> *There are no   a   I rate it five out of five.*
> – no frills, but does what cellphone needs to do. Rating 5/5.

5 1:37–1:38 With a partner, discuss how to expand these notes written by customers into full product reviews. Then listen and compare your versions with the recordings.

> **1**
> Hate this phone. Too small – can't open flip cover with one hand. No screen on outside to see caller identity. Reception – horrible. Drops calls probably 30% of time. Very long key delay, incredibly annoying. Anxiously awaiting day can upgrade and get rid of monstrosity. Rating 0/5.

> **2**
> Had phone about three weeks. Like size and design. Features good too. Easy enough to use, and survived couple of drops. However, alarm clock won't work anymore. Not too sure about internal antenna. Hate having full signal when making call, only to have dramatic drop when put phone to head. Everybody says telecom company's fault, not phone, or maybe just got bad one. We'll see. Going to try 9200 next. Rating 3/5.

Defining words

6 Complete these definitions by matching the noun combinations with the appropriate relative clause.

1 Decision-making tools are tools
2 Feature-packed spreadsheets are spreadsheets
3 An industry-standard battery package is a pack of batteries
4 Market studies are investigations

a) that have many different functions.
b) that companies conduct to identify customer needs.
c) that you evaluate choices and options with.
d) whose specifications comply with industry norms.

7 Finish these definitions by completing the relative clause.

1 Focus groups are groups _____ companies get product feedback _____ .
2 Consumer empowerment is an approach _____ gives consumers _____ .
3 A ring-pull can is a can _____ has a ring to open it _____ .
4 Complex text layout languages are languages _____ text layout is _____ .
5 Child-proof packaging is packaging _____ _____ can't open.
6 An award-winning design is a design _____ a jury has given an award _____ .
7 Portable document format (PDF) is a standard format _____ code can be read by all computers.
8 Household-cleaning products are products _____ you clean the house _____ .

Definitions game

8 In small groups, divide into As and Bs.

As: turn to page 111.
Bs: turn to page 117.

Internet research

Open an online dictionary by searching for the keywords *online dictionary*.
Search for the noun *information*. Is information countable or uncountable? What is its informal form? Which prepositions is it used with? What typical collocations and constructions is it used in?
Browse several online dictionaries and find out what other features they offer. Vote to find out which online dictionary the class prefers.

3 | Products and packaging

Brainstorming

1 What are the qualities of a good lesson, lecture or presentation? With a partner, draw up a checklist.

Listening for gist

2 🔊 1:39 Listen to Version 1 of a presentation of the Pingman, a new personal GPS tracking device which can be used to locate children, elderly people, animals or mobile staff. Compare the presentation with your checklist.

3 With a partner, discuss how Version 1 of the presentation could be improved.

Listening for detail

4 🔊 1:40 Listen to Version 2 of the presentation and tick the items on the checklist below as you hear them.

Introduction
- ☐ Hook, to get audience attention and interest
- ☐ Objective of the presentation
- ☐ Agenda, including timing and question etiquette

Body
- ☐ Background (past)
- ☐ Current situation (present)
- ☐ Forecasts (future)

Conclusion
- ☐ Summary of body
- ☐ Call for action
- ☐ Close

What other aspects of presentation technique have improved in Version 2?

5 Listen to Version 2 again and complete the expressions for introducing a presentation in the table below and for concluding a presentation in the table opposite.

Introduction		Expressions used in Version 2
Hook	Use rhetorical questions, surprising statistics, famous quotations or anecdotes to stimulate the audience, e.g.: *What would you do if … ?* *Why do our customers … ?* *Somebody once said …*	1 How _____ to know … ? 2 Did _____ that, on _____ … ?
Objective	Make sure everybody understands why they are present by clearly stating the goal, e.g.: *My objective today is …* *The goal of this meeting is …*	3 _____ this morning _____ the Pingman, … 4 The reason _____ is …
Agenda	Tell the audience your agenda and how you want to organize the meeting, e.g.: *My presentation is made up of three parts.* *I intend to begin by …* *I'll then go on to …* *Lastly, I want to …* *I'll take any questions at the end.*	5 _____ to interrupt me. 6 I've divided my presentation _____. 7 _____ of all, I'm going to … 8 _____, I'll be talking about … 9 _____, I'd like to present …

Conclusion		Expressions used in Version 2
Summary	Remind the audience of the most important points, e.g.: *I'm going to break off in a moment.* *In the first part, …* *In the second section, …* *In the third and final part, …*	10 I'd like to _____ the presentation 11 _____, I explained why … 12 _____, I presented the different specifications … 13 _____ but not _____, I have given you …
Call for action	Tell the audience what you want them to do, e.g.: *This is why we need your approval.* *This an opportunity that is too good to miss.*	14 These are _____ I am asking you to …
Close	Close the presentation and introduce what happens next, e.g.: *Thank you for listening.* *If you have any questions, I'll do my best to answer them.*	15 Thank you very much _____.

Internet research

Search for the keywords *presentation tips* to find answers to the questions below.

1 How long is a good presentation?
2 What should you research before a presentation?
3 What are the most important parts of a presentation?
4 What are the best ways to practise a presentation?
5 Which colours and fonts should you use in your slides?
6 How should you deal with hostile questions?
7 What's the latest presentation technology available?

Pronunciation

6 🔊 1:41 Decide where the speaker should pause in this extract from the presentation and draw a line for each pause. Before each pause, mark whether the speaker's voice should go up ↗| or down ↘|, as in the examples. Then listen and compare your answers.

I've divided my presentation into three sections. ↘| First of all, ↗| I'm going to remind you of the background to this project, and the current offer on the market. After that, I'll be talking about the prototype, the specifications, and the data we've collected from tests, focus groups and market studies. Finally, I'd like to present a business plan; this will show you why we expect a return on investment that is without precedent for our company. Is everybody happy with that agenda?

7 Underline the key syllables and key words which should be stressed, and draw a line between words which should be linked (‿), as in the example below.

I've divided my presentation into three sections. First of all, …

Listen again and compare your answers. Then practise reading the extract with correct intonation, stress and linking.

Presentation

8 In small groups, prepare the introduction and conclusion of a presentation of one of these new products to a group of department store buyers.

- a lightweight portable TV and DVD player with a 17-inch flexible screen that can be rolled up to fit in a pocket
- furniture which changes colour and temperature depending on the light and ambient temperature
- a T-shirt which displays a text message that can be modified from a PC or mobile phone
- your own product idea

Think about the following questions.

Hook:	What is the most surprising, exciting or unusual aspect of your product?
Objective:	Why are you making the presentation and what do you hope to obtain?
Agenda:	How will you organize your presentation and what will happen after the talk?
Summary:	What are the highlights of your talk?
Call for action:	What do you want your audience to do now?
Close:	How can you avoid an embarrassing silence at the end of your presentation?

9 In your group, present your introduction and conclusion and answer any questions. (Assume the body of the talk has been presented.) The rest of the class are the buyers. As a class, vote for the best product presentation.

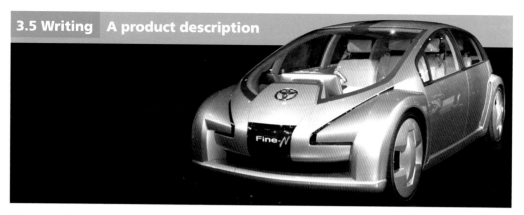

3.5 Writing A product description

Discussion

1 Identify the four features of this car and the four corresponding benefits to consumers. Then discuss the questions below.

> safe braking and cornering   alloy wheels   3.0l V6 engine   air-conditioned comfort
> power on demand   ABS   automatic climate control   head-turning good looks

1 What do you look for in a car – features or benefits? Why?
2 When you buy a computer, a mobile phone, or software, are you more interested in its features or benefits? What about other products?

Scan reading

2 Read the product description below and number the five sections in the box in the order they appear in the article.

> ☐ compatibility   ☐ background   ☐ details of features and benefits
> ☐ invitation   ☐ overview of benefits

OpenOffice.org 1.1

Great software – now better than ever

A An estimated 16 million + people have downloaded OpenOffice.org 1.0 in over 30 languages. OpenOffice.org is now proud to announce OpenOffice.org 1.1. More powerful, more compatible, more international, more accessible, more open than ever – and, best of all, this world-class software is still free!

A new approach to office productivity software

B OpenOffice.org 1.1 gives you everything you'd expect in office software. You can create dynamic documents, analyse data, design eye-catching presentations, produce dramatic illustrations and open up your databases. You can publish your work in Portable Document Format (PDF) and release your graphics in Flash (SWF) format – without needing any additional software. OpenOffice.org 1.1 is now available for more users than ever, with support for complex text layout (CTL) languages (such as Thai, Hindi, Arabic and Hebrew) and vertical writing languages.

C If you're used to using other office suites – such as Microsoft Office – you'll be completely at home with OpenOffice.org 1.1. However, as you become used to OpenOffice.org 1.1, you'll start to appreciate the extras that make your life easier. You can of course continue to use your old Microsoft Office files without any problems – and if you need to exchange files with people still using Microsoft Office, that's no problem either.

What's in the suite?

D WRITER – a powerful tool for creating professional documents. You can easily integrate images and charts in documents, create everything from business letters to complete books and web content.
CALC – a feature-packed spreadsheet. Use advanced spreadsheet functions and decision-making tools to perform sophisticated data analysis. Use built-in charting tools to generate impressive 2-D and 3-D charts.
IMPRESS – the fastest way to create effective multimedia presentations. Your presentations will truly stand out with special effects, animation and high-impact drawing tools.
DRAW – produce everything from simple diagrams to dynamic 3-D illustrations and special effects.
Find out more – try it today!
Click here to view an introduction to OpenOffice.org in Flash format!

Reformulating

3 R&D departments often focus on describing features, while marketing departments tend to describe benefits to consumers. Read the eight features described by R&D and underline their corresponding benefits in the text in 2.

1 International open source code application available to download (paragraph A)
   ... this world-class software is still free!
2 Fully integrated suite of office applications (paragraph B)
3 Supports PDF and SWF publishing without plug-ins (paragraph B)
4 Intuitive user interface (paragraph C)
5 Fully compatible with other document formats (paragraph C)
6 Image integration capability (paragraph D)
7 Built-in 2-D and 3-D charting tools (paragraph D)
8 Diagram and special effects functions (paragraph D)

4 Reformulate the product features of the Creole Audio Manager in terms of benefits.

1 Fully integrated multi-format audio and video player
   Creole gives you everything you'd expect from an audio player; watch and play video and music in all popular formats.
2 Downloadable shareware
3 Full PC and Mac compatibility
4 Music search, download and organizer features
5 Online radio and TV capability
6 Built-in CD-burning tool
7 Intuitive user interface and foolproof operation
8 Karaoke function

Internet research

The MP3 player market has huge potential for growth, and China wants its share. Search for the keywords *MP3 player market China* and write a short summary on your findings.

Writing

5 Write a product description of the Earworm2, a portable MP3 player, using the notes below. (Alternatively, use a product of your choice.) Focus on the benefits to consumers, adding any details you feel are appropriate.

Background	Over 30 million Earworm players all over the world New Earworm2 now available Smaller, lighter, stronger, more memory
Overview of benefits	Only 1 cm thick, less than 250 g, 40GBs: take your music everywhere you go – plays up to 20,000 songs
Compatibility	All popular music formats, PC, Mac, subscription services
Details of features and benefits	Attention-grabbing design Shockproof, water-resistant aluminium case 9 cm x 5 cm x 1 cm, 245 g 40 gigabytes storage = 20,000 songs 30-hour autonomy Built-in FM radio Built-in mic for voice recording Large 4 cm x 3 cm LCD screen Intuitive user interface and file management 2-year guarantee
Invitation	2-week no quibble money-back guarantee

3.6 Case study Big Jack's Pizza

Discussion

1 In one minute, list as many fast-food businesses as you can. How does each of them try to differentiate itself from its competitors?

Scan reading

2 Read the documents and answer the questions.

1. What sort of company is Big Jack's Pizza?
2. How many people are involved in the marketing meeting?
3. Who is Jack Jr?
4. What is Big Jack's USP (unique selling point)?
5. What proportion of Big Jack's customers eat in the restaurants?
6. What is the company's development strategy?
7. What is the biggest threat to the company?
8. What do customers like about Big Jack's?
9. What do they dislike?
10. What four changes is Jack Jr suggesting?

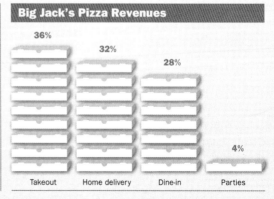

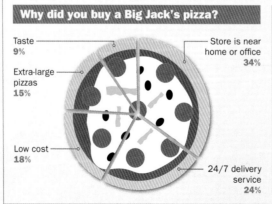

Big Jack's Pizza

Big pizzas, big value!

23 stores in Hong Kong, Kowloon and New Territories
dine-in, parties, takeout or 24/7 home delivery

Call us now on 2893 6161
Become a Big Jack's franchisee - call 2893 5468

Re: Marketing meeting tomorrow

Billie, Mick,

I've attached the latest figures and customer-feedback summary, which seem to confirm what we discussed last time. Restaurant sales are holding up but, as expected, our takeout and delivery revenues are down again this month.

If we want to defend our market share against Pizza Hut and the other international majors, and attract new franchisees, we desperately need to relaunch our product.

So, here's the agenda for the meeting:
1 a new, more exciting range of pizzas
2 new promotional ideas
3 a new or updated logo and color scheme
4 a new box for takeout and delivery

Looking forward to hearing your ideas on all these points tomorrow.

Jack Jr.

President & CEO

Why did you buy a Big Jack's pizza?

- Taste 9%
- Store is near home or office 34%
- Extra-large pizzas 15%
- Low cost 18%
- 24/7 delivery service 24%

Big Jack's Pizza Revenues

Takeout	Home delivery	Dine-in	Parties
36%	32%	28%	4%

Internet research

Search for the keywords *pizza box advertising* to find out how companies are using a new way to get their messages into the home.

Listening for gist

3 🔊 1:42 Listen to an extract from the marketing meeting at Big Jack's. What two decisions are made?

Listening for inference

4 Listen again and list the ten suggestions made by Billie and Mick. Which ones does Jack like?

5 Match the diplomatic phrases on the left with their real, more direct, meanings on the right.

1 Of course, but we can come back to that later?
2 Can we move on to point two?
3 Well, Billie, it's been done before, but I guess we could do that. Why not?
4 I'm sorry?
5 I'm not sure that's a direction we really want to go in.
6 That's more the kind of thing I had in mind.
7 I think you feel strongly about this?
8 Things have changed since Big Jack's time.
9 This is all very interesting, but ...
10 I trust you'll agree.

a) It's not a wonderful idea, but it's a possibility.
b) It's not a priority right now.
c) It's a bad idea.
d) I don't want to waste more time on this.
e) I know we disagree about this.
f) Big Jack's is old-fashioned.
g) What are you talking about?
h) It's not exactly what I wanted, but better than your previous ideas.
i) I've decided, whether you like it or not.
j) This isn't relevant.

Brainstorming and presentation

6 Work in small groups as consultants to Big Jack's Pizza and do the following tasks.

1 Read the brief below from Big Jack's Pizza.
2 Brainstorm and select the best ideas.
3 Prepare a presentation to the company's management.
4 Present your recommendations and take questions from the class.

Recurrent negative customer comments:

'The pizzas all taste the same.'

'Big Jack's is old-fashioned – it's time for a change.'

'The pizzas are too big; I can never finish them.'

'The slices slide around in the box and get stuck together.'

'No different from other pizza houses – same pizzas, same colors, same box, same price.'

Big Jack's Pizza wishes to strengthen its brand and improve its packaging. Please provide advice on the following points:

- a new range of fusion cuisine pizzas: exciting names needed for at least five pizzas
- new promotional ideas
- a new or updated logo, color scheme and slogan
- a new box or box design for takeout and delivery.

Estimated impact of implementing changes on packaging and advertising costs:

- change logo + 2%
- three-color printing + 1%
- four-color printing + 2%
- non-standard box shape + 2%
- non-standard box materials + 2%.

NB Big Jack's will not accept an increase of more than 5%.

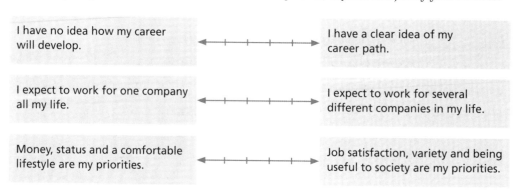

4.1 About business Career choices

Discussion

1 Mark your position on the scales below. With a partner, explain and justify your choices.

| I have no idea how my career will develop. | ←—+—+—+—→ | I have a clear idea of my career path. |

| I expect to work for one company all my life. | ←—+—+—+—→ | I expect to work for several different companies in my life. |

| Money, status and a comfortable lifestyle are my priorities. | ←—+—+—+—→ | Job satisfaction, variety and being useful to society are my priorities. |

Predicting and listening

2 🔊 2:01 You are going to listen to an interview with James Waldroop and Timothy Butler, business psychologists and directors of MBA career development programs at the Harvard Business School. Before you listen to Part 1, try to predict what they will say about the differences between:

1 careers ten or fifteen years ago and careers today
2 a vocation (or 'calling'), a career and a job.

Then listen and check your predictions.

Listening for detail

3 Listen to Part 1 again and answer the questions.

1 What does Waldroop say about the kind of contract:
   a) you had ten or fifteen years ago?   b) you have today?
2 What does Butler say is very dicey or unpredictable?

4 🔊 2:02 Listen to Part 2 of the interview and mark these statements *T* (true) or *F* (false).

1 It's wise to find a compromise between two competing needs. ☐
2 You can have several different values (e.g. earning a lot of money, having a satisfying lifestyle and influencing people) all at the same time. ☐
3 A good career choice is to do something you are good at. ☐
4 Choosing jobs that correspond to your interests is a good way to manage your career. ☐

Discussion

5 In small groups, discuss what these statements from the interview mean for your career.

1 'You are responsible for creating your own career within an organization.'
2 'The most common mistake that people make in their career decisions is to do something because they're "good at it".'

Scan reading

6 Read the article opposite and find which two tips can be summarized as:

1 Move towards your long-term goal in small, easy stages.
2 Make sure that preconceived ideas about success and failure are not preventing you from reaching your goals.

The words in grey are explained in the *Wordlist* on page 153.

Summarizing

7 Summarize each of the eight remaining tips in one sentence. In small groups, compare your sentences with other people and choose the best summary for each tip.

Internet research

In Part 2 of the interview with Timothy Butler, he refers to eight core business functions that correspond to life-interest categories. Search for the keywords "*job sculpting*" to find out what the eight business functions are, and how they are being used to retain valuable employees.

Ten Tips for Creating a Career That
LIGHTS YOUR FIRE

Have you ever found yourself so excited about something that the energy it generates just seems to pull you along? Imagine feeling that every day in the work you do. It's possible! Begin exploring your passions and discovering ways, big or small, to incorporate them into your life.

1 GET TO KNOW YOURSELF – Before you strike off in pursuit of a career that really lights your fire, take some time to do some serious self-exploration.

Make a list of all the things in your life that you have really enjoyed. It could be work or play, an event, a period of time in your life, etc. Pick one and start digging into the reasons why. Get beyond what you love doing, and break it down into the underlying characteristics. Think of it as identifying your passion's building blocks.

2 BRAINSTORM – Once you have a picture of the things that light your fire, brainstorm ways you could incorporate them into your life. Write them down alone or with friends, in one session or on a small pad of paper you carry with you. Above all, be creative. You never know what crazy idea is going to spark the Big One.

3 EXPLORE – Ask, ask, ask! Once you have identified some things you think you might be interested in, identify people who are knowledgeable in those areas and contact them. Explain that you are exploring your options and ask if you can pick their brains. You'll get some fantastic insights if you make this a habit, not to mention making some great contacts along the way.

4 BABY STEPS – The fear of jumping in the deep end of the passion pool keeps many people from swimming at all. Remember there's a shallow end too, so you can still enjoy splashing in the water. Look for baby steps you can take that will bring your passion into your life and keep you moving towards your long-term goal.

5 IDENTIFY YOUR OBSTACLES – What things are getting in your way? Make a list. Maybe they're real – financial obstacles, or perhaps the need for more training. Maybe they

are internal. What's stopping you? Fear? Self-doubt? Simple inertia? We all have voices in our heads that are always telling us 'You can't do that', 'You're not good enough', 'What will they think?', etc. Identifying and acknowledging those voices is the first step in taking their power away.

6 CREATE A PASSION POSSE – In my interviews with people who have followed their dream, the most commonly mentioned success factor has been the support of the people around them. Friends, family and colleagues can all be a great source of support and inspiration. It can be an informal support network, or a regularly scheduled meeting to exchange ideas and brainstorm solutions to challenges.

7 RE-EXAMINE YOUR DEFINITIONS OF SUCCESS AND FAILURE – What is your definition of success? Is it getting in the way? Our culture places a lot of emphasis on material accomplishments, status, etc. Unfortunately, that gets in the way of real happiness for a lot of people, who choose to stay on the treadmill in pursuit of that version of success. Perhaps you're not at a point where you can or want to change that definition of success. That's OK, don't. Instead, try identifying one or two less common ways of identifying 'success' – ones that come from the heart – and try to move towards them as well.

Our definition of failure, which tends to be all or nothing, also gets in the way. If you try something and it doesn't pan out, how do you see that? Is it a failure? Or is it an opportunity to learn? If you 'fail' in an effort to move toward your passion, it's not really failure. Think of it as a step in the right direction. Taking a longer term view can help with this.

8 MAKE A PLAN – Whether it's a high level overview or a granular action plan is up to you – you know how you work best. Creating a plan will force you to think things through and add some comfortable structure to something that can seem very up in the air and undefined.

9 ACT! TODAY! – The fact is, the time will never be right. Something is always going to be less than optimum. Don't wait! Do something right now that will move you toward your passion. What two things can you do right away that will start the ball rolling? They don't need to be earth-shattering, they just need to happen.

10 COMMIT TO MAKING IT HAPPEN – Let it out of your brain and into the open. Say, 'I am going to do this.' Say it out loud to yourself. Say it to a friend. Put it in writing and put it where you can see it. Once it's out in the open it will have room to grow. And that's exactly what you want!

Discussion

1 Rank these benefits from the most to the least desirable, in your opinion.

free medical insurance   company car   luncheon vouchers   profit-sharing   stock options
sports and social facilities   pension plan   free accommodation   Christmas bonus

Careers and employment

2 Put the events in Josef Gutkind's career in chronological order.

☐1 Before graduating, Josef **applied for** jobs in twenty companies.
☐ Josef **was offered a position** as a management trainee.
☐ He **attended a second interview** conducted by a panel of managers.
☐ He **found a new job**, but **was dismissed** after arguing with his boss.
☐ Two years later he **was appointed** Logistics Manager.
☐ He **was short-listed for** a second interview at Wilson Brothers.
☐ While he **was unemployed** Josef studied for a master's degree.
☐ When Wilson's got into difficulties, Josef **was made redundant**.
☐ In his early fifties he **took a sabbatical** to write a book.
☐ He **retired from business** and now lives in the south of France.
☐ Thanks to his enhanced CV, Josef **was hired by** a firm of consultants.
☐ The book was a best-seller, and Josef **resigned from** the firm.

3 Use the expressions in **bold** from the first five sentences above to complete these questions from a job interview. Change the verb form if necessary.

1 Could you tell me exactly why you _____ from OQP?
2 Was that before or after you _____ Quality Manager?
3 After the factory closed, was it difficult to _____?
4 Have you _____ jobs in other companies in the area?
5 Would you be available to _____ next week?
6 How would you feel if we _____ as a product manager?

4 Now correct these sentences from a biography. The words in **bold** have been mixed up.

1 Aisha's résumé was impressive; she was **dismissed** without even attending a first interview.
2 At the second interview, Aisha did so well that she was **made redundant** on the spot.
3 A few years later she wrote her first novel while she was **unemployed**; it sold only 400 copies.
4 Aisha was an unconventional journalist who preferred to work at night; after arriving four hours late for a meeting she was **hired**.
5 When the editor in her next job refused to publish a controversial article she had written, Aisha immediately offered to **retire** but the editor refused to let her.
6 However, when the newspaper was taken over by a larger competitor, Aisha was **short-listed**.
7 After difficult times while she was **on sabbatical**, she was finally able to live in comfort when her sixth novel became a best-seller.
8 She was 74 when she finally decided to **resign** from writing novels.

Internet
research

Search for the keyword *mentoring* to find out how a mentor can help employees with their personal development.

Collocations

5 In each set of five below, match a verb on the left with a noun on the right to make collocations for describing skills and qualities.

1	take	a)	a commitment to
2	make	b)	initiative
3	be	c)	good working relationships
4	work	d)	a good listener
5	build	e)	to strict deadlines
6	work	f)	a busy workload
7	make	g)	ownership
8	manage	h)	closely with
9	possess	i)	a valuable contribution to
10	take on	j)	strong negotiating skills

6 Use eight of the collocations in 5 to complete the sentences below. Change the verb form if necessary.

1 I enjoy taking initiative, and I keep my promises; when I _____ to a project, I always deliver.
2 I have a lot of experience in _____ both product development and sales teams, and can adapt to their different working styles.
3 I have excellent organizational skills, and I hate being late – so I have no problem with _____.
4 I liaise with government officials: fortunately, I _____.
5 I'm used to _____; I'm good at multitasking, and coping with pressure is no problem.
6 I often _____ of projects with multi-million dollar budgets.
7 I believe I can _____ any work group.
8 I _____, so I build good working relationships with colleagues.

7 Which two answers in 6 could you give to each of these questions?

a) Are you able to take responsibility?
b) Are you a good communicator?
c) Are you a good time manager?
d) Are you a good team worker?

Listening for gist

8 📀 2:03 Listen to an extract from a human resources review meeting. Mark these employees as high-fliers (+) or as concerns (-).

Rachel Ratcliff
Paul Stevens
Michael Diegel
Shane Garney

Taking notes

9 Listen again. For Rachel, Michael and Shane, take notes for each case on the problem, causes and possible solutions.

	Rachel	Michael	Shane
problem			
causes			
possible solutions			

Discussion

10 In small groups, decide what you would do about Rachel, Michael and Shane.

Present simple
She works in London.
permanent present
actions or situations

Present continuous
She's travelling in Asia.
temporary present
actions or situations

Present perfect simple
She's travelled 10,000 kilometres.
life experience up to now, or present result of a past action

Present perfect continuous
She's been visiting suppliers.
action in progress up to now

▶ Grammar reference page 124

4.3 Grammar   Present tenses

Test yourself: Present tenses

1 Present simple (*do / does*) or present continuous (*am / are / is doing*)? Identify and correct the 12 errors.

Jane Houseman is considering herself a happy woman. Based in London, she works as a project manager for Arbol Oil, a South American oil company which expands rapidly, especially in Asia. Jane loves travelling; at the moment she works on a project in China, which is meaning she is flying out to Beijing about once a month. She is already speaking fluent Spanish, and she learns Chinese. She isn't meeting the two other project managers in her department very often, because they are finishing a project in Saudi Arabia, but they all get on very well and are talking two or three times a week by telephone. Jane is also following an MBA course; she is submitting coursework by email and is attending three intensive weeks per year in London. Financially, Jane feels very lucky: right now, she is earning twice what most of her friends from university are bringing home, and the company is paying for her MBA. In many ways, Jane is believing she has the perfect job.

2 Present perfect (*have / has done*) or past simple (*did*)? Put the verbs in brackets in the correct form.

Jane (1) _____ (be) in her present position for six years. After she (2) _____ (leave) university, she (3) _____ (work) as a management trainee for four years in another oil company; she (4) _____ (never regret) the move to Arbol, since they (5) _____ (immediately put) her on their fast-track scheme for employees with the potential to become high-fliers. But today Jane faces a dilemma. In the last three weeks she (6) _____ (receive) no less than three proposals. First, her boss, an Argentinian, who Jane has always had an enormous respect for, suddenly announced his resignation. Jane (7) _____ (be) shocked and surprised, especially when, just a few days later, Arbol's HR Manager (8) _____ (call) to offer her the position. The second proposal (9) _____ (arrive) that same evening: Estelle, one of Jane's friends from the MBA course, who (10) _____ (already work) for several large multinationals, (11) _____ (invite) her to become a partner in a new consultancy. Last, but by no means least, Jane's boyfriend, Howard, (12) _____ (just ask) her to marry him. Not surprisingly, Jane has asked for more time to think about each of the proposals.

3 Present perfect simple (*have / has done*) or continuous (*have / has been doing*)? Put the verbs in brackets in the correct form. Each pair of answers (e.g. 1a and 1b) should have one simple and one continuous form.

Since she left university, Jane (1a) _____ (prefer) to live alone. For the last three years, she (1b) _____ (look) for a property to buy, and she (2a) _____ (just pay) a deposit on a small house near Heathrow airport. Suddenly she no longer knows if she is doing the right thing: all three of the proposals mean major changes in her lifestyle. She (2b) _____ (hope) for a promotion at Arbol; she (3a) _____ (try) to schedule an appraisal interview for months, and now she understands why her boss (3b) _____ (repeatedly postpone) it. But taking on her boss' job would undoubtedly mean moving to South America, probably losing the deposit on the house, and quite possibly losing Howard.

Howard is a divorcee with two young children; although Jane (4a) _____ (play) mum to the two kids, it (4b) _____ (never occur) to her that she might move them all to South America. On the other hand, Howard is a wonderful father; Jane has to admit to herself that she (5a) _____ (sometimes wonder) whether she should start a family before it's too late. And what about Estelle's proposal? Jane (5b) _____ (think) about running her own business ever since she was at school. After all, she (6a) _____ (not spend) most of her free time working on the MBA just to be a small cog in Arbol's big machine for the rest of her life! Jane sits down and pours herself another coffee. She (6b) _____ (already have) ten cups today, but she's no nearer a solution now than after the first cup.

Internet research

Search for the keywords *English grammar practice* to explore the many websites offering grammar explanations and exercises. In class, hold a vote to find your favourite grammar site.

Present perfect and past simple

4 You and your partner work for an international recruitment agency. Your clients are looking for:

1 a Spanish-speaking science graduate
2 an undergraduate with marketing experience
3 a graduate accountant, to be a future finance director
4 a French-speaking graduate in business
5 an arts undergraduate with experience in Asia
6 a Portuguese-speaking graduate with experience in sales.

You have each interviewed and tested five candidates. Exchange information with your partner to complete the tables and decide together which candidates are most suitable for each request.

Student A: use the information below.
Student B: turn to page 113.

Candidate	Graduation	Work experience	Management potential test
Mr Salmon	next summer, Chemistry	pullover sales in Mexico	B
Ms Bianco			
Mrs Grey	next June, Marketing	nurse in New York	B
Miss Rose			
Mr Da Silva	last December, MBA	own business in Brazil	C-
Mr Green			
Mr Schwartz	last October, Accountancy	banks in Geneva, Monaco, Portugal	A+
Miss Plum			
Ms Violeta	next spring, History	holiday club in Thailand	B
Mr Braun			

Listening: present perfect simple and continuous

5 🎧 2:04–2:13 Listen to ten situations and write down what has happened or has been happening in each. Then compare your ideas with a partner.

Asking questions

6 With a partner, take turns interviewing each other for a job.

Student A: turn to page 111.
Student B: turn to page 115.

4.4 Speaking Job interviews

Discussion

1 How would you answer the following interview questions?

1 Where do you see yourself in five years' time?
2 How would you manage working with someone who doesn't like you?
3 How do you motivate people to do their best?
4 What are your weaknesses?
5 Can you give an example of a situation you found stressful, and how you coped with the stress?

Listening

2 🔊 2:14–2:18 Listen to extracts from five job interviews A–E. Which candidate(s):

1 express the wish to make a long-term commitment?
2 give concrete examples from their experience?
3 ask questions to make sure they answer the interviewer's question?
4 structure the answer in two parts?
5 turn a question about a negative point into an opportunity to emphasize a positive quality?

3 Listen again and complete the useful expressions for answering job interview questions.

Asking for clarification / reformulating	I'm sorry, could you expand on what you mean by …
	Do you _____ , how do I …?
Playing for time	That's a very interesting question. I would say …
	That's a _____ question to _____; let's _____ _____ that …
Structuring your answer	I'd like to answer that in two ways: firstly, … secondly, …
	I think _____ _____ _____ important _____ to this _____.
Giving concrete examples	Let me give you an example of what I mean.
	Take … , for _____.
Validating your answer	Is that what you wanted to know?
	Does that _____ your _____?

4 The candidates in 2 used these expressions. Put the words in **bold** in the correct order.

1 I applied **what learned I.**
2 I'm able **being unpopular with to cope**.
3 I see myself **performing as top a a employee company in leading**.
4 I plan **experience to gain new and skills learn**.
5 I would be ready **more a move to position up with to responsibility**.
6 I realized that knowing **well you're how motivated essential doing is to staying**.
7 I'm aware **there that on that areas are can I improve**.
8 I don't feel **weaknesses I any have that significant**.
9 I would say **my organization is that one of strengths**.
10 I managed **on finish to the time project**.

5 Read the quotation and mark the interview questions a)–h) as type *1* or type *2* questions.

'The good news is that there are only two interview questions. That is, regardless of what you're asked, the employer really only wants to know:

1 What value can you add to my enterprise as an employee (and can you prove it)?
2 Why do you want this job?'

a) What are your strengths and weaknesses? ☐
b) Why do you want to work for us? ☐
c) What is your greatest achievement? ☐
d) How do you make sure things get done? ☐
e) Why do you want to leave your present job? ☐
f) Tell me about a time when you successfully handled a difficult situation. ☐
g) What sort of environment would you prefer not to work in? ☐
h) What are the most difficult kinds of decisions for you to make? ☐

With a partner, ask and answer the questions using expressions from 3 and 4, inventing any details as necessary.

Roleplay

6 With a partner, roleplay interviews for one of the jobs below.

Interviewer
Interview the candidate for the job they have chosen. Invent further information about the job as necessary. For each of your questions, note whether the answer is satisfactory or not. At the end of the interview, give the candidate feedback on how well they performed.

Candidate
Let the interviewer lead the conversation initially, but try to develop an exchange by asking questions about the job and the organization.

4.5 Writing A CV

Discussion

1 Discuss why you agree or disagree with the following statements about writing CVs or résumés.

1 You should always state your career objective.
2 You should list five or six people who can be contacted for a reference.
3 You should never use more than one page.
4 You should describe your experience first, then your qualifications.

Skim reading

2 Decide in what order you expect the following categories to occur in a CV. Then read the CV below to check.

☐ work experience ☐ references ☐ personal details ☐ qualifications
☐ voluntary roles / positions of responsibility ☐ general / additional skills

Robert Khan

Date of birth	29 April 1985
Nationality	British
Current address	27 Keats Road, London SE4 3KL
(until 30 June)	Tel: 020 8088 8965
Permanent address	247 Newmarket Road, Norwich NR4 1ET
	Tel: 01603 443143

EDUCATION

2004–2007	BA in Business Studies at Chelsea School of Business (Exam results to date 2:2; Expected final grade 2:1)
2001–2003	Norwich School: 3 'A' levels: Economics (A), Maths (B), History (C)
1997–2001	Norwich School: 10 GCSEs, including Maths and English

WORK HISTORY

Jan–June 2006	*Work placement, Atherton Consultants* I played an integral part in a team of consultants working on IS projects. This position required familiarity with networking solutions and Web design and involved liaising with a client's parent company in Germany.
July–Sept 2005	*Vacation Trainee, Jardine, White & Partners* I coordinated an office reorganization project.
2003–2004	*Sales Assistant, Kaufhaus des Westens, Berlin* I was responsible for managing the outdoor exhibition of camping equipment. I ran a language training programme for members of the department.

POSITIONS OF RESPONSIBILITY

2005–2006	*President of CSB Students' Union* I represented over 400 members in faculty meetings and organized and chaired conferences with visiting speakers.
2005 to present	*Captain of CSB Squash Team* I run training sessions and am responsible for organizing matches and motivating the team.

OTHER

	Fluent German Advanced computer literacy: Office software, networking and Web design 3rd trombone in the London Students' Jazz Orchestra Clean driving licence

REFERENCES

	See next page

Search for the keywords *résumé style* to find out about different résumé styles to consider, including *functional*, *skills* and *chronological* styles.

Reading for detail

3 Read the CV again. How has Robert formulated the following information in more appropriate language?

1　I sometimes phoned people in Germany.
2　I'm good with computers.
3　I was the contact for the removal company for the transfer to new offices.
4　I gave some colleagues some English lessons.
5　I spoke on behalf of 400 students in meetings with teachers.
6　I was the general assistant to the computer consultants.
7　I sold tents.
8　I had to learn how to set up a LAN.
9　I'm the only member of the team who believes we can win.
10　My job was to introduce the speakers and thank them at the end.

Ordering and reformulating

4 Using the headings in Robert Khan's CV as a model, decide where to put each piece of information below. Then write the CV, presenting the information appropriately and using relevant language and expressions.

- Voluntary work since 2005 – OUTLOOK, charity for disabled children – parties, visits, etc.
- Play violin in string quartet
- University basketball team – my job to bring drinks
- 2002–2004 Northern High School 'A' level Maths (A), Economics (B), French (B)
- Secretary, Newcastle Junior Chamber of Commerce in 2006 – minutes of meetings, monthly newsletter, etc. Sometimes phoned VIPs to invite to receptions, etc.
- June–Sept 2004 Holiday job, Newcastle Social Security; entered personnel data into new HR management software. Confidential, very boring. Visitor from Spanish government, three days.
- References – tutor, Mr. Bowers, Newcastle University, Mrs Broadbent, Principal, Northern High School
- Typing speed 90 wpm
- Justine Dominga Collier
- 14 Green Street, Newcastle NE13 8BH   Tel: 01879 122 7789
- Oct–Mar 2005 Internship Arbol Oil: finance department, small jobs, learned accounts software, email from S America
- Bilingual Spanish
- 4/11/86, Auckland NZ
- 2004–2007 BA Economics, Newcastle University (maybe 2:1 if I'm lucky)

5 Write (or update) your own CV.

4.6 Case study — Gap years and career breaks

Brainstorming

1 Brainstorm the advantages and disadvantages of taking a year off before or after university or in mid-career. How many different ways of spending a gap year can you think of?

Listening

2 🔊 2:19–2:24 Listen to six interviews with people who took a gap year and answer the questions.

1 When and where did they take their year out?
2 Were their experiences positive, negative or mixed? Why?

Scan reading

3 Read the advertisement and answer the questions.

1 Who can apply for a gap-year placement, and when?
2 What are the four benefits of a gap-year placement mentioned in the advertisement?
3 What kind of work is available?
4 Do you get paid / have to pay?
5 How do you apply?

Want to change the world,
or just want a change?

Whether you are still a student or already in work, a gap-year placement is a unique opportunity to broaden your horizons, enhance your CV and step back from your studies or career to decide what you want to do with your life. Perhaps more importantly, a gap-year placement is the chance to do something concrete and tangible to help people in need in underprivileged areas of the world.

Placements are designed for people over 17 years of age, and run for six or nine months throughout the world. All placements begin with an intensive orientation course to help you find your feet; for some countries, an optional ten-day intensive language course is recommended. Participants work as volunteers in sectors such as education, conservation, medical support and care work. Food and accommodation are provided, but participants pay their own travel costs.

To apply, choose your destination and complete and send in the application form (downloadable from our website www.gapyearplacement.org) together with your CV. Please note that, due to an increasing number of applications, places cannot be guaranteed. Shortlisted candidates will be invited to attend a selection interview in their country of residence.

Reading and discussion

4 Read the four descriptions of gap-year placements. With a partner, explain which one(s) you'd prefer to go on, and why. Why wouldn't you like to go on the others?

Writing and roleplay

5 You are going to take turns interviewing and being interviewed for www.gapyearplacement.org. First complete the application form, then follow the steps below.

---

application form
www.gapyearplacement.org

Name: _____

Current occupation: _____

A Describe your previous participation in any organization, your experiences in other countries and your contact with persons of other nationalities, races and cultures.

_____

_____

B What are your main reasons for spending a year abroad and why have you applied for a gap-year placement?

_____

_____

C What is your preferred destination and type of voluntary work?

_____

---

1 Divide into A Groups and B Groups of four students each.
2 Three students from Group A interview one student from Group B. At the same time, three students from Group B interview one student from Group A. Use the completed application forms above (and CVs, if available) for the interviews.
3 When the first interview is finished, a different person from each group goes to the other group to be interviewed. The interview panel will, therefore, be slightly different each time.
4 When all the interviews are finished, decide in your groups which candidates have been successful.
5 Group A and Group B join together and give the candidates feedback on why their applications have or have not been successful.

Care Work in South Africa

Population: 45 million
Official Language: 11 official languages, including English and Afrikaans
Placement: Schools for 4 to 18 year olds with special needs
Job: Classroom assistant in a special needs school, providing classroom support and working on an individual basis with children with mental and physical disabilities.
Working week: 45 hours, some evening duties.

Conservation in Malaysia

Population: 24 million
Official Language: Bahasa Melayu
Main Religion: Islam
Placement: Conservation work
Job: Various conservation projects: construction and maintenance of trails, identification of species, eco-tourism projects, organic farms, animal sanctuaries, turtle-conservation projects. Work is physically demanding.

Care Work in Costa Rica

Population: 4 million
Official Language: Spanish (Indian languages and Patois also spoken)
Main Religion: Roman Catholic
Placement: Care work
Job: Care-work placements in homes for children with disabilities or orphanages: assisting individual children, organizing activities, helping with lessons or assisting at meal times. Intensive Spanish language course recommended.

Teaching in Tanzania

Population: 37 million – over 129 tribes
Official Language: Swahili and English
Main Religion: Christianity and Islam
Placement: Teaching in primary or secondary schools
Job: Teaching five days a week: all subjects, including sport and drama. Participants must have excellent English. Four weeks' school holidays per year.

Review 3

Products and packaging

1 Fill in the missing vowels in these adjectives.

1 Today's marketplace is highly c_mp_t_t_v_.
2 Packaging has to be _ttr_ct_v_, _ff_ct_v_ and d_st_nct_v_.
3 Packaging is cr_t_c_l to make sure there is _ff_c__nt use of l_m_t_d shelf space.
4 An _r_g_n_l idea can turn out to be _mpr_ct_c_l for reasons of t_chn_c_l limitations.

2 Complete the sentences using words from the box.

| chance | communication | field | issues |
| needs | process | sale | solution | view |

1 Packaging is the manufacturer's last _____ to seduce the customer.
2 Many products are identical from the consumer's point of _____.
3 Most purchasing decisions are made at the point of _____.
4 The principal problem is a lack of _____ between the people involved in the design and development _____.
5 There are different groups of experts, all working in their own specialized _____.
6 Production people know nothing about consumer _____.
7 The manufacturing people deal with the technical _____ as and when they arise.
8 Our task forces can deliver an optimal _____ in one week, sometimes less.

3 In each set of four below, match a verb on the left with a noun on the right to make collocations about product development.

1 generate   the product onto the market
2 screen out   new ideas in focus groups
3 launch   specifications for the product
4 draw up   unfeasible or unprofitable ideas

5 conduct   production on a large scale after tests
6 draw   market studies
7 go into   sketches and build mockups
8 test   the product by using it in typical situations

4 Fill in the missing letters to complete these nouns about dimensions.

1 It's 45 cm **long**. = Its l_____ is 45 cm.
2 It's 31 cm **wide**. = Its w____ is 31 cm.
3 It's 8 cm **high**.   = Its h_____ is 8 cm.
4 It **weighs** 9 kg.   = Its w_____ is 9 kg.

5 Match each word in the box to its definition 1–5. Then translate the words into your language.

| benefit | feature | function | specification |
| USP (unique selling point) | | | |

1 The thing that makes a product special or different from others: _____
2 An important, interesting or typical part of something: _____

3 A detailed instruction about how something should be made: _____
4 An advantage that you get from something: _____
5 The job that something is designed to do: _____

6 Join the sentences using *who* (for people), *that* (for things) or *whose*.

1 Here's the email. I got it this morning.
Here's the email that I got this morning.
2 Here's the email. It arrived this morning.
_____
3 The team leader is an interesting man. He comes from Spain.
_____
4 The team leader is an interesting man. I met him yesterday.
_____
5 The team leader is an interesting man. His background is in IT.
_____

7 In the previous exercise, put brackets around any examples of *who* or *that* that are not necessary.

8 Make noun phrases from the following definitions.

1 A cycle for developing a product is a *product development cycle*.
2 A document that shows you have insurance for travel is a _____.
3 A concept for the design of packaging is a _____.
4 A product used for cleaning households is a _____.

9 Underline the correct word(s) in **bold** to make phrases for a product presentation.

1 After that, I'll **go / go on** to present …
2 And now, if you have any questions, I'll do my best to **answer / respond** them.
3 My **reason / objective** today is …
4 **Final / Finally**, I'm going to …
5 First of all, **I / I'll** talk about …
6 Thank you for **listening / your listening**.
7 I've divided my presentation **by / into** three sections.
8 Please **make / feel** free to interrupt me.
9 So, in summary, these are the **reasons / motives** why I am asking you to …

10 Put phrases 1–9 from the previous exercise into the order that you would probably hear them.

11 Rearrange the words to make diplomatic phrases used in a meeting.

1 can to that later come back we?
_____
2 we want to go in that's a direction I'm not sure.
_____
3 that's the more mind of thing I had in kind.
_____

Review 4

1 Finish each phrase about careers with the best collocation from the right-hand column.

1	make a career	application
2	reach your long-term	bonus
3	prefer money rather than job	choice
4	learn new	experience
5	gain	goal
6	get a performance-related	placement
7	send off a job	satisfaction
8	apply for a gap-year	skills

2 Fill in the missing letters in these words which all have a meaning similar to *goal*.

1 clear / annual / production / sales t_____s
2 limited / clear / specific / business o_____s
3 the overall / main / sole / underlying __m

3 Match each word in the box to its definition below. Then translate the words into your language.

> aptitude   background   experience
> know-how   knowledge   skill

1 Knowledge that you need to be able to do something: _____
2 Information that someone knows: _____
3 An ability to do something well, especially because you have practised it: _____
4 Knowledge or skill you get from being in different situations: _____
5 The type of education, experience and family that you have: _____
6 A natural ability to do something well or to learn it quickly: _____

4 The expressions in the box refer to losing your job.

> be dismissed   be fired   be laid off
> be made redundant   be sacked

1 Which three suggest it was your fault?
_____, _____, _____
2 Which of these three is more formal? _____
3 Which two expressions suggest it was not your fault?
_____, _____
4 Which of these two is British English? _____

5 Fill in the missing letters in these words about careers.

1 be sh___-li___d for a second interview
2 re___n from a job because you have a better offer in another company
3 a____d an interview on Friday morning
4 be app_____d to a more senior position after some time in the company
5 be h__ed by a company after a successful interview
6 a___y for a job in a company

6 Put each verb into the correct form: present simple (*do / does*), present continuous (*am / are / is doing*), present perfect (*have / has done*) or past simple (*did*). Each form is used twice.

'I'm really busy this morning – I (1) _____ (interview) three candidates for that sales job – the second one is outside now. Yesterday was even worse. I (2) _____ (interview) five candidates in two hours, and none of them were any good. Let me see, over the last ten days I think I (3) _____ (interview) sixteen candidates. Just imagine! And every time I (4) _____ (interview) someone there's a CV to read, questions to prepare, records to keep. It just never ends. Right now, I (5) _____ (need) a break. (6) _____ (anyone / see) that travel brochure about holidays in the Seychelles? I know I (7) _____ (put) it somewhere. Wait a minute. There's no-one here. I (8) _____ (talk) to myself.'

7 Put each verb into the correct form: present perfect (*have / has done*) or present perfect continuous (*have / has been doing*).

1 I _____ (write) my CV all morning, and finally I _____ (finish) it.
2 I _____ (write) four job applications this week. One day I must get lucky – I _____ (try) to find a job for ages.

8 Make nouns from the adjectives and verbs below.

1 strong (adj): _____
2 weak (adj): _____
3 responsible (adj): _____
4 perform (v): _____
5 commit (v): _____
6 achieve (v): _____

9 Use each noun from the previous exercise to complete these questions from a job interview. Some have a plural form.

1 What are your main functions and duties in your present job? What are your _____?
2 How does the company know you are doing a good job? How do they measure your _____?
3 What are the positive things you can bring to the team? What are your _____?
4 And what would you say are your _____? Come on, be honest now.
5 What is the one thing you are most proud of in your present job? What is your greatest _____?
6 If we offer you this job, what kind of _____ will you have to the company? Will you be looking for another job after a year or two?

5 | Making deals

Discussion

1 In small groups, discuss these questions.

1 Do you prefer shopping in a store or on a website? Why?
2 According to Jupiter Research, 'Less than 5% of people visiting a website ever turn into paying customers.' What can e-tailers do to make visitors actually buy products?

Scan reading

2 Compare your ideas about the second question in 1 with those in the article opposite. The words in grey are explained in the *Wordlist* on page 155.

Reading for detail

3 Read the article again and put these paragraph summaries in the correct order.

☐ Animated sales reps are cheaper than real people and can increase sales by one third.
☐ Though interactive discussion boosts sales, e-tailers have to be cautious.
☐ Only a very small percentage of visits to websites produce sales.
☐ Customer tracking is often badly perceived by online shoppers, who may prefer to shop privately.
☐ Live web chats with sales reps double online sales.
☐ Customer-tracking systems can provide help for customers when it is appropriate.

Roleplay

4 With a partner, roleplay newspaper interviews with a New York University researcher and an Overstock customer-service rep using information from the article opposite.

Student A: turn to page 112.
Student B: turn to page 116.

Student A: turn to page 112.
Student B: turn to page 116.

Listening

5 🔊 2:25 Listen to a chat show discussion about conversational agents and mark these statements *T* (true) or *F* (false).

1 Hermelinda's job is to help e-tailers increase their sales. ☐
2 Advertising on the Internet increases traffic but not necessarily sales. ☐
3 Small e-businesses can't afford conversational agents. ☐
4 Conversational agents are intelligent computer programs. ☐
5 Fifty per cent of customers are happy to talk to a machine. ☐
6 Giving customers more information increases the chance of making a sale. ☐
7 For customers, hearing a conversational agent speak and reading a website has the same effect. ☐

Discussion

6 In small groups, discuss the questions.

1 Would you prefer to interact with a conversational agent, to chat online with a real sales rep, or to browse without help? Why?
2 Do you think conversational agents are appropriate or useful for all e-tailing sites? Why (not)?
3 Suggest characters for online conversational agents on the following websites.

> Amazon (books)   Dell (computers)   Oréal (cosmetics)
> General Motors   The Tourism Authority of Thailand

Think about profession, age, looks and what they would be wearing.

Don't mind if I do ...

E-tailing:
It's all about service

Turning surfers into shoppers requires new levels of help online. The trick is providing it without seeming to be too pushy.

Today, most websites are easy to use and provide reliable and cost-effective shipping. But despite e-tailers' best efforts, lots of 'eyeballs' out there still aren't necessarily translating into sales. According to Jupiter Research, less than 5% of people visiting a website ever turn into paying customers. And if the rest have clicked through a paid search ad without buying anything, bringing them to the site actually costs the website money.

SMOTHERED WITH LOVE How to convert these window shoppers into paying customers? Overstock.com believes in customer service. It now has 60 highly trained customer-service reps, about 20 to 30 of whom staff a 24-hours-a-day department to answer customer questions via live web chats on the site. When a customer engages in a live chat with a sales rep, the average purchase doubles in value, Overstock has found. 'We're all about smothering the customer with love,' says Overstock CEO Patrick Byrne.

'... smothering the customer with love.'

Then there's LivePerson, a publicly-traded New York firm that makes customer-tracking software. What's most cool about LivePerson's technology is that it follows what customers are doing and can automatically flag and offer help to e-customers based on rules individual e-tailers set.

ANIMATED CHARACTERS Other small, private companies, like Oddcast in New York and Pulse in San Francisco, offer animated characters who act as sales reps on e-tail sites, drawing from a databank of voice answers to commonly asked questions. Oddcast's 'SitePal' has been adopted by many smaller retailers who can't afford as many live customer-service reps as Overstock. Software e-tailer Goldfish Software credits its animated sales rep with converting 33% more of its browsers into buyers.

OPPOSITES ONLINE Other sites are closely watching how people navigate a site, and testing out what pages or promotions work best with different customer groups. But seller beware: research done by New York University's Stern School of Business has found most shoppers consider tracking without their consent a violation of their privacy. When in a store, a customer has no expectation of privacy. But when someone is shopping online, he or she is usually at home or at work. A sales rep barging into your shopping experience can feel like an invasion of privacy. 'This is a lot about expectations,' says NYU Marketing Professor Eric Greenleaf. 'You feel like it's private when you're at home, as opposed to being in a store.'

RULES FOR CHATTING Overstock limits chats to about 10% of its customers, even though sales rise briskly with customers who are engaged in an interactive discussion of products. Says Tad Martin, Senior Vice-president for Merchandising and Operations at Overstock: 'We're taking the conservative approach right now. We don't want to be intrusive.'

5 | Making deals

Internet research

Search for the key words "principled negotiation" to find out about a popular approach to negotiation.

Discussion

1 'You can do everything in an e-store that you can do in a high-street store, except touch the product.' Do you agree? What can you do in an e-store that you can't do in a high-street store?

Collocations

2 Complete the collocations for negotiating by choosing the correct noun in the boxes for each group of three verbs.

the benefits   a price   an order   a proposal   the details   a discount

place		bring down		offer	
take	1 _An order_	quote	2 _a price_	ask for	3 _discount_
fill		state		grant	

see		sort out		make	6 _a proposal_
sell	4 _the_	discuss	5 _the details_	firm up	
explain	_benefits_	go over		reject	

fee   a compromise   negotiation   a deadline   a deposit   costs

subject to		pay		a monthly	
open to	7 _negotiation_	require	8 _a deposit_	an annual	9 _fee_
under		put down		an entrance	

hidden		meet		seek	12 _compromise_
extra	10 _costs_	miss	11 _deadline_	offer	
fixed		extend		find	

Listening

3 🔊 2:26–2:33 Listen to eight extracts from negotiations. Use one of the collocations in 2 to describe what is happening in each situation.

Then write two similar extracts illustrating two more of the collocations. Read them to a partner, who should try to identify the collocations you are referring to.

Pronunciation

4 🔊 2:34–2:38 Listen to these phrases you heard in 3. Each contains examples of /ə/(schwa), the neutral sound used for unimportant, unstressed sounds, for example the first and last sounds in the word *another*. Underline the /ə/ sounds in each phrase.

1   five hundred at 12 euros a box
2   two and a half thousand
3   an extra 2%
4   five or six weeks a year
5   We usually ask for 20% now.

Now practise saying the phrases with the correct pronunciation.

5 Put these steps in an e-tail transaction into the correct chronological order.

☐ The customer prices similar products on other sites.
☐ The product is shipped to the customer's address by mail or express carrier.
☐ The seller exchanges the product or gives a refund.
☐ The customer goes to the check-out and pays by credit card.
☐ The website records the transaction and generates an invoice.
☐ The customer selects a product and places it in a cart.
☐ The customer sends the faulty product back under guarantee.
☐ The customer's credit card account is debited.
☐ The customer clicks on the link to the seller's site.
☐ The prospective customer looks up the product on a search engine.
☐ The customer browses the site and identifies the product which interests him.
☐ The website sends an instruction to the warehouse to ship the product.

6 In each email, correct the words in **bold** which a computer virus has mixed up.

Dear Sir or Madam

I am writing to complain about the service from your lowlowprice.biz website. Last month I ordered a DVD; you then took three weeks to ship the (a) **site**. While I was waiting for delivery, I browsed another (b) **product**, which advertised the same DVD for only half the price. I have also priced the (c) **credit** on several other sites, all cheaper than yours. Finally, when I checked my bank statement, I noticed that you have debited my (d) **product** card twice! Please correct this error as soon as possible.

Mary Brotherton

Dear Ms Brotherton

Please accept our apologies for the errors you have experienced. Unfortunately our computer recorded your (a) **link** twice, and therefore generated two (b) **refunds**. Usually our prices are the lowest on the Web; when this is not the case, we are happy to give full (c) **product**. Please send the (d) **transaction** back and we will credit your account for the full amount. (Click on the (e) **invoices** below for the return address.)

Customer Service Department
www.lowlowprice.biz

Listening for detail

7 🔊 2.39 Listen to part of a negotiation and read the minutes below. Find the differences between the collocations in **bold** in the minutes, and the similar ones used in the negotiation.

- Ben (1) **got down to business** saying that although Jacky had (2) **pointed out the advantages** of the policy, he was not happy with certain issues. Jacky asked which (3) **questions** Ben wanted to **discuss**, and Ben asked him to (4) **clarify his comments** about returns.

- Jacky (5) **summarized the position**, saying that the policy only covered damage during shipping, and not damage caused by the customer. Ben asked for an extension of cover, and Jacky offered to (6) **make a proposal**, but at extra cost. Ben stressed that he was hoping to (7) **work out a solution**, but also threatened to (8) **consider other options**.

- Jacky suggested they (9) **break for coffee** while his team did a simulation. He reassured Ben that they would (10) **find an agreement**.

Discussion

8 Tell a partner about a time when you had difficulty reaching an agreement with someone. Talk about the different stages in the discussion, and if and what you eventually agreed.

5 | Making deals

First conditional
if + present simple,
(then) + *will* + *do*
likely future events

▶ Grammar reference page 126

Second conditional
if + past simple, *(then)* +
would + *do*
unlikely future events

▶ Grammar reference page 127

*recommend / suggest /
advise*
recommend / suggest
something
recommend / suggest
something *to* someone
recommend / suggest
(not) doing something
recommend / suggest
(that) someone *do*
something
advise someone *(not) to*
do something
advise (not) doing
something

▶ Grammar reference page 127

Test yourself: Conditionals

1 Choose the best form of the verb *go* to complete each sentence, using negatives and questions where necessary.

1 If the money was right, I _____ and work anywhere in the world.
2 We'll lose customers if we _____ down to our competitors' prices.
3 Unless we get a really good deal, we _____ to the conference this year.
4 They wouldn't agree to our request, unless we _____ some way towards their position.
5 If we paid cash, _____ (you) down to $25,000?
6 If you _____ to our competitors, you won't get a better deal than with us.
7 Providing the budget _____ over €500,000, we will accept.
8 If we pay all your expenses, _____ (you) over there to set up the system?

2 Decide in which example below a discount is a) possible b) probable c) sure.

1 If you increased your order, then we might consider offering a discount.
2 If you increase your order, then we will offer a discount.
3 If you increase your order, then we should be able to offer a discount.

3 Circle the word in **bold** which is best in each sentence.

1 Would you like to work abroad?
   Sure, **unless / only if / providing** it was in a nice, warm country!
2 I couldn't just stay at home all day, **unless / only if / providing** I found something really interesting to do.
3 I might consider it, but **unless / only if / providing** the money was really good.

Test yourself: *recommend / suggest / advise*

4 Correct these sentences by deleting one word from each as in the example.

1 What options would you recommend ~~me~~?
2 I suggest you to take the dust-proof control unit: it's specially designed for industrial environments.
3 Would you advise me choosing the 750W or the 1,000W motor?
4 We generally suggest you allowing for a little extra power.
5 We recommend you not exceeding 9,000 rpm in the first two weeks.
6 I would advise that you to check the oil level at least once a week.
7 Our parent company recommends it that we do not buy from non-ISO-certified suppliers.
8 In that case, I would suggest your Quality Manager to visit us before placing an order.

Reformulating

5 Reformulate these sentences using the **bold** words.

1 We can only deliver by 1 July if we receive a 30% deposit within ten days. (**unable**, **unless**)
We are unable to deliver by 1 July unless we receive a 30% deposit within ten days.

2 Our production manager will agree to make the changes, as long as you supply a prototype. (**willing**, **providing**)

3 We might consider a larger discount, on one condition: that you pay in advance. (**reluctant**, **unless**)

4 We would not wish to sponsor the exhibition unless we had a large stand in the entrance hall. (**prepared**, **but only if**)

5 Providing we can get the sub-components in time, we will be able to meet the deadline. (**unless**, **impossible**)

6 If, and only if, several other top CEOs were present, our president would agree to attend. (**as long as**, **available**)

Discussion

6 With a partner, ask and answer these questions, following the example.

1 Would you recommend working abroad for a few years and, if so, where?
I would certainly recommend it, providing it was a good career move and, personally, I would suggest going to an English-speaking country. What do you think?

2 Would you advise working for non-profit organizations and, if so, which ones?

3 Would you recommend that people work part-time?

4 How would you advise a manager who wants to be popular?

5 What do you suggest young people do to become millionaires?

Listening

7 🔊 2:40 Two colleagues in a sales department, Jan and Petra, are negotiating a list of responsibilities they have to share. Listen and write *J* (Jan) or *P* (Petra) next to the points they agree on.

☐ tennis tournament with customer
☐ conference in Madagascar
☐ presentation to 2,000 shareholders
☐ take holiday in August
☐ open office at 6am
☐ supervise intern for six months

☐ run exhibition stand in Kazakhstan
☐ team-building course in Siberia
☐ relocate call centre manager to India
☐ take holiday in January
☐ close office at 10pm
☐ share office with PR Manager

Negotiating

8 With a partner, try to negotiate an agreement on the remaining points in the list above.

5.4 Speaking   Negotiations – bargaining

Discussion

1 In one minute, negotiate the sale of your bicycle / computer / musical instrument / other item to a partner.

Did you win or lose the negotiation? Why? Is there always a winner and a loser?

Listening

2 2:41 Listen to Part 1 of a negotiation and answer the questions.

1 What does Harry Petersen's company do?
2 What services are included in the package Ingrid's company offers?
3 How does Harry intend to deliver products?
4 How will Holman Multimedia charge for their services?
5 What are the advantages for Harry of working with Holman Multimedia?
6 What is the next step?

3 2:42 Listen to Part 2, Version 1. What important mistake does Harry make?

4 2:43 Listen to Part 2, Version 2 and answer the questions.

1 How has Harry improved on Version 1?
2 What conditions does Ingrid ask for to:
   • bring down the monthly fee?
   • guarantee a maximum down time of 24 hours per month?
   • have the site up and running by next month?
3 What do Harry and Ingrid agree?
4 How does Ingrid avoid the question of penalties?

5 Complete the useful phrases for bargaining from Part 2, Version 2 of the listening.

1 I _____ be able to bring it down a little, but _____ a three-year contract.
2 _____ to agree to a three-year contract, _____ guarantee a maximum down time of 24 hours per month.
3 ... so _____ guarantee less than 24 hours per month, _____ our platinum service level.
4 I suppose _____ do it, providing _____ a year's fees in advance.
5 ... let's _____ difference.
6 I can pay six months in advance _____ the site online in two months.
7 ... if you _____ – here, here and here – _____ the champagne ...

Internet research

Search for the keywords *cross cultural negotiation* to find out how cultural differences affect international negotiations.

6 Look at the table below showing sentences from negotiations and the categories they belong to. Decide on the correct category for each sentence in 5, and add the sentence numbers to the table. The first one has been done for you.

Tentative offers	Counteroffers	Firm offers	Compromising
I might consider reducing the price if you increased your order. • 1	It would be difficult for me to increase my order unless you guaranteed the price for two years. • •	I am ready to sign a contract today if you can guarantee the price for two years. • • •	Would you agree to a compromise? Is that an acceptable compromise? •

Which tenses are used in the condition (*if / unless*) clauses of the tentative offers, counteroffers and firm offers above, and why?

Pronunciation

7 🔊 2:44–2:46 Stressing keywords is important in making clear that your first offers are tentative and hypothetical. <u>Underline</u> the two keywords that are stressed in each of these examples.

1 I might possibly be able to bring it down a little, but only if we had a three-year contract.
2 I might consider reducing the price, if you increased your order.
3 I'd be reluctant to agree to a three-year contract, unless you could guarantee a maximum down time of 24 hours per month.

Listen and check your answers, then practise saying each sentence.

Negotiating

8 Work with a partner to negotiate the following situations. Change roles for the second negotiation.

1 Student A: You have to give a presentation to the sales team tomorrow morning, but you booked an important client meeting at the same time. Ask B to give the presentation for you.
   Student B: This is the second time this has happened in two months. You think A should be more organized, so if you agree, negotiate something valuable in return.
2 Student A: You have to work with an auditor on Friday afternoon, but your boss has booked you on an all-day training course. Ask B to look after the auditor for you.
   Student B: You were planning to take Friday afternoon off as you are going away for the weekend, so if you agree, negotiate something valuable in return.

Use the following format to structure your negotiations:

Student A	Student B
Ask a favour.	Make a tentative offer.
Make a counteroffer.	Make a firm offer.
Propose a compromise.	Agree, go back to the beginning, or break off negotiations.

9 With a partner, practise negotiating an e-tailing package.

Student A: turn to page 113.
Student B: turn to page 117.

5 | Making deals

Discussion

1 Discuss your views on mailshots and spam. Mark your position on the scale.

| They make good business sense. | ←——┼——┼——┼——┼——→ | They're a waste of money. |

Scan reading

2 Read the proposal below and answer the questions.

1 What service does the proposal offer?
2 What benefits does it offer?
3 How much does the service cost?
4 Why should the customer choose this provider?

Dear Mr Bellows,

Thank you for taking the time to talk to me by telephone today. As agreed, please find below a proposal for our PZpay merchant account, which I believe will resolve all your online payment problems.

Your website currently generates five to ten orders per day. You expect this to increase steadily with the introduction of a new range of products. You are looking for a flexible, inexpensive and transparent payment system which will allow you to deal directly with your customers and control your cash flow.

We recommend the PZpay Pro small business merchant account, which can process up to 75 orders per day. If your sales volume were to expand more quickly than anticipated, you would be able to upgrade to PZpay Corporate with no additional set-up fee.

PZpay Pro will gain prestige and respect for your e-business, since customers will make their credit card payments directly on your website. PZpay is totally transparent, giving you total control of your sales, cash-flow and administration fees. In the unlikely event of a dispute with a customer, you alone would decide whether to refund your customer's payment. Our charges are amongst the lowest on the market, meaning that your business will be more profitable from day one.

We provide everything you need to set up PZpay on your website within 48 hours. Should you however encounter any difficulties, our helpline is available 24 hours a day, seven days a week to assist you.

With more than 1,800 satisfied members in 26 countries, PZpay is the fastest-growing merchant account provider on the Web. I will be happy to put you in touch with other PZpay users in your region.

The monthly fee for PZpay Pro is just $12, with minimum transaction fees of only $10. You will find full details of our terms and conditions in the attached quotation.

We look forward to having you as a member: to apply, simply fill out the application form at http://pzpay.com. If you have further questions, please feel free to call me.

Sincerely yours,

Internet research

Search for the keywords *how to write direct mail* to find out more about writing to sell.

Analysis

3 Read the proposal again and number these sections in the order they appear in the proposal.

☐	**Solution**:	State the options you recommend, and any contingency plans.
☐	**Benefits**:	Sell your solution by pointing out its advantages for the customer.
☐	**Introduction**:	Refer to previous contact with your customer, state the purpose and contents of the document and summarize the objective of the proposal.
☐	**Conclusion**:	Encourage the customer to take the next step.
☐	**Qualifications and references**:	Justify your ability to do the job.
☐	**Process and schedule**:	Explain procedures, lead time and after-sales service.
☐	**Needs / background**:	Review the reasons for the proposal and the customer's needs.
☐	**Costs**:	Give a breakdown of the investment, or refer to a separate quotation.

Writing

4 Your small business designs and builds multimedia websites. In small groups, supply suitable endings / beginnings for these options and contingencies.

1 If you would like to see similar projects we have managed, _____.
2 In the unlikely event that you were less than 100% satisfied with the result, _____.
3 Should you require on-site support, _____.
4 _____, I would be delighted to organize a demonstration on your premises.
5 _____, we would provide a replacement while your server was repaired.
6 _____, our engineers can perform an upgrade on-site.
7 _____, we require a deposit of 25%.

5 Read the notes from a sales meeting with a prospect, and write a proposal to supply a new website. Invent any details as necessary.

Prospect
Ms Nash-Williams

Company
'Poster Passion' – they sell posters of pop stars, rock bands, sports, etc. by mail order and via the Internet. Customers are mostly teenagers.

Needs
Current website was designed by a friend five years ago – very static and boring. No movement, no sound. Basically just a catalogue and price list.
Sales are dropping – competitors have more interactive sites. Wants something more exciting with music, guided tour, etc. Perhaps games to attract visitors?
Give details of how we work, references, prices, etc.
Very concerned about after-sales – explain how we support them if anything goes wrong.

Discussion

1 Some companies reward their best sales staff with gifts, trips or additional pay, hoping that such benefits will serve as an incentive to improve sales. What do you think are the advantages of such sales incentive programs? Are there any disadvantages?

Reading

2 Read the memo and answer the questions.

1 Who can go on the incentive trip?
2 Is this the first time the company has organized such a trip?
3 When and why was the memo sent?
4 What sort of customers does the St John's Beach Club aim to attract?

Ashton Pharmaceuticals – Memo

To: All sales reps

Re: Incentive trip

Just a quick reminder that our top ten performers will win an all-expenses paid holiday for two in the sun. As usual, our destination is the Caribbean, and this year we have chosen the St John's Beach Club in Antigua (see attached brochure). So if you haven't yet made it into the top ten, and you want to be on the beach this December, there's still time to record really excellent figures in Q4!

Good luck!

Malcolm Roberts

Sales Director

Listening for detail

3 2:47 Listen to a conversation between Malcolm Roberts and Loretta Harding, CEO of Ashton Pharmaceuticals. Mark these statements *T* (true) or *F* (false), and say why.

1 The conversation takes place in Malcolm's office. ☐
2 Malcolm and Loretta are going on the trip. ☐
3 Charles is probably the CFO. ☐
4 Last year's budget was about $26,500. ☐
5 Malcolm is going to negotiate with the St John's Beach Club. ☐
6 There will be between 22 and 26 participants. ☐
7 Malcolm hopes to stay in Antigua for ten nights. ☐

4 Listen again and complete these sentences.

1 Loretta would get to know the sales team better if _____
2 If they only talked to one travel agent, _____
3 Loretta thinks the agents may give a free upgrade if _____
4 If they can negotiate a really good package, Malcolm _____
5 They'll stay longer than a week if _____

Negotiating

5 Divide into travel agents (A) and buyers (B). Each buyer negotiates with two different travel agents to get the best possible deal for Ashton Pharmaceuticals' incentive trip to the St John's Beach Club. When you have finished negotiations, compare your scores to see who got the best deal.

Student A: turn to page 111.
Student B: turn to page 115.

Antigua

- **Population: 67,000**
- **Language: English**
- **Climate: Tropical**
- **14 miles long, 11 miles wide**
- **365 beaches, pure white sand, turquoise water**
- **Several international casinos**

St John's Beach Club

- **Four-star luxury accommodation on the beach**
- **Gourmet food in our three restaurants**
- **Three pools, beach bar, night club**
- **Sailing, scuba-diving, squash and tennis included**
- **Team-building events and competitions**
- **Group benefits for bookings of ten rooms or more**

Discussion

1 Brainstorm a list of groups of people a company has a responsibility towards. What conflicts of interest are there between the different groups?

Scan reading

2 Read the credo below and identify the four groups of people that Johnson & Johnson prioritize. The words in grey are explained in the *Wordlist* on pages 155–156.

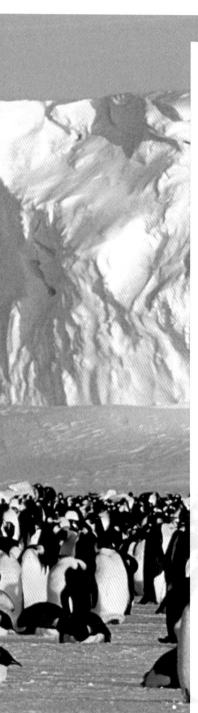

The Johnson & Johnson group manufactures health care products in over 200 companies in 57 countries. Their Credo, first written in 1943, has been a model for corporate social responsibility (CSR) policies for over 60 years.

Our Credo

We believe our first responsibility is to the doctors, nurses and patients,
to mothers and fathers and all others who use our products and services.
In meeting their needs everything we do must be of high quality.
We must constantly strive to reduce our costs
5 in order to maintain reasonable prices.
Customers' orders must be serviced promptly and accurately.
Our suppliers and distributors must have an opportunity
to make a fair profit.

We are responsible to our employees,
10 the men and women who work with us throughout the world.
Everyone must be considered as an individual.
We must respect their dignity and recognize their merit.
They must have a sense of security in their jobs.
Compensation must be fair and adequate,
15 and working conditions clean, orderly and safe.
We must be mindful of ways to help our employees fulfil
their family responsibilities.
Employees must feel free to make suggestions and complaints.
There must be equal opportunity for employment, development
20 and advancement for those qualified.
We must provide competent management,
and their actions must be just and ethical.

We are responsible to the communities in which we live and work
and to the world community as well.
25 We must be good citizens – support good works and charities
and bear our fair share of taxes.
We must encourage civic improvements and better health and education.
We must maintain in good order
the property we are privileged to use,
30 protecting the environment and natural resources.

Our final responsibility is to our stockholders.
Business must make a sound profit.
We must experiment with new ideas.
Research must be carried on, innovative programs developed
35 and mistakes paid for.
New equipment must be purchased, new facilities provided
and new products launched.
Reserves must be created to provide for adverse times.
When we operate according to these principles,
40 the stockholders should realize a fair return.

Internet research

Search for the keywords *Starbucks bean stock* and *Starbucks standards business conduct* or *CSR* find out more about the social performance of other companies.

Reading and discussion

3 Read Johnson & Johnson's credo again and discuss who should decide what is meant by:

1 maintaining reasonable prices (line 5)
2 making a fair profit (line 8)
3 fair and adequate compensation (line 14)
4 just and ethical actions (line 22)
5 our fair share of taxes (line 26)
6 a fair return (line 40).

4 Discuss the questions relating to Johnson & Johnson's credo opposite.

1 Which 'good works and charities' (line 25) should multinational companies support?
2 What kind of 'civic improvements' (line 27) should the company encourage?
3 How should the company protect 'the environment and natural resources' (line 30)?
4 Are there any points in the credo you disagree with or items you would like to add?
5 Does a credo really change the way a company operates or is it just good PR?
6 Do small businesses have the same responsibilities as multinationals?

Listening for gist

5 🔊 2:48–2:50 You are going to hear an interview on NPR (National Public Radio), a US news provider, with author Marc Gunther, who believes corporate America is changing for the better.

Part 1
Listen to Part 1 and complete the summary.
Marc Gunther is interested in companies that treat employees well, (1) _____ and (2) _____. Nowadays, businesses work closely with (3) _____ and many employees are like (4) _____. Starbucks, for example, gave away its bean stocks to (5) _____.
The Bush administration does not see (6) _____ as a man-made problem. However, US utility companies are (7) _____ and transportation companies are changing from (8) _____ to (9) _____.

Part 2
Listen to Part 2 and answer the questions.

1 Tick the reasons that motivate companies to be responsible, according to Marc Gunther.
☐ profitability   ☐ altruism   ☐ recruitment
2 Tick the reasons that motivate employees.
☐ They want to enhance shareholder value.
☐ They want to define the company's goals.
☐ They want their jobs to have meaning.
☐ They want to make the world a better place.
3 How do Southwest Airlines prioritize the three groups they have responsibility towards?
4 What is the theory behind this choice?
5 What example does Marc Gunther give of how this works?

Part 3
Listen to Part 3 and decide if the following statements are *T* (true) or *F* (false).

1 In the 50s and 60s American corporations believed it was their duty to take care of their employees and customers. ☐
2 In the 70s and 80s corporations no longer wanted to take care of employees and customers. ☐
3 Marc Gunther believes the short-term model of the 70s / 80s is sustainable for businesses and for society. ☐

6 | Company and community

Vocabulary Meetings, ethical behaviour and social performance

Meetings

1 Match up the phrases you might use in a meeting.

1	I have received two	a) a copy of the agenda?
2	Has everybody received	b) the meeting.
3	If we can't agree, I think we should take	c) apologies for absence.
4	It's getting late, so I propose we close	d) the agenda.
5	I think this would be a good time to break	e) a vote.
6	We have lots to discuss, so let's stick to	f) for lunch.
7	It's five past nine, so I'd better open	g) side-tracked.
8	Can we start by approving	h) any other business.
9	We seem to have reached	i) handout.
10	That's interesting, but I think we're getting	j) the meeting.
11	I'll just give out this	k) a unanimous decision.
12	Before we finish, we need to deal with	l) the minutes of the last meeting?

2 Which phrases would you probably use:

1 at the beginning of a meeting? ☐☐☐☐   2 at the end of a meeting? ☐☐

Adjectives

3 Match the adjectives in **bold** in the article with the definitions below, as in the example.

ELASTIC
ETHICS

It was Groucho Marx who said that if people didn't like his principles, he had others.

And unfortunately, business people and companies are not always as **reliable** or as **trustworthy** as we would like. Product descriptions are frequently not as **accurate** as they could be, for example when listing ingredients used in foodstuffs. Service is not always as **prompt** as we expect, even in so-called fast-food restaurants. But it is perhaps in the world of advertising where ethical standards seem to be the most elastic. Advertisements are frequently **deceptive** and often **confusing** or deliberately **misleading**, sometimes making extravagant promises. No doubt advertisers are neither more **dishonest** nor any less **altruistic** than the rest of us; they do not often make obviously **false** claims. It's just that, like Groucho, they sometimes seem a little too economical with the truth.

1 immediate or quick — *prompt*
2 willing to do things which are not honest
3 intended to make someone believe something that is not true
4 appearing different from the way it really is
5 able to be trusted as honest
6 dependable
7 complicated, not easy to understand
8 not true
9 having a selfless concern for others' well-being
10 correct or true in every detail

"We could advertise it as 100% salt free."

Collocations

4 Finish these extracts from a guide to corporate social responsibility by completing each one with verbs from the box that collocate with the words in **bold**.

> contribute   identify with   think   supporting

PRO-ACTIVE SOCIAL PERFORMANCE

For most companies, rather than (1) _____ a different **charity** each year on an ad hoc basis, it is preferable to (2) _____ **long-term**. It can be very valuable for a company to (3) _____ **an issue** which is related to its business, and to (4) _____ **funds** regularly.

> recognizing   uphold   obey   respecting

ON-GOING SOCIAL PERFORMANCE

Obviously a fundamental of HR management is that companies should always (5) _____ **the law**. But above and beyond that requirement, they have a moral duty to (6) _____ **standards** of common decency. This means for example (7) _____ **human dignity** when there are problems, and (8) _____ **merit** when staff perform especially well.

> negotiate   acknowledge   compensate   limit

DAMAGE LIMITATION

The company's first duty in the case of an accident is to (9) _____ the **impact** of the problem on its staff and on the community. It is then essential to (10) _____ **the problem**: nothing less than total transparency will do. After the crisis has passed, management should allow sufficient time to (11) _____ **a settlement** which will satisfy all parties and (12) _____ **the victims** properly.

Internet research

Search for the keywords *Rhonda Abrams* to read more about Rhonda and her advice for entrepreneurs.

Listening for detail

5 🔊 2:51 Listen to a presentation entitled *Doing well by Doing good* given to an audience of entrepreneurs by Rhonda Abrams, columnist, author and consultant. Tick the expressions you hear.

- ☐ respect the environment
- ☐ play a positive role in
- ☐ obeying the law
- ☐ an honest, responsible business
- ☐ have a competitive edge over
- ☐ be involved in community causes
- ☐ responsibility to your customer
- ☐ act with integrity and honesty toward
- ☐ environmental policies
- ☐ get in trouble with regulatory agencies
- ☐ face lawsuits or fines
- ☐ misleading, confusing, or even false advertising or sales techniques
- ☐ treats employees, customers and suppliers fairly

Discussion

6 Rhonda Abrams talks about 'being a good corporate citizen'. What specific practices and policies do you suggest this involves in:

- R&D, production and quality?
- marketing and sales?
- HR?
- purchasing?
- finance?

Refresh your memory

The passive
be + past participle
it does ➔ *it is done*
it is doing ➔ *it is being done*
it did ➔ *it was done*, etc.
Used when the person who does the action is obvious or unknown

▶ Grammar reference page 128

Reported speech
I've finished!
He said he had finished.

direct	reported
present	➔ past
past	➔ past / past perfect
present perfect	➔ past perfect
will	➔ would

When you report what someone said, move the original tense back in time

▶ Grammar reference page 129

Test yourself: The passive

1 Change these active sentences to the passive to avoid mentioning the agent.

1 Your company sometimes releases illegal levels of nitrates into the river.
2 Your department is making too many mistakes at the moment.
3 Unfortunately, you made a poor decision in hiring unqualified staff.
4 Our sub-contractors were employing children to make T-shirts in Asia.
5 Several anonymous journalists have accused us of industrial espionage.
6 My boss and several other managers had warned the company about the risks.
7 We can avoid conflict with the unions by making small concessions.
8 The authorities might ask you some delicate questions.
9 The Board, the Plant Manager and the trade unions all agreed that production staff should work a four-day week.
10 Head Office have decided that they're going to make 300 employees redundant.

Test yourself: Reported speech

2 Complete the extracts from a report of a public meeting about a pollution problem.

1 'Nitrate levels in the local water supply are slightly higher than normal.'
CEO Ben Straw announced that _____
2 'It is possible that the factory is responsible.'
Mr Straw admitted _____
3 'There was a small chemical leak last Friday.'
Plant Manager Jane Lee explained _____
4 'We have taken measures to ensure that this situation cannot reoccur.'
Mrs Lee reassured the meeting that _____
5 'We are negotiating a settlement with the town council.'
Mr Straw said _____
6 'We will announce full details in a press statement in a few days' time.'
He promised the meeting that _____
7 'Has there ever been a problem like this before?'
Mrs Green, a local resident, asked if _____
8 'No, I can not remember any other leaks in 30 years at the factory.'
Mrs Lee replied that _____
9 'When do you plan to re-open the factory?'
Pat Holz, a union representative, enquired when _____
10 'As soon as possible, but some staff may be laid off for a few days.'
Mr Straw warned that _____

3 Read the following extracts from an interview with the CEO of a multinational oil company. Report the phrases in **bold** using the verbs in brackets, as in the example.

1 'I repeat what I said a few moments ago: **my company does everything it can to limit the impact of our activities on the environment**.' (emphasize)
The CEO emphasized that the company did everything it could to limit the impact of its activities on the environment.
2 'I really can't accept that. You need to understand that **developing countries are extremely grateful for the investment and the jobs that we bring**.' (argue)
3 'I think there's a slight misunderstanding here. Yes, **we do make fair profits and pay good dividends, but we've never exploited our employees**.' (explain)
4 'Yes, that's a fair point: **we can, and we will, do more to develop sources of alternative energy** such as wind, wave and solar power.' (accept)
5 'Well, we have little or no influence on government policy on taxation, but no, **I do not feel that higher petrol prices will reduce traffic and pollution**.' (comment)

Internet **research**

Read the business pages of an online newspaper to find interesting comments and quotes from people and companies in the news. Tell a partner what was said.

4 Read the four extracts from newspaper reports. Then say who made the twelve statements below and explain how you know this. What phrases helped you?

CEO KLAAS ROOS announced an end to manufacturing in Europe, informing shareholders that labour costs could not be justified, and explaining that Asian textile imports could no longer be matched for price.

Speaking to our reporter on the spot, Ms Gronko explained that all villagers forced to leave their homes by the new road would be compensated. Asked to what level, she replied that she was unable to give a figure, but added that discussions were being held with local representatives.

Journalists are reported to have been refused entry to Plazachem's Tashkent plant after leakages of toxic chemicals were described by workers. Employees claimed that health and safety regulations had not been applied for the last five years, and that several fatal accidents had occurred. Plazachem management declined to comment.

Asked how the company intended to compensate the victims of the accident, Mr Sanchez answered that no decision had yet been reached. Emphasizing the complexity of the legal situation, he suggested negotiations may be protracted.

1 'It's just too expensive.'
2 'It's dangerous: people have died.'
3 'We're still talking.'
4 'It could take years.'
5 'I don't know.'
6 'It's really not simple.'
7 'It's too early to say.'
8 'They will be paid.'
9 'We are closing down.'
10 'Your request has been denied.'
11 'We can't compete.'
12 'I'm afraid he's unavailable.'

Listening and reporting

5 🔊 2:52–2:57 A manufacturing plant in Kassra, a small town in Algeria, has just made 100 people redundant. Listen to six extracts from a conversation between Geoffrey Bullard, the Plant Manager, and Leila Belabed, a member of the mayor's staff. For each extract, decide how Leila reported to the mayor, using appropriate verbs, as in the example.

1 *I complained that 100 people had been made redundant and I reminded Mr Bullard that he had promised to create jobs for the town.*

6 Explain these formal announcements to a foreign visitor in informal language.

1 Protective glasses must be worn beyond this point.
You have to wear special protective glasses from this point onwards.
2 Visitors are requested to use the stairs while the lift is under repair.
3 Customers are advised that no refunds will be made without a receipt.
4 Deposits will only be refunded after the return of all equipment to reception.
5 All meetings are transferred to the training centre during redecoration of the conference room.
6 Only expenses which have been approved by a manager will be reimbursed.

Roleplay

7 With a partner, roleplay a conversation between a dissatisfied customer and a salesperson. First decide what the customer bought, and make a list of promises the salesperson made. Use reporting verbs from the boxes, as in the example.

- Verbs with *me*, e.g. *you told me* (*that*)...
  tell   promise   assure   ask

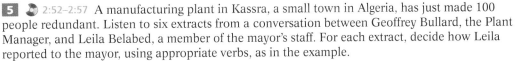
- Verbs without *me*, e.g. *you said* (*that*)...
  say   guarantee   claim   explain   imply   state

A: *I'm very dissatisfied with this car. You promised me it would do 160 kilometres per hour!*
B: *No, sir. I'm sorry, you asked me if it would do 160, and I said it would, but only downhill with the wind behind you.*

6.4 Speaking Meetings – teamwork

Discussion

1 Discuss how acceptable you find the following gifts from a seller to a corporate buyer.

> a corporate pen   lunch in a good restaurant   a free sample of the product
> a case of champagne   a free weekend 'seminar' on a yacht   cash   employing a relative

Listening

2 🎵 2:58 The management committee of an eastern European manufacturer of electrical components have called a meeting to discuss a problem: one of their buyers, Mr Vieri, has been accepting regular gifts from a supplier.

Listen to Version 1. How does one member of the committee, Stanislas, behave inappropriately? List five ways.

3 Listen again and write down six examples of Stanislas's inappropriate language.

4 🎵 2:59 Listen to Version 2 of the meeting. What are the differences?

5 Complete the expressions Stanislas uses in Version 2.

1 Sorry to _____.
2 Would you _____, (Anna)?
3 Sorry, (Anna), I don't see _____.
4 Well, I feel _____ (we should dismiss Mr Vieri).
5 I'm afraid _____, (Jon).
6 Yes, but, wouldn't you _____ (his behaviour was unethical)?

6 Reorder the words in **bold** in these useful expressions for meetings. They were all used in Version 2 of the meeting.

1 **that to brings next the point us** on the agenda.
2 **that tend think I to** we need …
3 **but I point your see** you can't just dismiss someone …
4 **think don't that you** everyone should have a second chance?
5 **we're think side-tracked getting I** here.
6 **just come here in I could**?
7 **have on views do any you** this issue?
8 **say you when** this issue, **mean you do** our policy on gifts?

7 Put the expressions from 5 and 6 into the appropriate category below.

Giving an opinion	Asking for opinions	Managing the discussion
In my opinion, …	What's your feeling?	Do we all agree on that, then?
It seems to me that …		Perhaps we should break for coffee.
		Could we come back to this later?

Disagreeing tactfully	Interrupting	Asking for clarification	Persuading
I agree up to a point, but …	Sorry, but could I just say …	So, are you saying that … ?	Isn't it the case that … ?

Internet research

What are the essentials of a successful meeting? Search for the keywords *"golden rules of meetings"* to find out.

8 With a partner, hold short meetings on the four issues below. Follow the structure provided. Take turns being A and B.

1 A vodka manufacturer offers to sponsor your end-of-year party. Do you accept?
2 One of your suppliers uses child labour in Vietnam. What should you do?
3 Advertisements for your product show only slim, beautiful people. Is that OK?
4 Ethnic minorities and the disabled are under-represented in your firm. What can you do?

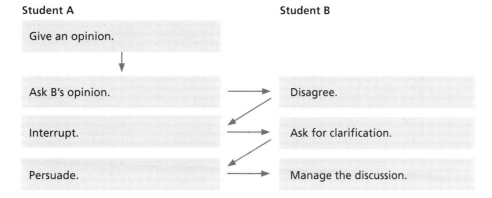

Student A	Student B
Give an opinion.	
Ask B's opinion.	Disagree.
Interrupt.	Ask for clarification.
Persuade.	Manage the discussion.

9 Work in small groups. Hold a management meeting to decide what to do in the following cases of employee misbehaviour in your company. For each case, discuss:

- what action to take.
- what corporate policy to adopt (if any).
- how you will implement your decisions.

Case 1

Mike Ho, a buyer in your purchasing department, accepted cash from suppliers in return for buying large volumes at high prices.

Case 2

Marieta Myska, a sales manager, obtained confidential information about government contracts by having a relationship with a civil servant.

Case 3

Joseph Fisher, a project manager, used company resources and equipment to run a club for disabled children at weekends.

6.5 Writing Reports and minutes

Discussion

1 Why should companies invest time and money in community projects?

Brainstorming

2 How many different alternatives can you think of for the words in the box?

but	and	so	say	tell	think

Skim reading

3 Mirratec Industries, a subsidiary of a multinational manufacturer of compressors for refrigerators and air-conditioning units, has a plant in the small Polish town of Bychawa. Read the report which Mirratec sent to Head Office, and the minutes of a management committee meeting at Head Office, and answer the questions.

1 What are the arguments for and against involvement in the community centre project?
2 What did a) Head Office and b) Mirratec decide?

Bychawa Community Centre project

EARLIER this year Mirratec was asked to invest in a project to build a Community Centre in Bychawa. As a rule, group policy is to give encouragement but only limited financial support to such community projects. However, a meeting was held by managers and staff at the plant and in this case it was thought that the benefits to the company's image justified more active and extensive support, in particular after the recent difficult negotiations with the local authorities over the access road to the new workshop. Moreover, it was felt that employee involvement in the project would bring substantial benefits in terms of motivation and job satisfaction. Consequently, it is recommended that the company should contribute 50% of the funding; in addition, selected employees should be assigned to manage key areas of the project during work time, such as design, fund-raising and construction.

Naturally, the project will require a high level of commitment from our staff in order to complete all stages on time. The community centre will be officially opened in September, and it is hoped that department managers will be able to reduce staff workloads for the duration of the project.

In conclusion, it is believed that the community and the company will derive numerous benefits from the project and that overall, the company's image within the community will be greatly improved. It is expected that an ongoing close relationship with the community will have a positive effect on two strategic areas of our development, namely expansion of our manufacturing facilities and recruitment of our workforce locally.

Minutes of the Management Committee meeting, 15 April
Attendees: Jan Navratil, MD; Ines Caba, Production; Christopher Taberley, Finance

1. Bychawa Community Centre. JN reported that the plan had been favourably received at Head Office. Even so, there were concerns about the size of the investment and the project's impact on productivity. But he stressed that group management were aware of the need for good relations with local communities, and would support Mirratec's decision. Consequently, JN felt that they should go ahead.

    IC agreed that it was important to improve public relations, but emphasized the risks involved for production, for example, absenteeism and quality issues. She claimed that the project could become an excuse to take time off work, especially during the construction phase in the summer.

    CT reminded the meeting that only a small number of employees would be concerned. Obviously department managers would have to organize cover for any absences. In other words, production should not be affected. Furthermore, managers of other departments were very happy with the project on the whole. In brief, he suggested that the benefits in developing team spirit were clearly far greater than any potential risk to productivity.

    Finally, it was agreed that the project should be approved.

Internet research

Search for the keywords *email ethics* and make notes about ethical practice in electronic communication. Write a short report on your findings, using some of the linking words you studied in this module.

Scan reading

4 Read the report and the minutes again. <u>Underline</u> the linking words and complete the table.

Function	Linking words
Addition	besides, mo_____ , in ad_____ , fur_____
Conclusion	lastly, in c_____ , f_____
Consequence	so, therefore, c_____
Contrast	but, h_____ , e_____ s_____
Equivalence	that is to say, n_____ , in o_____ w_____
Example	for instance, s_____ as, f_____ e_____
Generalization	in most cases, as a _____ , on the w_____
Highlighting	mainly, chiefly, in p_____ , es_____
Stating the obvious	of course, n_____ , ob_____ , cl_____
Summary	to sum up, o_____ , in b_____

Writing

5 Replace the inappropriate linking words in **bold** with a better choice from 4.

Josiah Wedgwood was a pioneer in social responsibility, building a village for his workforce in 1769. **For instance**, his products combined technology with classical culture. More than a century later, George Cadbury developed social housing for his chocolate factory workers. **As a rule**, Cadbury's became one of Britain's most respected companies. Both men were pioneers of corporate social responsibility. **Overall**, they were also accused of paternalism.

Today, sustainable development policies aim to manage the effects of business on employees, the community, and, **on the whole**, on the environment. Multinationals like Shell are focusing on the idea of being good neighbours, **naturally**, by consulting local stakeholders before beginning new projects which may affect them.

Reading for detail

6 Read the quote below and identify five more impersonal structures used in the report in 3 to express the views of Mirratec's management.

'… **it was thought that** the benefits to the company's image justified more active and extensive support … '

7 Choose an appropriate reporting verb from the box and report Christopher Taberley's statements below, as in the example. The verbs in the box were all in the minutes in 3.

report ~~agree~~ suggest stress claim

1 Yes, I have to say that you are quite right that productivity is a concern.
   Christopher agreed that productivity was a concern.
2 On the other hand, you mustn't forget that only a small number of staff will be directly involved.
3 As a matter of fact, most department managers don't expect any problems.
4 I've heard there's a similar project in Greece where they've actually improved productivity.
5 I'm pretty sure team spirit will be much better when the community centre has been built.

Listening and writing

8 🔊 2.60 Listen to a discussion of the second point on the agenda of the meeting in 3. Take notes. Then, with a partner, write a short summary of the discussion and decisions.

6 | Company and community

Internet research

Search for the keywords *automobile recycling contamination* to find out more about the risks and perspectives in this industry.

6.6 Case study | Phoenix

Discussion

1 Would you like to have a recycling centre near your home? Why (not)?

Reading

2 Read the Internet page about Phoenix and answer the questions.

1 What kind of corporate image does the company try to project?
2 What do you imagine working at Phoenix is like?

PHOENIX
Australia's leading independent vehicle recycling specialist

- Home
- Spare parts
- Recycling
- Jobs with Phoenix
- About us
- Contact

Every year almost a million of Australia's ten million cars reach the end of their useful lives. Phoenix provides a valuable community service by recycling over 75% of each vehicle.

Phoenix's mission is to protect and preserve Australia's unique ecology. We take special care to ensure that hazardous materials and toxic substances are processed safely and securely with minimum risk to the environment or the population.

At all our recycling centres across Australia, we believe in being good neighbours. We believe it is our duty to treat customers, employees and suppliers fairly, to respect the local environment and to be involved in community causes.

Roleplay preparation

Divide into three groups: Port Katherine Planning Department, Port Katherine Residents' Association, and Phoenix. Use the activities opposite (3, 4 and 5) to gather information for your group, in preparation for a public meeting (6 opposite) to discuss the choice of site for a new recycling centre in Port Katherine. You will need to make a presentation at the meeting summarizing your views, stating which site you prefer and why, and explaining why the other sites are not appropriate. You should also be prepared to ask the other groups questions, and argue against their proposals if they conflict with your interests.

Listening

3 ♪ 2:61 Listen to part of a meeting at Phoenix's head office in Sydney and answer the questions.

1 Why is Port Katherine a good choice for Phoenix's new site? Give four reasons.
2 What are the pros and cons of sites A, B and C from your group's point of view?
3 What do you think 'Operation Charm and Diplomacy' is?

Reading and discussion

4 In your groups, prepare for the public meeting by reading a message and answering some questions.

Group A – Port Katherine Planning Department: turn to page 112.
Group B – Port Katherine Residents' Association: turn to page 114.
Group C – Phoenix: turn to page 117.

5 Read the agenda. Then, in your groups, prepare your presentation and strategy for the public meeting.

Roleplay

6 Roleplay the public meeting using the agenda above.

Writing

7 Write a short report on the meeting.

Port Katherine Planning Department: write to Duncan Gillespie at the Lord Mayor's Office.
Port Katherine Residents' Association: write to your members.
Phoenix: write to your head office in Sydney.

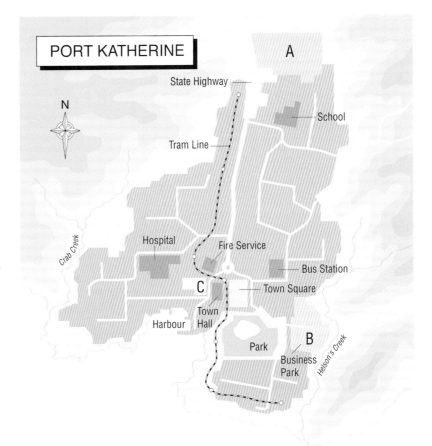

PORT KATHERINE

Agenda

1 Welcome and introductions
2 Opening presentations
   • Phoenix
   • Port Katherine Planning Department
   • Port Katherine Residents' Association
3 Questions and discussion of the three possible sites
4 Summary and conclusion

Review 5

Making deals

1 Complete these paragraphs about e-tailing using the words in the box.

> approach   browsers   databank   expectation
> eyeballs   merchandising   purchase   search ads
> website   web chats

1 Most visitors to a (a) _____ don't actually buy anything, so simply having lots of (b) '_____' doesn't mean there will be lots of sales. In fact, if the site attracts visitors through paid (c) _____ on Google or Yahoo, then bringing them actually costs money.

2 Customer service reps answer customer questions via live (a) _____ on the site. When a customer engages in live chat with a sales rep, the average (b) _____ doubles in value.

3 But instead of real customer service reps, many smaller e-tailers use animated characters that draw on a (a) _____ of answers to commonly asked questions. E-tailers hope that the animated characters will turn (b) _____ into buyers.

4 When someone is shopping at home, they have an (a) _____ of privacy. Ted Martin, senior vice-president for (b) _____ and operations at Overstock.com, said: 'We're taking the conservative (c) _____ right now, we don't want to be intrusive.'

2 Complete this sentence about e-tailing using these words: *consent, privacy, tracking, violation*.

Research shows that most online shoppers consider _____ their navigation of a site without their _____ to be a _____ of their _____.

3 In each set of four below, match a verb on the left with a noun on the right to make collocations about an e-tail transaction.

1 look up   on a link to get to the seller's site
2 pay   the product you want in a cart
3 place   a product on a search engine
4 click   by credit card

5 browse   the customer's credit card
6 debit   the product from the warehouse
7 send back   the site to find any interesting products
8 ship   a faulty product under guarantee

4 The collocations below are useful in negotiating. Cross out the one verb in each group that does *not* collocate with the noun.

1 **fill / offer / place / take** an order
2 **ask for / be entitled to / find / offer** a discount
3 **discuss / go over / put on / sort out** the details
4 **make / put forward / put back / reject** a proposal
5 **extend / meet / miss / take** a deadline
6 **look for / meet / seek / reach** a compromise

5 Complete each sentence with a collocation from 4 above.

1 If you fail to do something by the agreed time, you _____ the _____.

2 If you tell a retailer you want to buy something from them, you _____ an _____.

3 If you finally get agreement after both sides had different starting points, you _____ a _____.

4 If you automatically have the right to a lower price, for example because of the quantity you are ordering, then you _____ a _____.

6 Look at the seven alternatives in **bold** below. Cross out the three that can never be used.

If we **increase / increased / will increase / would increase** our order, **do you give / will you give / would you give** us a discount?

7 Which version of the sentence in 6 is appropriate if you want to show you are unsure about increasing your order (it's just a possibility)? Write the whole sentence:

_____

8 Which version of the sentence in 6 is the most common – you are just asking a simple question? Write the whole sentence: _____

9 Complete the bargaining phrases in this dialogue using the pairs of words in the box.

> providing + agree   if + increased   unless + guaranteed

Supplier: I might consider reducing the price (1) _____ you _____ your order.
Customer: It would be difficult for me to increase my order, (2) _____ you _____ the price for two years.
Supplier: I might be able to guarantee the price, (3) _____ you _____ to a five-year contract.

10 Underline the correct answer in **bold**.

1 What do you **recommend / recommend me**?
2 What do you **advise to do / advise me to do**?
3 I **suggest / suggest you** ordering 500 pieces initially, and then perhaps more later.
4 I **advise that you / advise you** to order 500 pieces initially.
5 I **suggested him / suggested to him** that he should order 500 pieces initially.

11 Complete the extracts from a business proposal using the words in the box.

> agreed   available   below   charges   lowest
> replacement   require   unlikely   should   wish

1 As _____, please find _____ a proposal to install a series of photocopiers.
2 _____ you require on-site support, our engineers are _____ seven days a week.
3 In the _____ event of a breakdown, we would provide a _____.
4 Our _____ are amongst the _____ on the market.
5 If you _____ to place an order, we _____ a deposit of 25%.

Review 6

Company and community

1 Read the examples of corporate social responsibility then answer the questions below.

The company should ...
- enhance shareholder value.
- recognize employees' merit.
- give fair and adequate compensation.
- provide clean and safe working conditions.
- provide new equipment and new facilities.
- carry on research and develop innovation.
- encourage civic improvements.
- support good works and charities.
- protect the environment and natural resources.
- avoid exploiting developing countries.
- build a sustainable business.

And employees need to ...
- have a sense of security in their job.
- have equal opportunity for jobs and development.
- feel free to make suggestions and complaints.
- feel they can align themselves with the company's goals.

Find a word above that means:

1   the profit that a company makes for its investors (two words): _____ _____
2   money paid because someone is injured or has lost their job: _____
3   rooms and equipment that are provided for a particular purpose: _____
4   organizations that give help to people who need it: _____
5   the land, water and air that people live in: _____
6   treating someone unfairly in order to get a benefit for yourself: _____
7   capable of continuing for a long time: _____
8   a situation in which people have the same chances as everyone else (two words): _____
9   things you say or write when you are not happy: _____
10 agree with and support publicly (_____ yourself with): _____.

2 Complete the sentences about ethical behaviour using a phrase from each column.

The company should ...

1 acknowledge any problem	common decency.
2 act with integrity	any problem.
3 compensate victims	that exists.
4 limit the impact of	which satisfy everyone.
5 negotiate settlements	for any damage caused.
6 obey the law or	staff perform well.
7 recognize merit when	towards employees.
8 uphold standards of	face a lawsuit or fine.

3 Complete the remarks of a chairperson at various stages of a meeting. Use the words and phrases in the box.

any other business	apology for absence
approving the minutes	break for coffee
close the meeting	come back to this
getting side-tracked	have any views
introduce the first item	see your point
stick to the agenda	take a vote
unanimous decision	wouldn't you agree

Beginning
Good morning, ladies and gentlemen. Is everyone here? I have received just one (1) _____ from Celia. OK, I think we can begin. Let's start by (2) _____ of the last meeting. Any comments? They're quite straightforward, I think. Good. Now, there is a lot to discuss today, so let's try to (3) _____. OK, who is going to (4) _____?

Middle
That's interesting, but I think we're (5) _____. Could we (6) _____ later? OK. Now, Antonio, we haven't heard from you. Do you (7) _____ on this issue? ...
Thank you, Antonio. I (8) _____, but you have to consider the impact on our budget. (9) _____ that there will be substantial costs if we do as you suggest? ...
OK, there seems to be a consensus, so we don't need to (10) _____. This would be a good time to (11) _____.

End
Good, I think we've reached a (12) _____ on this. Before we finish we need to deal with (13) _____. Does anyone have any other issue that we haven't discussed? OK, I think we can (14) _____.

4 Put each verb in brackets into the correct form, active or passive. The first two are present simple and the last four are past simple.

'The company (1) _____ (try) to limit its impact on the environment as much as possible. However, sometimes mistakes (2) _____ (make). It is true that some radioactive waste (3) _____ (lose) in transit last week, somewhere on the Swiss-German border. But I am pleased to report that we (4) _____ (take) action immediately. The driver of the truck (5) _____ (find), and we (6) _____ (dismiss) him after completing our enquiries. Press reports that he had been drinking heavily and thought he was in Austria are completely exaggerated.'

5 Find pairs of linking words / phrases with the same meaning.

as a rule	clearly	consequently	especially
finally	in addition	in particular	in brief
in conclusion	in other words	moreover	obviously
on the whole	that is to say	therefore	to sum up

6 Which two words / phrases from 5 would you use to:

1   add a second point to support your argument?
2   highlight one fact or point?
3   make a generalization?

7 Mergers and acquisitions

Discussion

1 How is a merger like and unlike a marriage?

How are mergers and acquisitions perceived by:

- employees?
- shareholders?
- customers?
- the general public?

Skim reading

2 Read the article opposite and answer the questions.

1 Who are the students and why do they want M&A classes?
2 What lessons do they learn?
3 What are good reasons for mergers and acquisitions?
4 What are the wrong reasons?

Reading for detail

3 Read the article again. The words in grey are explained in the *Wordlist* on page 157. With a partner, discuss why these statements are T (true) or F (false).

1 Every year over 500 mergers and acquisitions in the US fail to deliver increased value. ☐
2 American executives are keen to get a share in multi-billion dollar takeovers. ☐
3 Executives wishing to attend M&A courses have to have an MBA. ☐
4 Experienced managers tell attendees about typical mistakes they have made. ☐
5 Because of the risks, business school professors do not recommend mergers. ☐
6 Shareholders can often only judge the success of their CEO's acquisitions policy several years after a takeover. ☐
7 Austin says that empire-building, diversification and increasing debt are the wrong reasons for a merger. ☐
8 According to Austin, many CEOs embark on mergers and acquisitions for irrational, emotional reasons. ☐

Listening for gist

4 🔊 3:01 Listen to an interview with Bernard Degoulange, an M&A specialist at Banque de Reims, who talks about choosing targets for acquisition. What are the five Gs?

Listening for detail

5 Listen again and answer the questions.

1 According to Bernard Degoulange, what is the best reason for a merger?
2 Explain how he uses the example of champagne and whisky to show why external growth is necessary.
3 Explain each of the points summarized by the five Gs.
4 What opportunity does a merger offer the competition, and why is it possible?
5 Why is a merger a traumatic period according to Bernard Degoulange?
6 How does he say companies should help people get through this trauma?

Discussion

6 You are the owners of Bradburgers, a hamburger restaurant in your town. With your five employees, you have established a reputation for fast, good quality food, and the business is making a good profit. One of your competitors in the next street is Kadri's Kebabs, which sells takeaways and delivers kebabs to homes and offices. There are fifteen employees. Kadri and his two brothers are excellent cooks, but poor managers; their kebab house is losing money, and is up for sale. What are the pros and cons of taking over the business? Think about the five Gs in particular.

Lessons in M&A

SOME 1,500 TO 2,000 mergers and acquisitions are completed per year worldwide, of which around half are in the US. With deals worth astronomical sums, ($25bn for HP-Compaq, $35bn for Daimler-Chrysler, and $77bn
5 for Exxon-Mobil,) it comes as no surprise that American executives are queuing up to go back to school for M&A classes. And although it's true that improving earnings and asset growth are not the only goals in takeovers, the fact that many mergers result in a net loss of value suggests
10 that schooling is sorely needed!

Every year hundreds of executives attend M&A courses at prestigious institutions from New York to L.A. In these 'open enrolment' classes, the only condition of attendance is your, or rather your company's, ability to pay the fees:
15 as much as $1,000 per day. At least that seems to demonstrate that the B-schools know something about improving earnings!

So what do you learn in a week with America's top finance professors? 'We aim to equip participants with
20 techniques based on best practice in the key areas of merger activity performance,' says Ted Austin from the Delaney School of Business. 'We cover all aspects of the conception, planning, due diligence, negotiation and integration stages.' Austin also draws on case studies and
25 guest speakers to illustrate some of the most common acquirer errors: over-valuation, over-confidence, 'under-communicating', and underestimating the value of your newest assets – the people in the company you've just bought. In the turmoil of integration, your best engineers
30 and managers may be more susceptible to attractive offers from the competition.

There is no doubt that M&A is a risky business. With a 70% plus failure-rate, you might think that B-school professors would do well to discourage their students
35 from launching takeover bids. But you'd be wrong. Austin describes some of the other (good) reasons for mergers and acquisitions: 'I suppose the most popular reasons invoked in CEOs' messages to shareholders are developing synergies and making economies of scale – these are
40 sometimes conveniently long-term goals! Other objectives may be increasing market share; cross-selling, when for example a bank can sell insurance to its existing clients; diversification, if a company is perceived to be too dependent on a niche market; or quite simply taking on
45 debt, the so-called poison pill, in order to make itself a less attractive target for would-be buyers.'

The bankers, brokers and lawyers will be pleased to know there are still many good reasons to merge. But what about the wrong reasons? 'They mainly involve excessive
50 pride or arrogance on the part of management,' says Austin. 'Wanting to build too big an empire, too quickly, and overextending the financial, commercial and human capacity of the organization.
55 These courses aim to help executives bring their CEOs back down to earth: learning to follow your head rather than your heart is the key lesson in avoiding very expensive mistakes.'

7.2 Vocabulary Business performance

Discussion

1 Match these newspaper headlines with the extracts they belong to. Decide why the headlines are good or bad news.

① **Titanic Enterprises go under**

② Air New Zealand in the black

③ **OLDIES RECORDS COVER COSTS**

④ HONECKER LTD. GO TO THE WALL

⑤ BRIZAL COFFEE BREAK EVEN

⑥ **Marks & Engsel go bankrupt**

⑦ **LIVERPOOL F.C. IN THE RED**

⑧ Predictor Inc. make a profit

ⓐ After a series of expensive transfer deals the club has failed to meet financial goals.

ⓑ The cooperative has run out of capital and had to close all its branches.

ⓒ The music firm was a hit with investors as record revenues matched expenses.

ⓓ S American shareholders had grounds for optimism as news filtered through of a probable return to profitability.

ⓔ Catastrophic results in E Europe led to the company's collapse on the Berlin stock exchange.

ⓕ The futurology specialists will report a miraculous return on investment at tomorrow's AGM.

ⓖ Profitability soared as sales of flights to rugby internationals took off.

ⓗ As the company's stock sank to rock-bottom, chairman Leonard Caprio described it as 'only the tip of the iceberg'.

Giving financial information

2 Mark sentences 1–8 and a)–h) from a financial report ↗, ↘, or → to show whether the words in **bold** indicate an increase, a decrease, or stability. Which two phrases mean something else?

1 Last year our billings **rose** by 45%. ↗
2 Variable costs **are falling**.
3 The book value of our assets **has jumped**.
4 We expect fixed costs **to stabilize**.
5 In 2001 our stock **slid** to a record low.
6 Production costs **fluctuate** over the year.
7 Liquidity will **dip** if payments are late.
8 Liabilities **reach a high** when business is slow in August.

a) Our overheads should **level off**.
b) Our shares **slumped** during the crash.
c) Our turnover almost **doubled**.
d) Cost of sales **varies** from month to month.
e) Our debt **peaks** at the end of summer.
f) The value of our buildings and equipment **has climbed**.
g) Our operating costs **are dropping**.
h) Cash flow **will deteriorate** if we allow customers more credit.

Now match sentences 1–8 to those with similar meanings a)–h).

3 Choose the correct label a) or b) for each graph.

①	②	③	④
$3M / $2M	30% / 20%	25 / 10	50% / 30%
a) Sales increased by $3M.	a) There was a decrease of 10%.	a) Prices fell by €15.	a) There was a rise of 30%.
b) Sales increased to $3M.	b) There was a decrease to 10%.	b) Prices fell to €15.	b) There was a rise from 30%.

Internet research

Search for the keywords *bulls bears* to find out about two types of stock market investors. What other 'animals' can you find on the stock markets?

4 Match the causes and effects in each set of four below.

1 There was a **considerable improvement** in the company's image
2 We plan to acquire new technology;
3 As a result of its strategic alliances,
4 A wave of corporate raids resulted in
5 After the merger, our profitability will **improve significantly**
6 Due to lower labour costs,
7 They saw **a slight increase** in sales
8 Share prices often **go up sharply**

a) as a result, debt will **grow slightly**.
b) the company enjoyed **moderate growth**.
c) **a sudden surge** in redundancies.
d) thanks to a joint venture with a prestigious American corporation.
e) profits will **shoot up dramatically**.
f) as a consequence of their diversification into new markets.
g) because of rumours of hostile takeovers.
h) as a result of economies of scale.

5 The phrases in **bold** in 4 describe different degrees of change. Put them in order from smallest (-) to largest (+).

Verb + adverb	-	+

Adjective + noun	-	+

6 Complete the sentences below using phrases in the box. Sometimes there is more than one possible answer.

> as a result   as a result of   resulted in   thanks to   due to
> as a consequence   as a consequence of   because of

1 The FTSE 100 fell again _____ increasing economic uncertainty.
2 Rumours of a merger _____ Tenzin Pharma gaining 6%.
3 Nidden PLC has successfully resisted a raid; _____ its price has levelled off.
4 Henry Halen climbed quickly _____ excellent third quarter results.
5 Profit warnings from several computer companies _____ significant drops in price.
6 JTL Holdings' Brazilian subsidiary went bankrupt. _____ its stock fell to £22.

Which five phrases explain causes? Which three introduce effects?

Listening for detail

7 3:02 Listen to a radio stock market report and complete the graph of Fraxis Corp's share-price history.

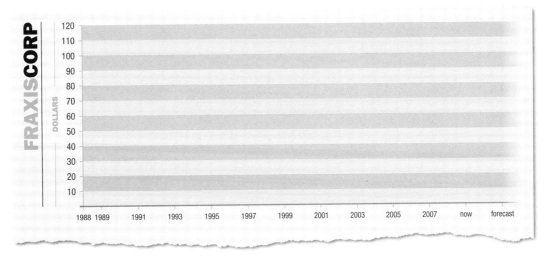

Presenting

8 With a partner, practise describing the information in a graph.

Student A: turn to page 112.
Student B: turn to page 116.

Refresh your memory

Future forms
will + do
I'll open the window.
instant decisions,
predictions, future facts
going to + do
It's going to rain.
plans & intentions,
prediction based on
present situation
is / are doing
I'm seeing the doctor at 10.30.
fixed arrangements for
the future

▶ Grammar reference page 130

Expressing likelihood

▶ Grammar reference page 131

7.3 Grammar | Future forms and expressing likelihood

Test yourself: Future forms

1 Underline the best future forms (*will* or *going to*) in the dialogue.

A: What do you think of Artip Laboratories? Iticom are meeting Artip's Board of Directors: they (1) **will / are going to** make a takeover bid.
B: I know. But Artip are losing millions. Everybody can see what's coming: they (2) **will / are going to** go bankrupt.
A: Iticom obviously don't agree. Perhaps they think that with new management and fresh capital, Artip (3) **will / are going to** have a second chance.
B: Hm. Well, I'm sure they're wrong. Anyway, I've already discussed it with my broker. (4) **I'll sell / I'm going to sell** my Iticom shares.
A: Really? You're sure? In that case, maybe (5) **I'll sell / I'm going to sell** mine, too.

2 Decide which sentence in each pair uses the wrong future form (in **bold**) and correct it.

1a) Kylton Electronics **are launching** a new home entertainment system on the 15th.
 b) Hundreds of journalists have blocked a whole week, because Kylton **will fly** them to Hawaii for the launch.
2a) The system's specifications are top secret; Kylton **will not release** any details until the launch.
 b) Experts believe the product **is** taking the home-entertainment market by storm next quarter.
3a) 'Lots of celebrities are coming to our launch party,' said a distributor. 'Everybody will be here except the President, because he **will attend** a conference in Italy.'
 b) 'We **are going to fly** 20,000 units in the day before the launch.'
4a) Kylton have already threatened they **are prosecuting** any pirates.
 b) However, copycat products **will** no doubt **be** on sale by December.

Test yourself: Expressing likelihood

3 Match the two parts of the forecasts and estimate how probable it is that each event will happen, from 0% (= totally impossible) to 100% (= absolutely certain).

50%	1 We have **a 50/50 chance**	be sold.
20%	2 **We're unlikely to**	of success.
	3 **There's no way** my boss	get a better offer.
	4 Artip **will definitely**	will agree.

	5 Costs are rising: **it's possible** our competitors	will deliver by next week.
	6 It's going to be a tough negotiation, but they **might just**	will put their prices up.
	7 It's in everybody's interest: the merger **will definitely**	accept our offer.
	8 **There's not much chance** our suppliers	go ahead.

	9 You did a good job: you're **almost certain to**	find common ground.
	10 Their cultures are different, but I suppose they **could**	come down.
	11 Wait a few months, the asking price is **bound to**	'll meet the deadline.
	12 There's **a good chance** we	get a raise.

	13 It's **highly likely that** taxes	get the job.
	14 It's still uncertain, but they **may**	will increase.
	15 Chris has all the right qualifications: she's **likely to**	increase.
	16 In the months to come, we **fully expect** sales to	announce a merger.

Internet research

Search for the keywords *Alvin Toffler* to find out about this leading futurist and his company's work

Discussion

4 Work in groups of three. You are futurists. Choose a column each, A, B or C. Prepare a one-minute presentation discussing the likelihood of each event happening by 2050. Using the expressions in **bold** in 3, take turns to present your views, answer questions and defend your ideas.

A	B	C
Everyone will work from home.	Everyone will go back to university every ten years.	Nobody will work more than three days a week.
There will be a single world currency.	Mobile cities will be built on the oceans.	Virtual offices will be accessible from anywhere in the world.
There will be hotels and conference centres on the moon.	The majority of senior managers will be women.	Chinese will be the language of business.

Listening

5 3:03 Listen to a conversation between two friends at a party, and mark the future events in the box *U* (unlikely) or *P* (planned).

☐ go freelance ☐ start evening classes ☐ stay at Artip ☐ find a new job
☐ Artip take-over ☐ read the job ads ☐ give up smoking and drinking
☐ retrain as a marketing assistant

Which arrangement has Ashley forgotten to mention?

Discussion

6 With a partner, discuss your plans, intentions and hopes for the future. Talk about:

- the rest of the day
- this evening
- tomorrow
- the weekend
- next week
- next month
- next holidays
- next term
- next year
- your next job
- the next 25 years
- your retirement. (It's never too soon to plan ahead!)

7.4 Speaking Presentations – visuals

Discussion

1 Mark these presentation tools *E* (essential) or *N* (non-essential) to a good presentation, then compare with a partner and explain your choices.

- [ ] a laptop
- [ ] a video projector
- [ ] a DVD player and TV
- [ ] a laser pointer
- [ ] a flip chart and pens
- [ ] a blackboard and chalk
- [ ] an overhead projector
- [ ] a set of handouts
- [ ] a 35-mm slide projector
- [ ] presentation software

Listening for gist

2 3:04–3:08 Listen to five presentation extracts A–E. Match each extract to one of the guidelines below.

- [ ] Don't put too much data on slides: no more than six lines of text, and no more than six words per line.
- [ ] Too many visuals confuse the audience: don't overload them with slides.
- [ ] Don't be too technical: adapt to the target audience, and don't read out text on slides.
- [ ] Help the audience to understand by introducing, highlighting and explaining the most important information.
- [ ] Check all materials and equipment, and have backups for everything.

3 3:09 Listen to a better presentation and decide which pair of slides (A, B or C) is being described.

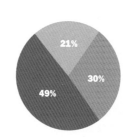
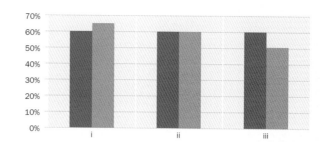

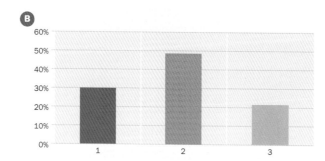
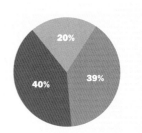

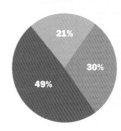
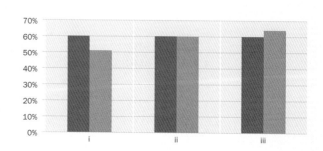

Internet research

What do the terms *vertical* and *horizontal integration* mean? Find out about current trends in vertical integration in the music, drinks or TV industries.

Listening for detail

4 Listen again and complete the expressions for presenting visuals. The expressions are numbered in the order you will hear them.

Introducing a slide or visual	Highlighting
I'd like you to look at this slide.	**As** the graph **shows**, …
(1) **My next** _____ _____ two charts …	(2) **As you will** _____ in the pie-chart, …
(4) **Let's** _____ at the second chart.	(5) **As you can** _____, after a merger …
Contrasting	Explaining and interpreting
In contrast to …	(7) **The** figures _____ to _____ that …
(3) _____ **to** almost half who said …	(8) **This is** _____ **to** a perceived drop …
(6) _____ it remains about the same.	(9) **The results** _____ **that** retailers …
(10) **as** _____ **to** manufacturers …	(11) **This is the** _____ **of** improved …

Presenting visuals

5 The pie-chart shows how typical Americans spend their income.

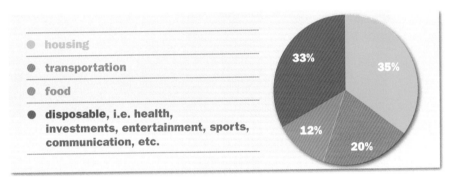

- housing
- transportation
- food
- disposable, i.e. health, investments, entertainment, sports, communication, etc.

33% 35% 12% 20%

Draw two pie-charts, showing how you use your income today, and how you think you might use it in twenty years from now. In small groups, present your charts using the framework below.

- Introduce the first chart.
- Highlight points of interest.
- Explain anything unusual.
- Interpret what your chart says about you and your lifestyle.
- Repeat the four steps above for your second chart, and contrast the second chart with the first.

Pronunciation: Linking

6 3:10–3:13 Words beginning with a vowel are linked to the previous word, as in the example in 1. Mark the links in the other three sentences in the same way.

1 Customers were asked if service had deteriorated as a result of the merger.

2 Only a third of customers noticed an improvement.

3 Customer satisfaction falls by an average of almost 9%.

4 This is essentially due to a drop in levels of service after a merger.

Listen and check your answers. Practise saying the sentences, pronouncing the linked words or groups of words as one continuous sound.

Presentation

7 Work in groups of three. Your company, which manufactures tennis racquets, is looking for a suitable takeover target in order to diversify and accelerate growth. Each person will present one company: decide together which is the best candidate for acquisition.

Student A: turn to page 111.
Student B: turn to page 113.
Student C: turn to page 117.

Discussion

1 Decide which two of the following you would *not* expect to find in a presentation slide. Why not?

different fonts   italics   bullet points   photos   footnotes
sound effects   paragraphs   backgrounds   logos   bold text

Reading and analysis

2 Read the three presentation slides. Which is the best way of presenting the information, and why?

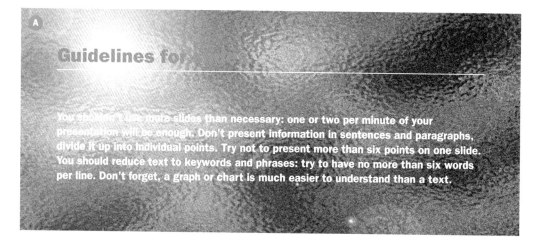

Guidelines for

You shouldn't use more slides than necessary: one or two per minute of your presentation will be enough. Don't present information in sentences and paragraphs, divide it up into individual points. Try not to present more than six points on one slide. You should reduce text to keywords and phrases: try to have no more than six words per line. Don't forget, a graph or chart is much easier to understand than a text.

B

Guidelines for slides

- 1–2 slides per minute of presentation
- Information in points, not complete sentences
- Maximum six points per slide
- Reduce to key words and phrases
- Maximum six words for each point
- Graphs and visuals wherever possible

C

Guidelines for slides

- 1–2 slides / minute
- info in points
- max 6 / slide
- keywords only
- max 6 words
- visuals best

Writing

3 Underline the key words in each extract to include on a slide about writing presentations. Then reduce each point to six to eight words.

1 One of the most challenging aspects of writing a presentation is the need to organize the information in a logical way.
2 Choose attractive background and text colours that are comfortable for the audience to read.
3 Presentation software can be fun to use. Be creative, but do not include too many effects which may distract your audience from your content.
4 Make sure the text is large enough that the audience can read it easily from the back of the room. Also, use a standard font that is not too complicated or distracting.
5 Use positive statements like 'The figures show...' rather than vague language like 'The data could possibly suggest ...'.

4 Reduce this presentation extract to five points on one slide.

> 'I'm here this morning to present the three possible scenarios which, in our discussions with the bank and our consultants, we have identified as the three most realistic futures for our company. Our first option is to do nothing: we know that the market is becoming more and more competitive, but if we are careful, we can continue to survive – at least for some years. Our second option is to borrow money to invest in new technologies in order, hopefully, to develop new, high-margin products for our existing customers, and for new markets. The third and final scenario is to launch a takeover bid to acquire Iticom, who already have the technology we need to enter those new markets immediately. Ladies and gentlemen, after carefully considering all the options, it is this third scenario which I intend to recommend. It is, of course, a high-risk scenario, but it is a scenario which holds enormous potential for our company.'

Taking notes and writing slides

5 3:14 Listen to a presentation about Galway Software. Take notes on the strengths, weaknesses, opportunities and threats the speaker has identified, and his proposal. Then write slides to illustrate the presentation.

Writing slides

6 Plan a short presentation on a subject of your choice and write a maximum of six slides. Exchange slides with a partner and give each other feedback.

7.6 Case study Calisto

Discussion

1 Calisto, IMM and Reysonido sell musical instruments in Central America. Look at the figures and compare the three businesses.

	FY	FY -1	FY -2
IMM	(M$)	(M$)	(M$)
Sales	21	20	25
Cost of Sales	10.5	10	12.5
Total Operating Expenses	8	9	10
EBIT	2.5	1	2.5
CALISTO	(M$)	(M$)	(M$)
Sales	15	18	20
Cost of Sales	7.5	9	10
Total Operating Expenses	9	9	9
EBIT	(1.5)	0	1
REYSONIDO	(M$)	(M$)	(M$)
Sales	10	11	12
Cost of Sales	4	4.4	4.8
Total Operating Expenses	6	6	6
EBIT	0	0.6	1.2

Reading

2 Read the newspaper article and answer the questions.

1 How has Dylan achieved its impressive growth?
2 What effect has it had on the market?
3 Which company has adapted best to the new market leader?

Dylan rocks instrument market

New figures yesterday confirmed the meteoric rise of Dylan Instruments to number one in Central America's musical instrument market (see charts). Panama-based newcomers Dylan, who have modelled their business on PC direct sales giant Dell, have pushed former market leader Instrumentos Musicales Mejicanos (IMM) into second place. Under the charismatic leadership of CEO Abejundio Dylan, the firm has used slick marketing and aggressive discounting to capture market share from all its competitors. 'We aim to have 50% of the local market in two years' time,' trumpets Dylan. Competitors like IMM, Calisto and Reysonido are considering alliances to ensure their survival; several smaller players have already gone out of business.

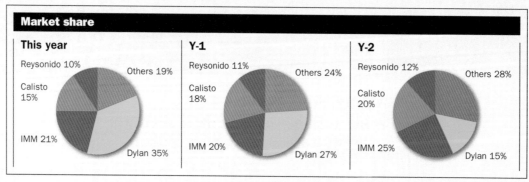

Market share

This year
Reysonido 10%
Others 19%
Calisto 15%
IMM 21%
Dylan 35%

Y-1
Reysonido 11%
Others 24%
Calisto 18%
IMM 20%
Dylan 27%

Y-2
Reysonido 12%
Others 28%
Calisto 20%
IMM 25%
Dylan 15%

Listening for gist

3 🔊 3:15 Listen to a presentation by Calisto's President to the Board of Directors and list the company's six options in column 1 of the table.

Options	Notes
1 Cut jobs	– same strategy as _____ – would reduce operating expenses by _____ %
2	– same strategy as _____ – would reduce production costs by _____ % – would increase operating expenses by _____ per year
3	– next year's sales: _____ – cost of sales would increase to _____
4	– price: _____ – advantages: _____ – disadvantages: _____
5	– price: _____ – bonus: _____ – repayments: _____ – combined sales: _____
6	– sell off our _____

Listening for detail

4 Listen again and complete the notes on Calisto's six options in column 2 of the table above.

Discussion and presentation

5 In small groups, meet as consultants to Calisto's Board of Directors.

1 Review Calisto's six options, as well as your own ideas, and decide what strategy you will recommend.
2 Prepare a presentation outlining your recommendations to the Board, using slides to structure and support your arguments.
3 Give your presentation. Yours will be in competition with those of other groups. As Calisto's Board of Directors, the class should ask questions and vote for the best presentation.

Internet research

How can smaller companies compete with a dominant market leader? Search for the keywords *"Avis: We Try Harder"* to read about how Avis took on a giant.

8.1 About business Export sales and payment

Discussion

1 How can selling your product in other countries be more difficult than at home? With a partner, list four aspects of export sales where there may not be a level playing field.

Scan reading

2 Read the article opposite from a trade magazine. Which four export mistakes did Eisenhart Games make?

Reading for detail

3 Read the article again. The words in grey are explained in the *Wordlist* on page 158. Which eight lessons does Vincenti say exporters have to learn?

Listening for detail

4 🔊 3:16 Listen to an interview with James Sullivan, a sales manager with Nehling and Hynes, an American credit agency, and answer the questions.

1 Which two kinds of service do credit agencies provide?
2 How large is Nehling and Hynes' database, and why is this important?
3 How are credit ratings useful?
4 What proportion of European and US firms purchase credit insurance?
5 Which advantage does credit insurance give Daryl Vincenti in Saudi Arabia?
6 On average, how much does international credit insurance cost?

Reading for detail

5 Read this extract from a guide to methods of payment in international trade. Put the methods in order from the safest (1) to the riskiest (4) from the exporter's point of view.

☐ **Open account**
Goods are shipped directly to the buyer, with a request for payment.

☐ **Advance payment**
Payment is expected by the exporter, in full, before goods are shipped.

☐ **Bills for collection**
A bill of exchange is sent from the exporter's bank to the buyer's bank. When the buyer agrees to pay on a certain date, they sign the draft. The documents and goods are released to the buyer against this acceptance.

☐ **Letters of credit (L/Cs), also known as documentary credits (DCs)**
Documentary credit is a bank-to-bank commitment of payment: the buyer's bank guarantees that payment will be made when the shipping documents are found to be in compliance with terms set by the buyer.

Discussion

6 As the exporter, decide what methods of payment in 5 you would require from these customers.

1 The buyer is a well-known company in a large country in western Europe. This is a first order but you hope the buyer will become a regular customer.
2 The buyer is in a country where currency exchange is controlled by the government. Requests for foreign currency payments must be justified by supporting documents.
3 The buyer is a new customer in a country with a fragile economy and a poor credit rating.
4 The buyer is a large North American company with a reputation for slow payment.
5 The buyer is one of your suppliers in a neighbouring country.
6 The buyer represents a small company in a developing country and is a personal friend.

7 You and a friend design and sell your own line of T-shirts at rock concerts. You have been very successful in your own country, and now several contacts in other countries have expressed interest in your product. What problems do you anticipate if you start to export, and what solutions can you suggest?

Pinball wizard
learns from mistakes

At Chicago-based Eisenhart Games, Daryl Vincenti is known as the 'export wizard'. Over the last three years, the pinball machine
5 manufacturer has developed a profitable new market in the Middle East. 'Times are hard for pinball in the US,' says Vincenti. 'Competition from video games
10 and computers has hit small manufacturers like us really hard, so we have to find new markets.' Eisenhart now has some 35% of a growing Middle East market, but
15 it hasn't been easy. 'We made a lot of mistakes at the beginning,' confesses Vincenti, 'but we learned fast. We're now starting to work in S E Asia, and things are
20 much easier because we've taken important lessons on board in the Middle East.'

Vincenti puts using a good credit agency at the top of his
25 lessons learned list. 'When you've invested time, effort and money in making an export sale, you want to get paid! After wasting a lot of time chasing payments, a friend
30 introduced me to Nehling and Hynes. We learned that by using a credit agency to check out your customer's creditworthiness and to insure against non-payment, you
35 can make export virtually risk-free.'

Other lessons learned centred on adaptability. 'Be flexible: you have to learn to think outside the box,' says Vincenti. 'And
40 don't assume that what works well in your domestic market will automatically go down well in another. You should also be prepared to modify your
45 product specifications to meet local conditions, and to focus on different aspects of the marketing mix. In the Middle East, for example, price is not everything.
50 We started out trying to sell on price: we soon learned that over there, image, quality and service are all more important.'

Vincenti also stresses that
55 would-be exporters should make a firm commitment to export, but focus on one market, rather than trying to sell all over the world. 'You don't succeed in export
60 markets by giving them a couple of hours a week when things are slow at home. You have to put in a lot of time, get out there and meet your customers, and manage
65 your local distributors proactively – if you don't, it's "game over".' Eisenhart learned the hard way when they signed an exclusive deal with an agent in the Gulf;
70 at the end of the first year, sales were zero, and the agent had disappeared without trace.

A final lesson is to remember that appearances can be
75 deceptive, warns Vincenti: 'One day we received a 15-word fax in approximate English from what seemed to be one man and a camel somewhere out in the desert. We
80 thought it was a joke, but a week later we decided we should answer it anyway. They're now our biggest customer.'

'... at the end of the first year, sales were zero, and the agent had disappeared without trace.'

8 International trade

Collocations

1 Choose one keyword from the box to complete each group of verb–noun collocations.

conditions	a payment	a deal	goods	an application	an invoice
4	6	5	2	3	1

issue		provide		submit	
settle	1 _____	load	2 _____	vet	3 _____
query		ship		approve	

state		negotiate		make	
meet	4 _____	make	5 _____	meet	6 _____
comply with		sign		chase	

Decide whether the buyer or the seller carries out the actions above.

Phrasal verbs

2 Put the words in these guidelines for exporters in the correct order. Each sentence contains a phrasal verb.

1 check customer's your on creditworthiness up new
2 doubts insurance if you take about getting have out paid
3 behind their customers do not get payments with let
4 as invoices soon become they chase as overdue up
5 act getting your difficulties quickly if customer is into

3 Match each definition to the correct phrasal verb in 2.

a) get something officially from a specialist organization
b) moving towards a particular condition or situation
c) find out information about something or someone discreetly
d) find out what is being done about something
e) fail to do something at the right time

Internet research

What is a thesaurus and when is it useful? Search for the keyword *thesaurus*. Then, in an online thesaurus, search for the nouns *credit*, *cash* and *trade*. For each noun, find synonyms, antonyms and common collocations.

Listening

4 3:17–3:21 Listen to five conversations about export issues. Use vocabulary from 1 and 2 to say what is happening in each.

Collocations

5 Combine the nouns on the left with those on the right to make as many two-word collocations as possible.

credit	claim	loyalty	line	portfolio
insurance	policy	sales	insurance	card
customer	terms	period	credit	

6 Use collocations from 5 to complete these sentences.

1 Frequent-flyer schemes, free gifts and credit are all ways of developing _____.
2 To avoid cash-flow problems, sales teams need to be given a clear _____.
3 An _____ provides cover in case of an accident.
4 Because old customers leave, a sales person must constantly be looking to add to their _____.
5 _____ reduces the risk of default on export payments.
6 After the fire, the company filed an _____ for compensation.

Defining words

7 With a partner, practise defining words relating to business transactions.

Student A: use the information below.
Student B: turn to page 117.

Give Student B definitions for 1, 2, 4, 6, 7 and 9 across. Student B will give you definitions for 1, 3, 5 and 8 down and 10 and 11 across to help you complete the crossword.

1 (across) H A V E D O U B T S
2 (across) M A K E A N A P O L O G Y
3 (down) P
4 (across) R E C O N S I D E R A P O S I T I O N
5 (down) S
6 (across) T A K E P R E C A U T I O N S
7 (across) M A K E A N O F F E R
8 (down)
9 (across) S E N D A R E M I N D E R
10 (across)
11 (across)

in
periods
the morning, July, the winter, 2007, the 80s

on
days and dates
Monday, the 17th, New Year's Day

at
times and special times
3pm, breakfast, the weekend, Christmas

Ø
expressions with *last, next, ago, yesterday, tomorrow*

▶ Grammar reference page 132

8.3 Grammar   Prepositions

Test yourself: Prepositions

1 Use each preposition once to complete the schedule.

during	within	at	from	in	until	by	for	after	on

Preliminary studies will be carried out (1) _____ January to June of next year. (2) _____ this period, the exact scope of the work will be evaluated, and a definitive quotation will be submitted (3) _____ 15 June latest. The customer will then have (4) _____ mid-September to study the proposal. After signature of the contract, work will begin (5) _____ 1 October and is expected to continue (6) _____ 18 months. A deposit of 20% will be payable at signature (7) _____ September; thereafter, invoices will be issued (8) _____ one week of completion of each stage of the project, for payment (9) _____ 90 days. The final 15% will not be invoiced until (10) _____ reception of the completed building.

2 Complete the story with appropriate prepositions. Sometimes no preposition is needed.

1 On vacation in Kenya, a buyer with IBM heard _____ a small new factory and called _____ a salesman.
2 She asked _____ the salesman if his components conformed _____ American norms.
3 She insisted _____ seeing the workshop and commented _____ the poor working conditions.
4 Nevertheless, the salesman succeeded _____ convincing her to consent _____ a trial order.
5 He told _____ the buyer that she could rely _____ him to organize everything.
6 She returned to the US, looking forward _____ receiving the components, but after several weeks she had heard nothing _____ Kenya.
7 Eventually she rang _____ the factory and complained _____ the manager.
8 The manager apologized politely _____ the delay, but explained that he was still waiting _____ a report on the new customer's creditworthiness.

3 In these guidelines for exporters, the nouns in **bold** are in the wrong sentence. Find the correct noun for each statement.

1 International negotiators should always show **responsibility** for other cultures.
2 Transparency in all dealings with foreign governments is essential to **involvement** in export.
3 Exporters should remember that certain countries levy special **effect** on imports.
4 Any **success** in illegal trading practices can permanently damage a company's image.
5 Late payment can have a very damaging **taxes** on a company's cash-flow.
6 The seller's bank may have **solution** to information about the buyer's creditworthiness.
7 In a confirmed documentary credit, the seller's bank takes **respect** for obtaining payment.
8 Bills of exchange and letters of credit are no **need** for careful credit checks.
9 Credit ratings and reports are a practical **access** to the problem of evaluating risk.
10 Credit insurance can eliminate the **substitute** for letters of credit.

Listening for detail

4 🔊 3:22 Listen to the conversation between Paul, a manager, and his assistant, Jenny. Complete the schedule with the times or time periods, using the appropriate prepositions.

1 Jenny is picking up tickets
   this evening, before 6.00.

2 Jenny is dropping tickets off at office

3 Paul's flight leaves

4 Check-in opens

5 Finance meeting finishes

6 Paul's kids go to bed

7 Paul is staying in the States

8 Paul is attending six meetings

9 Paul's return flight leaves

10 Paul is preparing the Merosom pitch

11 Merosom announce their decision

12 Paul will read files for New York meetings

Internet research

Search for the keywords *"how to become a millionaire"*. As you read, make a list of five words followed by a dependent preposition, which you feel are useful to learn.

Dependent prepositions

5 Delete the verb in each group that does not have the same dependent preposition as the other three, and write in the preposition, if any.

1 agree	~~ask~~	consent	refer	(*to*)
2 comply	sympathize	resort	associate	(_____)
3 vote	pay	allow	object	(_____)
4 depend	rely	insist	attend	(_____)
5 result	invest	borrow	succeed	(_____)
6 suffer	emerge	hear	account	(_____)
7 discuss	apply	look	apologize	(_____)
8 consist	react	approve	think	(_____)
9 access	call	comment	tell	(_____)
10 insure	fight	protect	conform	(_____)

Listening for gist

6 🔊 3:23–3:32 Listen to ten short dialogues and use a word from the box to describe what the people are discussing. Be careful to use the right preposition.

> access   apologizing   aptitude   complying   damage   dependence
> hearing   insuring   investing   satisfaction

Speaking

7 Work in groups of three. You are going to hold a conversation about one of the subjects below.

- how to become a millionaire
- how to persuade a bank to lend you money
- how to get promotion

- how to find and keep customers
- how to manage professional stress
- how to manage your boss

Student A: turn to page 113.
Student B: turn to page 115.
Student C: turn to page 117.

8.4 Speaking   Negotiations – diplomacy

Discussion

1 Read the information in the box, then with a partner discuss whether the countries and regions below are *L* (low-context) or *H* (high-context) cultures.

	Low-context cultures	High-context cultures
Focus of negotiations	problem-solving, deadlines are important	relationship-building, time is flexible
Communication style	direct, verbal, few non-verbal signals	indirect, dislike conflict, avoid saying no
Business organization	individuals more important than the group	group harmony more important than individuals

- ☐ China
- ☐ Middle East
- ☐ USA
- ☐ Latin America
- ☐ Australia
- ☐ UK
- ☐ N Europe
- ☐ Japan

What does this mean for international negotiators?

Listening for gist

2 🔊 3:33–3:35 Listen to three negotiation extracts. What went wrong in each case? Think about high- and low-context cultures, as well as the actual phrases used.

3 🔊 3:36–3:38 Listen to alternative versions of the three negotiations. How do the negotiators avoid misunderstandings?

Listening for detail

4 Listen to the alternative versions again and complete the phrases below. Phrases are numbered in the order you hear them on the recording.

	Extract 1	Extract 2	Extract 3
Checking understanding	1 Correct me if _____, but you seem to be _____ that ...	4 Have I _____ right? 5 Would I be right _____ that ... ?	8 If I've understood _____ ...
Correcting misunderstandings	2 I'm afraid there _____ a slight _____.	6 I'm sorry, that isn't _____.	9 Perhaps I haven't _____.
Reformulating	3 Let me _____ another _____.	7 What I was _____ was ...	10 Allow me _____. 11 What I _____ ...

Diplomatic language

5 Match the direct remarks 1–4 to the diplomatic forms that were used in the listening.

Direct	Diplomatic
1 I'm not ready to make a decision.	a) Perhaps we should talk again in a few days?
2 This project is totally unrealistic.	b) I think we might need more time to explore all the implications.
3 Let's finish the meeting now.	c) We would be very happy to give you the same terms as Auckland, if you were in a position to order the same volume.
4 We won't pay for shipping unless you give us a bigger order.	d) I'm afraid we feel there are still quite a large number of difficulties to face in this project.

Internet research

Search for the keywords *high low context polychronic culture* to find out more about Edward T Hall's work on culture and communication.

6 Complete the summary.

Diplomatic language often uses:

- modal verbs like *could*, _____, _____, _____
- softening adverbs like *maybe* or _____
- qualifiers like *a bit*, *rather*, *a little* or _____
- introductory warnings like *I'm sorry*, *actually*, _____
- (negative) questions rather than statements.

7 'Translate' the direct remarks into diplomatic language, and vice versa.

Direct	Diplomatic
1	I'm sorry, but wouldn't it be easier for everybody if we held the meeting here rather than in Colombia?
2 If you don't want to do business, just say so!	
3	Actually, I was wondering whether you might possibly reconsider your position?
4 So you don't want to sell us your products?	
5	I'm sorry, but couldn't we start a little earlier than 11am tomorrow? We might find we would make a bit more progress.
6 That's not true. I never said that!	
7	To be perfectly honest, I'm inclined to think that business trips aren't quite as useful as everybody says they are.
8 So you don't trust us to pay?	

Negotiating

8 With a partner, take turns to choose a subject and hold short negotiations following the chart below. Be diplomatic!

1 buying worldwide rights to your partner's movie script
2 buying advertising space on your partner's car
3 buying worldwide rights to using your partner's name
4 buying equity in your partner's business

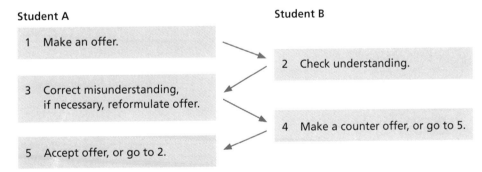

Student A
1 Make an offer.
3 Correct misunderstanding, if necessary, reformulate offer.
5 Accept offer, or go to 2.

Student B
2 Check understanding.
4 Make a counter offer, or go to 5.

8 International trade

Discussion

1 Answer the questions below, then compare your answers with a partner.

1 What is your philosophy on credit?
   a) never borrow money   b) use credit in moderation   c) get as much credit as you can
2 If you have to ask someone to repay money they owe you, how do you feel?
   a) embarrassed   b) angry   c) nothing, it's only money
3 What would you write to remind someone they owe you money? Why?
   a) a text message   b) an email   c) a letter

Reading and analysis

2 Read the emails below. Which email is:

a request? ☐   a reminder? ☐   a refusal? ☐   a final demand? ☐

Highlight the phrases which helped you to decide.

---

1 According to our records, our invoice number 061704 for €15,789 is now overdue. If, however, this invoice has already been settled, please disregard this email.

---

3 Further to our email of 23 May, we have still not received payment for the outstanding sum of €15,789. We regret to inform you that we are suspending all shipments until this outstanding balance has been settled.

---

2 In answer to your enquiry of 2 September about trading on open account, we regret to inform you that we are unable to agree to your request due to your insufficient credit rating. We hope you will understand the reasons for this decision, and we trust that we can continue to do business together as in the past.

---

4 As we now intend to place regular orders with your company, we would appreciate being able to trade on open account. We are confident this arrangement will be to our mutual benefit, and we look forward to an early reply.

---

3 Make complete sentences by using one phrase from each column. The first one has been done for you.

1 I am writing to enquire	agree to	which is still outstanding.
2 I am afraid group policy	the sum of €21,552	to extend credit terms of 60 days.
3 We are pleased to	whether you would be able	of this outstanding balance.
4 May I remind you that	your early settlement	the terms you propose.
5 We wrote to you on 4 November	does not allow us	to our legal department.
6 Would you let us	regarding the balance of €12,650	is still outstanding?
7 We would appreciate	but to pass the matter on	as soon as possible?
8 We shall have no alternative	know your decision	to give more than 30 days' credit.

Which sentences are used in:

a request? ☐ ☐   a reminder? ☐ ☐   a refusal? ☐
an agreement? ☐   a final demand? ☐ ☐

Internet research

If your customers are slow payers, one way to improve cash-flow is factoring. Search for the keywords *factoring receivables* to find out how factoring works, and its advantages and disadvantages.

4 Which is the most polite form, a) or b)?

1a) In view of the increase in our volume of business, …
  b) Considering how much more business we're giving you, …
2a) About the longer credit you asked for, …
  b) With regard to your request for improved credit terms, …
3a) Re: your letter dated 31/1, …
  b) Further to your letter of 31 January, …
4a) We look forward to receiving your order.
  b) We expect you to order quickly.
5a) We're giving you a week to pay, …
  b) Unless we receive payment within seven days, …
6a) We would like to apologize for the delay in sending the enclosed cheque.
  b) We are sorry we took so long to send the enclosed cheque.
7a) This was an unfortunate oversight due to circumstances beyond our control.
  b) We forgot, but it wasn't our fault.
8a) We can assure you that it will not recur.
  b) Don't worry, it will never happen again.

5 Complete the emails using vocabulary from 2, 3 and 4.

1 In _____ of the increase in our volume of _____, I am writing to _____ whether you would be prepared to _____ credit terms of 60 days.
Would you let us _____ your decision as soon as _____?

4 May I _____ you that the sum of €101,000 is still _____ on your account?
We would appreciate your early _____ of this outstanding _____.

2 With _____ to your request for improved credit _____, I am afraid that group _____ does not _____ us to extend more than 30 days' credit.

5 We would like to _____ for the delay in sending the _____ cheque. This was an unfortunate _____ due to circumstances beyond our _____, and we can assure you that it will not _____.

3 _____ to your email of 17 July, we are pleased to agree to the _____ you propose, and we look _____ to receiving your order.

6 We wrote to you on 11 April _____ the balance of €15,550 which is still _____. Unless we receive payment _____ seven days, we shall have no _____ but to pass the matter on to our _____ department.

Which email is:

a request? ☐   a reminder? ☐   a refusal? ☐
a final demand? ☐   an apology? ☐   an agreement? ☐

Writing

6 Work in groups of three to write and reply to requests and reminders.

Student A: turn to page 113.
Student B: turn to page 115.
Student C: turn to page 116.

8.6 Case study | Jeddah Royal Beach Resort

Discussion

1 Brainstorm a list of services which large hotels can charge for in addition to accommodation.

Reading for detail

2 Read the extract from a business magazine and answer the questions.

1. How does giving credit increase room revenues and attract more clients?
2. Why do luxury hotels prefer to issue their own credit cards rather than be paid by VISA, MasterCard, American Express, etc.?
3. What are the advantages for the customer of a 'cashless resort'?
4. Who is Riaz Hussain and what are his responsibilities?

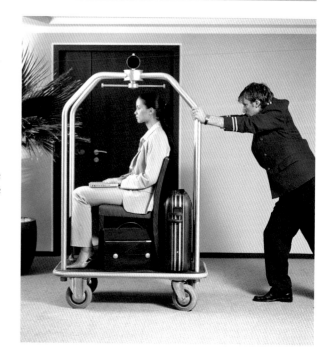

THE JEDDAH ROYAL BEACH RESORT

THE JEDDAH Royal Beach Resort is one of Saudi Arabia's newest and most luxurious hotels. In a fiercely competitive market where foreign corporations provide 75% of revenues, every hotel from the five-star palace to the one-star motel needs to increase room revenues to be able to invest in new facilities to attract new clients. One of the major incentives in the armoury of modern hotel marketing is credit. The Royal Beach, like many of its competitors, has its own credit manager, whose job is to manage the credit which the hotel uses to encourage customers to spend freely on additional services.

One of Riaz Hussain's first innovations as Credit Manager was to introduce an in-house credit card to the Royal Beach. Such credit cards are increasingly popular, allowing hotels to develop customer loyalty as well as to avoid paying commission to credit card companies. The Royal Beach advertises itself as a 'cashless resort': customers are able to use their electronic membership card to make reservations via the Internet, to speed up check-in and check-out, and to pay for a host of services including accommodation, telephone and fax, restaurant and bar bills, leisure activities, limousines, airline tickets and even cash advances with no exchange problems. With its own boutiques, nightclub, beach, water sports and golf course, it's easy for guests from all over the world to spend several days in the sun (and perhaps several weeks' salary!) with nothing more than their plastic smart card in their pocket.

Riaz Hussain's responsibilities include vetting corporate and individual applications for credit, following clients who reach or exceed their credit limits, and organizing debt recovery from indelicate guests, or their corporate sponsors, who 'forget' to settle their bills.

Listening for detail

3 🔊 3:39 Listen to a conversation between Riaz Hussain and Frederick, the front office manager at the Jeddah Royal Beach Resort, and complete the customer database entries.

Customer:

Ms Koepple

Company:

Company credit rating:

good / average / poor / unknown

Current credit limit:

0

Credit limit requested:

Notes:

Customer:

Mr Kobayashi

Company:

Company credit rating:

good / average / poor / unknown

Current credit limit:

Credit limit requested:

Notes:

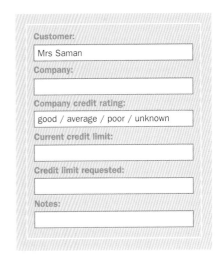

Customer:

Mrs Saman

Company:

Company credit rating:

good / average / poor / unknown

Current credit limit:

Credit limit requested:

Notes:

4 Listen again and answer the questions.

1 Why doesn't Riaz like having rock groups in the hotel?
2 If Ms Koepple leaves today without paying, how much will the hotel lose?
3 How much credit is Riaz prepared to allow her?
4 Why does Frederick think Mr Kobayashi is a difficult customer?
5 Why is Frederick suspicious of him?
6 What happened with Mrs Saman's company last year?
7 Why are Mrs Saman and her brother important for the hotel?

Discussion

5 Look at the chart showing the Jeddah Royal Beach Resort's customer payments. Describe the trends for:

1 cash payments 2 short credit periods 3 longer credit periods 4 uncollectibles.

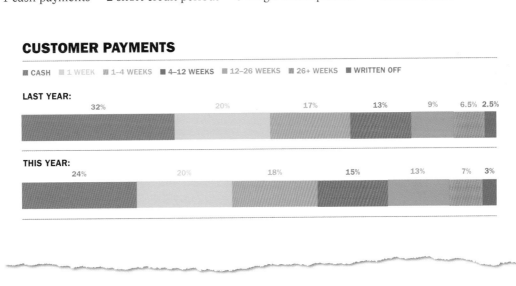

CUSTOMER PAYMENTS

■ CASH ■ 1 WEEK ■ 1–4 WEEKS ■ 4–12 WEEKS ■ 12–26 WEEKS ■ 26+ WEEKS ■ WRITTEN OFF

LAST YEAR:

| 32% | 20% | 17% | 13% | 9% | 6.5% | 2.5% |

THIS YEAR:

| 24% | 20% | 18% | 15% | 13% | 7% | 3% |

6 With a partner, decide:

1 how the trends in payments can be explained
2 how the hotel can improve its cash flow
3 how Riaz Hussain should deal with each of the three customer applications in 3.

Then change partners, and compare and explain your decisions.

Writing

7 Write a short letter to each customer explaining your decision.

Review 7

Mergers and acquisitions

1 Match each word or phrase about finance in the box to its definition below.

acquisition	assets	due diligence
economies of scale	fixed costs	liabilities
liquidity	merger	turnover	variable costs

1 full investigation of a company's activities and finances
2 the amount of money that a company owes
3 the process of combining two companies to form a bigger one
4 something that someone buys (especially a company that has been bought by another company)
5 costs that alter directly when the business alters its level of output (e.g. raw materials, components, labour costs for factory workers)
6 costs that do not alter when the business alters its level of output (e.g. rent, marketing, management salaries)
7 things such as money, buildings or equipment that a person or company owns
8 measure of a company's ability to quickly convert assets into cash
9 reductions in the cost of producing a unit of a product that occur as the output increases
10 total amount of money coming into a company from sales (usually given as an annual figure)

2 Find words or phrases from the box in 1 that have the same or similar meanings to the following.

1 cost of sales / direct costs: _____
2 overheads / indirect costs: _____
3 cash-flow: _____
4 debts: _____
5 revenue / income: _____

3 Match the words in the box to their definitions (and extra information) below.

| climb | dip | deteriorate | fluctuate | jump |
| peak | rise | slide | soar | stabilize |

1 become higher (literally: to move up using your hands and feet)
2 become less (literally: to put something into a liquid and quickly lift it out again)
3 change frequently, especially from a high level to a low one and back again
4 stop changing and become steady
5 get worse (opposite: improve)
6 get worse gradually (literally: to move smoothly and quickly across a surface)
7 increase (opposite: fall)
8 increase quickly to a high level (literally: to fly high in the sky)
9 increase suddenly and by a large amount (literally: push your body off the ground using your legs)
10 reach the highest point before becoming lower (the noun means 'the top of a mountain')

4 Read this sentence:

There was a _____ increase in sales.
Make adjectives that can go in the empty space using the letters and meanings given.

(**Clue**: the letter in bold is always the first letter.)

1 _____ ab**c**deeilnors (large)
2 _____ aac**d**imrt (sudden and surprising)
3 _____ adee**m**ort (neither big nor small)
4 _____ ah**p**rs (sudden)
5 _____ acfgiiinn**st** (large or noticeable)
6 _____ ghil**st** (small in size)
7 _____ dden**su** (quick and unexpected)

5 Look at one way to show 'cause ➜ effect':

*The new technology we bought last year **resulted in** a significant increase in productivity.*
Now show 'effect ➜ cause' using these words to complete the gaps: *a, as, because, due, of, of, result, thanks, to, to.*

The increase in productivity last year was _____ _____ / _____ _____ / _____ _____ / _____ _____ _____ _____ the new technology we bought.

6 Complete the sentences using the most appropriate form: *will, be going to* or the present continuous. Use contractions (*I'll, I'm*) where possible.

1 (describing your plans) Next year _____ (we / enter) the Croatian market by buying a small local firm.
2 (making a promise) Don't worry, _____ (you / have) the goods by the end of the week.
3 (giving details of a fixed arrangement) _____ (I / meet) Barbara from 9:00 to 10:00 at her office, and I should be back around 10:30.
4 (making an instant decision) Is that my mobile phone ringing? I'm sorry, _____ (I / turn) it off.

7 Complete this presentation extract using the words and phrases in the box.

resulted in	as a result of	seem to suggest
whereas	however	let's move on
next slide shows	notice from the chart

... OK, (1) _____.
My (2) _____ our administration costs one year after the merger. You will (3) _____ that the figures (4) _____ no noticeable impact on costs (5) _____ the merger. But this hides the real situation. Initially, the merger (6) _____ many large compensation payments for managerial staff who lost their jobs, and this increased costs. (7) _____, over the longer term salary costs are coming down as a result of the cuts. Next year we expect administration costs to be 2.3M, (8) _____ this year they will be about 2.9M.

Review 8

International trade

1 In each set of four below, match a verb on the left with a noun on the right to make phrases about export sales.

1 Don't sell — proactive with local distributors.
2 Be — a firm commitment to export.
3 Make — outside the box.
4 Think — on price rather than quality.

5 Trade — an exclusive deal.
6 Sign — time, effort and money.
7 Be prepared — on open account.
8 Invest — to modify product specifications.

9 Ask — payments can be done by the credit agency.
10 Chasing — a credit agency about a customer's creditworthiness.
11 Focus on — that what works in your domestic market will also work abroad.
12 Don't assume — one market, rather than trying to sell all over the world.

2 Find a word in 1 that means:

1 the ability of a company to repay debts: _____
2 trying hard to get something you want: _____

3 The collocations below are used in international business transactions. Cross out the one verb in **bold** in each group that does not collocate with the noun.

1 **issue / reach / settle / query** an invoice
2 **assume / provide / load / ship** goods
3 **chase / comply with / state / meet** conditions
4 **negotiate / reach / sign / state** a deal
5 **check in / check out / check up on** a customer's creditworthiness
6 **fall behind with / get behind with / move behind with** payments

4 The words in **bold** below are all in the wrong places. Put them in the correct places.

After the exporter and foreign customer finally (1) **check up on** a deal, the exporter will (2) **comply with** the goods and (3) **reach** an invoice. The exporter must (4) **issue** all the conditions in the contract, and if they do they can expect to be paid on time. It is a waste of time if they have to (5) **ship** customers who (6) **chase** payments. If there is a problem with payment, the exporter can use a credit agency to (7) **get behind with** a customer's creditworthiness.

5 Complete the text with these time prepositions: *at, during, from, in, until, within.*

(1) _____ the 90s we worked with a series of different local agents. (2) _____ 2002 we started using APL, and they have been our exclusive agent (3) _____ that time (4) _____ now. They are very good at collecting payment from local customers, and we give them the discretion to ask for payment (5) _____ either 60 or 90 days. They forward to us all payments they have collected, after taking their commission, and we receive money from them (6) _____ the end of every month.

6 Put the words in the diplomatic sentences into the correct order.

1 Direct: I'll explain it again if you want.
Diplomatic: *it let me way another put.*
_____

2 Direct: You are not convinced.
Diplomatic: *wrong me if you correct but I'm saying that seem to be you are not convinced.*
_____

3 Direct: You are wrong!
Diplomatic: *I'm a slight misunderstanding there seems to be afraid.*
_____

4 Direct: You don't understand!
Diplomatic: *I clear myself haven't made perhaps.*
_____

5 Direct: You want to withdraw from the project, right?
Diplomatic: *you would be saying I right in that want to withdraw from the project?*
_____

7 Use the words in brackets to make the direct sentences more diplomatic.

1 We need more time. (I think / might)
_____
2 There are still many difficulties. (I'm afraid / quite a large number)
_____
3 We must renegotiate parts of the contract. (perhaps / should / one or two)
_____
4 That will be very expensive. (won't / rather)
_____

8 Complete this email sequence using the words and phrases in the box.

further to   according to   regret to inform
pass this matter   now overdue   early settlement
have no alternative   outstanding balance

Email 1 (Reminder)

(1) _____ our records, our invoice number KL788 is (2) _____. The total sum is €25,600. We would appreciate your (3) _____ of this (4) _____.

Email 2 (Final demand)

(5) _____ our email of 14 June re invoice KL788, we have still not received payment for the outstanding sum of €25,600. We (6) _____ you that we (7) _____ but to (8) _____ to our legal department.

9 Match the words *outstanding* and *overdue* to their definitions below.

1 not paid when expected; late: _____
2 not yet paid: _____

10 Which of the two words from 9 has a second meaning of 'excellent and impressive'?

Additional material

1.2 Vocabulary

Defining words (page 9, exercise 8)

Student A

Give Student B definitions for 1, 3, 5, 7 and 9. Student B will give you definitions for 2, 4, 6, 8 and 10 to help you complete the crossword.

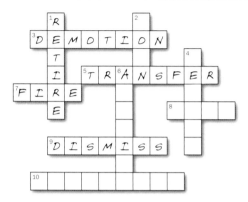

1.3 Grammar

Telling a story (page 11, exercise 5)

Student A

Put the story in order by matching the pairs of ideas. Then, without looking at the book, tell your partner the story in your own words, using appropriate past tenses.

1	Two engineers had recently been promoted,	a	so they called down to him:
		b	'Can you tell us where we are?'
2	After a while, the wind became stronger,	c	so they decided to celebrate with a flight in a balloon.
3	By the time they had managed to regain control,	d	they realized they were lost.
		e	and the balloon went out of control.
4	A man was walking along a road below them,		
5	'Excuse me, sir, we're lost!'		
6	After he had thought for a while,	f	Third, his answer was perfectly useless!'
7	'You're in a balloon!'	g	'That man must be a manager.'
8	As the man was walking away, one engineer said to the other:	h	the man looked down, looked up again, and then shouted:
9	'Why?'	i	and walked away down the road.
10	'Three reasons. First, he took a long time to answer. Second, he was perfectly correct.	j	asked the other engineer.

1.3 Grammar

Giving advice (page 11, exercise 7)

Student A

1 You have recently started work with a well-known firm of management consultants. Ask your partner for advice about the problems below, and react to their suggestions. Use the expressions in the box to help you.

1 You work from 8am to 7pm every day but you can never finish your work.
2 You find it difficult to set goals.
3 Your clients don't take you seriously: they think you're too young for the job.
4 Every time you call a friend, your colleagues give you black looks.
5 You have lots of ideas to share in meetings, but your boss keeps interrupting you.

> I'm having problems with ... Can you give me any advice?
> Do you have any ideas about how to ...?
> What do you suggest I do about ...? I just can't seem to ...
> What would you do?
> I see what you mean, (but ...) You've got a point, (but ...)
> You may be right, (but ...)
> OK, point taken. Yes, you're quite right.

2 Your partner will tell you about their problems. Suggest two or three alternatives for each problem. Use the expressions in the box to help you.

> Have you tried –ing ...? Have you considered –ing ...?
> How about –ing ...?
> Have you thought of –ing ...? You could ...
> Why don't you ...? You might want to ...

1.4 Speaking

Roleplay (page 13, exercise 10)

Student A

1 You are a new employee at the R&D laboratory of a Finnish electronics company. You come from Brazil. You find the atmosphere in the company miserable: people work alone, mostly in silence, so you try to make them happy by being friendly, sharing sweets and biscuits, and singing songs. You have a lot of work: because you work best in the evening, you stay late to finish it. You think the centre would be more productive if everyone relaxed and enjoyed their work. Your supervisor, Student B, has asked you to attend an informal meeting: this is an opportunity for you to explain your ideas and give B some helpful advice.

2 You are Student B's supervisor at a large travel agency in Australia. You are worried about B because he/she refuses to communicate with other members of staff and hardly speaks in staff meetings. You have given B a lot of responsibility because you feel he/she has excellent potential, but he/she is not sharing the work with the team. The travel business has a reputation for extreme stress, and you are concerned that B is trying to do too much. Australians value teamwork and consider sports and social events an integral part of corporate life. Hold an informal meeting with B to advise him/her on how to relate to colleagues and achieve a better work-life balance.
Start the meeting by asking B if he/she is enjoying the job.

1.6 Case study

Roleplay (page 17, exercise 6)

Problem holder A: Tokyo

You are experiencing culture shock in Tokyo. After two months in the marketing department of a large electronics company, you feel that you have achieved nothing. Your job description is very general; you spend most of your time processing answers to long market survey questionnaires. You are a very creative person, but when you suggest new ideas at meetings, they are usually met with silence. One colleague was very upset because you drew attention to a mistake in his presentation.

Your apartment is very small and your journey to work takes 90 minutes each way. After a long day at work, your colleagues do not understand that you do not have time to go to the restaurant with them. You would like to learn Japanese to communicate better, but when you meet Japanese people socially, they always want to speak English. You feel you are wasting your time and learning nothing.

2.1 About business

Debate (page 18, exercise 8)

For

You are going to take part in a debate. Try to convince the other group of the benefits of outsourcing call centres to developing countries like India. As well as your own ideas, refer to the following:

Outsourcing enables companies to:
- reduce costs
- be more competitive by offering customers lower prices and better service
- preserve jobs in production
- benefit from more competent and more motivated staff
- bring new technology to developing countries
- help developing countries to improve their economies.

2.4 Speaking

Improving a conversation (page 24, exercise 4)

Read this conversation aloud with your partner, then decide how the conversation could be improved and practise your improved version.

Helpline: Yes?
Customer: Oh, hello. Is that Autosales?
Helpline: Yes.
Customer: Oh, good. Well, I'm calling about the new car I bought last week. It won't start.
Helpline: Oh.
Customer: Well, can you do something about it?
Helpline: I'm new here. I don't know much about cars, actually.
Customer: Well, could you put me through to someone who does?
Helpline: No.
Customer: What do you mean, 'no'?
Helpline: I mean, no, I can't. There's nobody else here.
Customer: Well, can I leave a message?
Helpline: Yes, all right. What's your name?
Customer: It's McCready. Alistair McCready.
Helpline: Er, McWhat?
Customer: No, McCready. That's M-C-C-R-E-A-D-Y.
Helpline: Got it.
Customer: All right. Well, I'll be expecting your call. Goodbye.
Helpline: Don't hold your breath!

2.4 Speaking

Giving instructions (page 24, exercise 1)

Student A

Without saying what it represents, give Student B instructions to draw the symbol in grid 1. Student B will then give you instructions to draw another symbol in grid 2.

1

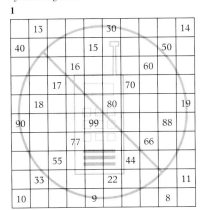

	13			30			14
40			15			50	
		16			60		
	17			70			
	18			80			19
90			99			88	
		77			66		
	55			44			
	33			22			11
10			9			8	

2

A			B			C	
	D			E			F
	G			H			
		I			J		
K			L			M	
	N			O			P
	Q			R			
		S			T		
U			V			W	
	X			Y			Z

2.5 Writing

Writing (page 27, exercise 5)

Student A

You work in the Accounts Department at Relopharma, a medium-sized pharmaceuticals company. Compose and send business email 1 below, using appropriate style. When you receive an email from another student, read it, then answer it following the instructions in 2. Continue in this way until you have written and sent four emails.

1 You have a problem with the accounts payable database — some entries are disappearing. It looks like some kind of virus, but your anti-virus software hasn't detected any problems. Write an email to your colleague, Student B, in Information Systems, explaining the problem and asking for help.

2 You have received an email about an invoice from Student C at Nakisoft, a software supplier. You have no records of this invoice in your database. Write an email to Student B asking them to confirm the purchase and, if appropriate, to obtain a duplicate invoice.

3 You have received another email from Nakisoft about software training. Write to Student B to complain: the week in question is impossible because you have to close the accounts.

4 You have received an email from Nakisoft about a patch. Write a reply to Student C explaining that the link on their website doesn't work.

3.3 Grammar

Definitions game (page 37, exercise 8)

As

Help the other team guess the noun combinations below by giving definitions using a relative clause. If you want to make it more difficult, use synonyms instead of the exact terms in the noun combinations.

1 vertical writing languages
2 a management consultancy firm
3 a customer satisfaction survey
4 pilfer-proof packaging
5 stress-raising automation
6 a sandwich degree course

4.3 Grammar

Asking questions (page 49, exercise 6)

Student A

1 You are interviewing Student B for a job at your sports club. Ask B the right questions to obtain the answers below. Score one point for each correct answer you receive.

1 At weekends.
2 Since I was at school.
3 Several years ago.
4 During the holidays.
5 No, only a few weeks.
6 The Economist.
7 For two years.
8 No, not yet.
9 In the next six months.
10 No, I haven't.

2 You are being interviewed for a job at Student B's community arts centre. Answer the questions they ask.

5.6 Case study

Negotiating (page 69, exercise 5)

Student A (travel agent)

Negotiate the best deal possible with the customer (Student B). Your standard price is $150 per person per night: this includes all meals, drinks, snacks, activities and sports (except golf). Remember you are in competition with other travel agents for the same product.
Score points as indicated for each item below.

Item	Points
Cost per person per night	
• more than $140	2
• $120 – $140	0
• less than $120	-5
Upgrade to executive suite, per person, per night	
• $50	2
• $25	1
• $10	-2
Number of participants	
• 22	1
• 24	2
• 26	3
Number of nights	
• 7	1
• 8	2
• 9 or more	3
Free access to golf course	-1

7.4 Speaking

Presentation (page 91, exercise 7)

Student A

Present the three slides on Ultraxport and explain why this company would be a good acquisition.

1

Ultraxport
• Chain of sports stores
• Turnover €50M
• Strong brand recognition
• Strategy: low margins, aggressive growth
• Estimated price: €100M

2

Ultraxport — Sales & Earnings (M€)
Sales
Earnings
Y - 1   Y0   Y + 1   Y + 2

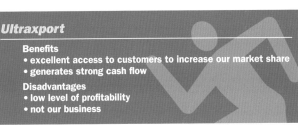

3

Ultraxport
Benefits
• excellent access to customers to increase our market share
• generates strong cash flow
Disadvantages
• low level of profitability
• not our business

2.5 Writing

Writing (page 27, exercise 5)

Student B

You work in the Information Systems Department at Relopharma, a medium-sized pharmaceuticals company. Compose and send business email 1 below, using appropriate style. When you receive an email from another student, read it, then answer it following the instructions in 2. Continue in this way until you have written and sent four emails.

1 You want your software supplier, Nakisoft, to organize training on a new software tool for your Accounts Department as soon as possible. Write an email to Student C at Nakisoft asking them to contact Student A in your Accounts Department with dates for the training.

2 You have received an email from your colleague, Student A, in Accounts, about a software problem. You think it could be a virus. Write an email to Nakisoft explaining the problem and asking them to contact Student A directly to resolve the problem.

3 You have received another email from Student A about an invoice. Write an email to Student C at Nakisoft apologizing for the delay and asking them to send you a duplicate invoice.

4 You have received another email from Student A about training. Reply to Student A explaining that there is no alternative.

5.1 About business

Roleplay (page 58, exercise 4)

Student A

1 You are a researcher at NY University's Stern School of Business, and an expert in e-tailing. Answer B's questions, adding details and opinions.

2 You are a journalist interviewing an Overstock customer-service rep. Ask for information and opinions about:
- Overstock's strategy for increasing sales
- how live chat works
- Overstock's policy on customer privacy
- your own question.

6.6 Case study

Reading and discussion (page 81, exercise 4)

Group A – Port Katherine Planning Department
Read the email you have received and answer the questions.

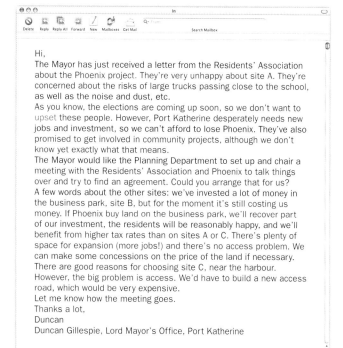

> Hi,
> The Mayor has just received a letter from the Residents' Association about the Phoenix project. They're very unhappy about site A. They're concerned about the risks of large trucks passing close to the school, as well as the noise and dust, etc.
> As you know, the elections are coming up soon, so we don't want to upset these people. However, Port Katherine desperately needs new jobs and investment, so we can't afford to lose Phoenix. They've also promised to get involved in community projects, although we don't know yet exactly what that means.
> The Mayor would like the Planning Department to set up and chair a meeting with the Residents' Association and Phoenix to talk things over and try to find an agreement. Could you arrange that for us?
> A few words about the other sites: we've invested a lot of money in the business park, site B, but for the moment it's still costing us money. If Phoenix buy land on the business park, we'll recover part of our investment, the residents will be reasonably happy, and we'll benefit from higher tax rates than on sites A or C. There's plenty of space for expansion (more jobs!) and there's no access problem. We can make some concessions on the price of the land if necessary.
> There are good reasons for choosing site C, near the harbour. However, the big problem is access. We'd have to build a new access road, which would be very expensive.
> Let me know how the meeting goes.
> Thanks a lot,
> Duncan
> Duncan Gillespie, Lord Mayor's Office, Port Katherine

1 Who is the email from?
2 What is your role at the meeting?
3 Why is it important to keep the residents happy?
4 Why is the Phoenix project important for the town?
5 Which is the best site from your point of view?

Presenting (page 87, exercise 8)

Student A

1 Present Chanco's stock market history using the information from the graph, explaining causes and effects.

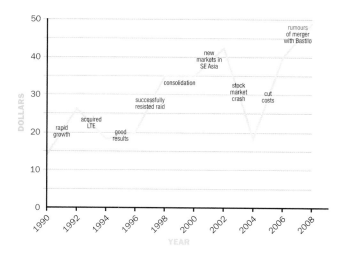

2 Listen to B's presentation of Bastilo Corp. and complete the graph.

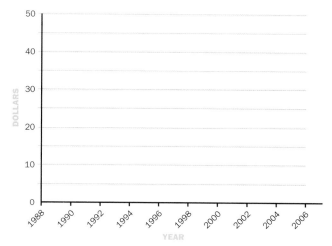

4.3 Grammar

Present perfect and past simple (page 49, exercise 4)

Student B

You and your partner work for an international recruitment agency. Your clients are looking for:

1 a Spanish-speaking science graduate
2 an undergraduate with marketing experience
3 a graduate accountant, to be a future finance director
4 a French-speaking graduate in business
5 an arts undergraduate with experience in the Far East
6 a Portuguese-speaking graduate with experience in sales.

You have each interviewed and tested five candidates. Exchange information with your partner to complete the tables and decide together which candidates are most suitable for each request.

Candidate	Graduation	Work experience	Management potential test
Mr Salmon			
Ms Bianco	last October, Maths	car sales in Argentina and Brazil	A+
Mrs Grey			
Miss Rose	next summer, Languages	marketing in Australia and Japan	A
Mr Da Silva			
Mr Green	last November, Physics	call centres in California and Florida	B+
Mr Schwartz			
Miss Plum	last September, Business	financial services in Mexico and Quebec	B
Ms Violeta			
Mr Braun	last September, Finance	computing and accounts in China	C-

5.4 Speaking

Negotiating (page 65, exercise 9)

Student A

Harry Petersen's application service provider, Holman Multimedia, has gone out of business, taking with it Harry's site which was turning over a thousand dollars per day.

Harry needs to hire a new provider. This time he is determined to negotiate a contract which will protect his business if there are problems. Harry has asked you to negotiate with another supplier, Easytail. He has given you a list of points to negotiate below. You win if you obtain more 'Ideals' than 'Unacceptables'.

	Ideal	Acceptable	Unacceptable
Set-up time	< 3 weeks	3 weeks	> 3 weeks
Cost	less than Holman	same as Holman	more than Holman
Payment terms	> 30 days	30 days	< 30 days
Contract	6–12 months	12–18 months	> 18 months
Penalties if site is offline	> 50% of average turnover	50% of average turnover	< 50% of average turnover
Penalties if contract is broken	50% of turnover for 2 months	50% of turnover for 1 month	< 50% of turnover for 1 month

7.4 Speaking

Presentation (page 91, exercise 7)

Student B

Present the three slides on Piezoteknik labs and explain why this company would be a good acquisition.

8.3 Grammar

Speaking (page 101, exercise 7)

Student A

Choose six words from the list below and write them on separate small pieces of paper. Hold a conversation with Students B and C on one of the topics listed on page 101. The goal is to use all six words in the conversation. The first person to use all their words (with the correct preposition) is the winner.

hear (v)   conform (v)   rely (v)   look forward (v)   respect (n)
responsibility (n)   dealings (n)   substitute (n)   object (v)   depend (v)

8.5 Writing

Writing (page 105, exercise 6)

Student A

You work at Red Sea Products Inc, a manufacturing company in Saudi Arabia. Compose and send business email 1 below, using appropriate style. When you receive an email from another student, read it, then answer it following the instructions in 2. Continue in this way until you have written and sent four emails.

1 You have worked for several years with Beefeater Shipping Corp (Student B), who ship your products all over the world. You currently pay them at 60 days, and you almost never pay late. However, your own customers are paying more and more slowly. Write to Beefeater asking them to increase your credit period to 90 days.

2 You have received an email from Canada Import Co (Student C), one of your best customers. Reply, agreeing to their request, but reminding them politely that they haven't paid a bill from last quarter.

3 You have received a reply from Beefeater to your request in 1. Send a cheque and an apology, or ask for more time, explaining why you can't pay for the moment.

4 You have received a reply from Canada Import to your reminder in 2. If they sent a cheque, send a friendly reply, thanking them for the payment and reminding them that your payment terms for open account trading are strictly 30 days and no more. If they didn't send a cheque, send a final demand threatening legal action, and suspending the decision to trade on open account.

1.2 Vocabulary

Defining words (page 9, exercise 8)

Student B

Student A will give you definitions for 1, 3, 5, 7 and 9 to help you complete the crossword. Give Student A definitions for 2, 4, 6, 8 and 10.

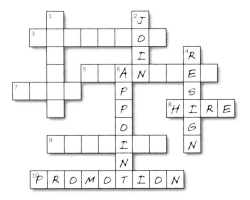

1.3 Grammar

Telling a story (page 11, exercise 5)

Student B

Put the story in order by matching the pairs of ideas. Then, without looking at the book, tell your partner the story in your own words, using appropriate past tenses.

1. A young business student was interviewing a rich old businessman, ————
2. The old guy replied, 'Well, son, times were hard,
3. 'I invested that nickel in an apple,
4. 'When I had polished that apple all day,
5. 'The next day, after I had invested those ten cents in two apples,
6. I continued this system for a month,
7. 'And that's how you built an empire?'
8. 'Heavens, no!' the man replied.

a. and I started to polish it.'
b. I sold it for ten cents.'
c. and asked how he had made his money.
d. and I had spent everything except my last nickel.'

e. the boy asked.
f. 'Then my wife's father died and left us two million dollars.'
g. by the end of which I'd accumulated a fortune of $1.37.'
h. I spent the entire day polishing them and sold them at five o'clock for 20 cents.

1.3 Grammar

Giving advice (page 11, exercise 7)

Student B

1 Your partner will tell you about their problems. Suggest two or three alternatives for each problem. Use the expressions in the box to help you.

Have you tried –ing …?	Have you considered –ing …?
How about –ing …?	
Have you thought of –ing …?	You could …
Why don't you …?	You might want to …

2 You have recently started work in a government department. Ask your partner for advice about the problems below, and react to their suggestions. Use the expressions in the box to help you.

1. Your boss doesn't trust you: she checks every document you write and always manages to find something wrong.
2. You are frustrated by all the procedures you have to respect: even the simplest tasks seem to take a long time.
3. The atmosphere in the office is very sombre: your colleagues are all much older than you.
4. You find it difficult to sleep at night because your job is so stressful.
5. You hate writing reports, but it's an important part of your job.

I'm having problems with …   Can you give me any advice?
Do you have any ideas about how to …?
What do you suggest I do about …?   I just can't seem to …
What would you do?
I see what you mean, (but …)   You've got a point, (but …)
You may be right, (but …)
OK, point taken.   Yes, you're quite right.

1.6 Case study

Roleplay (page 17, exercise 6)

Problem holder B: Birmingham

You were hoping that the UK would be an exciting centre of popular culture, but after two months in Birmingham, you are not enjoying life. You live several miles from the city centre, and seem to spend a lot of your time on dirty, uncomfortable buses. The weather is depressing; cold, grey and wet, and the food is bland and fatty with few fresh vegetables. You caught a cold soon after you arrived and it seems impossible to get rid of it.

People at work are friendly, but the local accent is really difficult to understand. You are finding it difficult to make friends with English people, mainly because their idea of having a good time is going to a noisy, smoky pub and drinking as much as possible, or watching football, which you hate. You are starting to feel lonely and depressed; you are seriously thinking of giving up and going home.

2.1 About business

Debate (page 18, exercise 8)

Against

You are going to take part in a debate. Try to convince the other group of the disadvantages of outsourcing call centres to developing countries like India. As well as your own ideas, refer to the following:

Outsourcing makes customers angry due to:
- language and cultural problems
- operators not having sufficient local knowledge.

Outsourcing is responsible for:
- job losses in industrialized countries
- exploitation of desperate workers in developing countries
- emphasizing inequalities between north and south / east and west
- encouraging unrealistic expectations in the developing world.

6.6 Case study

Reading and discussion (page 81, exercise 4)

Group B – Port Katherine Residents' Association

Read part of a letter your association has sent to the Mayor, and answer the questions.

> … deeply concerned about plans to build a recycling centre on a site close to our school and a quiet residential area. The idea of monster trucks on a narrow road used by small children to walk to school is frankly terrifying and completely irresponsible.
>
> Moreover, the risks and nuisance to the school and the surrounding residents from noise, smoke, fumes and dust are totally unacceptable, not to mention the fire hazard and risk of soil contamination from so many flammable and toxic materials. The residents are prepared to take whatever measures are necessary to resist the choice of site A.
>
> If the recycling centre must be built in Port Katherine (surely Perth, as a large industrial city, would be better for business?), site C is clearly a far more logical and environmentally rational choice. This site is in an industrial environment, on land which is currently derelict and worthless, with the appropriate fire and emergency services close by, and offers the added advantage of convenient transport by sea as an ecological and economical alternative to monster trucks. As for the choice of site B, surely it would make the business park less attractive to other, less industrial, companies?
>
> As the elections approach, we, the residents of Port Katherine, trust that you will take the necessary measures to ensure that …

1. How do the members of your association feel about the environment?
2. What does your association have in mind when it says 'whatever measures are necessary to resist the choice of site A'?
3. Why do you think the Mayor and the Planning Department have to take your association seriously?
4. Which is the best site from your point of view?
5. What are your objectives at the meeting?

2.4 Speaking

Giving instructions (page 24, exercise 1)

Student B

Student A will give you instructions to draw a symbol in grid 1. Without saying what it represents, give Student A instructions to draw the symbol in grid 2.

1

	13			30			14
40			15			50	
		16			60		
	17			70			
18			80				19
90			99			88	
		77			66		
	55			44			
	33		22				11
10			9			8	

2

A			B			C	
	D			E			F
	G			H			
		I			J		
K			L			M	
	N			O			P
	Q			R			
		S			T		
U			V			W	
	X			Y			Z

2.5 Writing

Writing (page 27, exercise 5)

Student C

You work at Nakisoft, a small company specializing in accountancy software. Relopharma is your biggest customer. Compose and send business email 1 below, using appropriate style. When you receive an email from another student, read it, then answer it following the instructions in 2. Continue in this way until you have written and sent four emails.

1 You have not received payment for your invoice 6695 KF for software you supplied four months ago. Write a polite email to Student A in Relopharma's Accounts Department asking if there is a problem.

2 You have received an email from your customer, Student B, in Relopharma's Information Systems Department. Write an email to Student A telling them that, as requested by Student B, you have set up the training for week 52.

3 You have received another email from your customer, Student B. The problem is caused by a Trojan which is undetected by anti-virus software. The solution is to download a patch from your website and install it on each PC. Write an email to Student A explaining what to do.

4 You have received an email from Student B about an invoice. Write a reply to Student B attaching the document requested.

4.3 Grammar

Asking questions (page 49, exercise 6)

Student B

1 You are being interviewed for a job at Student A's sports club. Answer the questions they ask.

2 You are interviewing Student A for a job at your community arts centre. Ask A the right questions to obtain the answers below. Score one point for each correct answer you receive.

1	Yes, I am.	6	Yes, almost.
2	By bus.	7	Tomorrow morning.
3	Three times a day.	8	Yes, several times.
4	Business English.	9	No, not at the moment.
5	A long time ago.	10	Since the beginning of the year.

5.6 Case study

Negotiating (page 69, exercise 5)

Student B (buyer)

Negotiate the best deal possible with the travel agent (Student A). Remember you cannot exceed a global budget of $28,000. Score points as indicated for each item below.

Item	Points
Cost per person per night	
• more than $140	0
• $120 – $140	2
• less than $120	4
Upgrade to executive suite, per person, per night	
• $50	0
• $25	1
• $10	3
Number of participants	
• 22	0
• 24	2
• 26	3
Number of nights	
• 7	0
• 8	1
• 9 or more	3
Free access to golf course	1

8.3 Grammar

Speaking (page 101, exercise 7)

Student B

Choose six words from the list below and write them on separate small pieces of paper. Hold a conversation with Students A and C on one of the topics listed on page 101. The goal is to use all six words in the conversation. The first person to use all their words (with the correct preposition) is the winner.

> insist (v)   comment (v)   complain (v)   apologise (v)   effect (n)
> involvement (n)   access (n)   demand (v)   attend (v)   result (v)

8.5 Writing

Writing (page 105, exercise 6)

Student B

You work at Beefeater Shipping Corp, an international freight forwarding company. Compose and send business email 1 below, using appropriate style. When you receive an email from another student, read it, then answer it following the instructions in 2. Continue in this way until you have written and sent four emails.

1 You have recently shipped several containers of goods bought by Canada Import Co (Student C) from your customer Red Sea Products Inc (Student A) to your warehouse in New York. Canada Import were supposed to collect the containers two months ago, but they are still in your warehouse. Write to Canada Import, reminding them about the containers and offering to ship them to Canada for $1.20 per mile per container, payment at 30 days.

2 You have received an email from Red Sea Products. Reply, agreeing to their request, but reminding them politely of an invoice for $10,000 which is overdue.

3 You have received a reply from Canada Import to your email in 1. Write a reply, either agreeing to or refusing their request, and reminding them that the space their containers are occupying in your warehouse is costing you money, so you need a quick decision on your offer to ship them to Canada.

4 You have received a reply from Red Sea Products to your reminder in 2. If they sent a cheque, send a friendly reply, thanking them for the payment and reminding them that the new terms of 90 days mean strictly 90 days and no more. If they didn't send a cheque, send a final demand threatening legal action, and suspending the decision to increase the credit period to 90 days.

1.4 Speaking

Roleplay (page 13, exercise 10)

Student B

1 You are Student A's supervisor at the R&D laboratory of a Finnish electronics company. In Finland, people like to concentrate hard on their work so that they can finish early and go home to enjoy sports and leisure activities. You have called Student A to an informal meeting because some members of your team have complained about him/her: they say that they can't organize the work efficiently because A always arrives late. He/she disturbs their concentration by talking loudly to friends on the phone, singing and whistling. He/she eats and drinks in the lab, which is against company rules, takes long breaks and wears unsuitable clothes. Hold an informal meeting with A to advise him/her on how to adapt to the local work culture.

Start the meeting by asking A if he/she is enjoying the job.

2 You are a new employee at a large travel agency in Australia. You come from Vietnam, where modesty and discretion are highly valued. You feel that some of your Australian colleagues have no respect for management: they are always giving their personal opinions in meetings, they call everybody by their first names, even managers, and spend more time talking about rugby or cricket than working. Your supervisor, Student A, is a demanding manager who has set your department ambitious objectives; you are trying to do your best to compensate for your colleagues' inefficiency, so you work late in the evenings and at weekends. Consequently, you have no time to socialize with other people in the company. You are not sleeping enough, so you have to drink a lot of coffee to stay awake, and you feel very stressed. Take the opportunity of the meeting your supervisor has asked for to suggest, respectfully, that your colleagues should take their work more seriously.

1.6 Case study

Roleplay (page 17, exercise 6)

Problem holder C: Chicago
After two months in Chicago you feel miserable and exhausted. You come from a small, quiet town in the country. The noise and the speed of life in Chicago are driving you crazy. You work in an enormous open-space office in a large insurance company, where you are constantly disturbed and find it impossible to concentrate. Your manager is not satisfied with the quantity of work you are producing and told you very directly that you weren't working hard enough.

You feel stressed out and are suffering more and more from severe headaches. You would like to go and walk in a park to relax after work, but it's too dangerous to walk the streets at night. You live at the YMCA. Your neighbours and colleagues are very friendly, and they are always inviting you out in the evenings and at weekends, but they want to go dancing or play sports and you just need to rest and relax.

5.1 About business

Roleplay (page 58, exercise 4)

Student B

1 You are a journalist interviewing a researcher from NY University's Stern School of Business. Ask for information and opinions about:
- the problem of visitors who just browse websites without buying
- customer-tracking software and customer privacy
- animated sales reps
- your own question.

2 You are an Overstock customer-service rep. (Overstock sells well-known brands of consumer goods at discount prices.) Answer A's questions, adding details and opinions.

7.2 Vocabulary

Presenting (page 87, exercise 8)

Student B

1 Listen to A's presentation of Chanco and complete the graph.

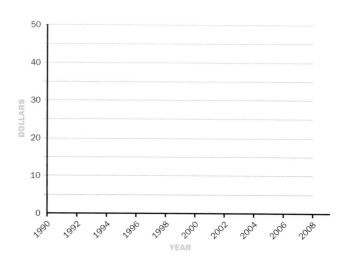

2 Present Bastilo's stock market history using the information from the graph, explaining causes and effects.

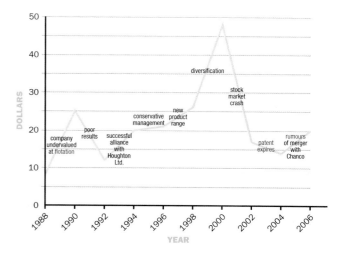

8.5 Writing

Writing (page 105, exercise 6)

Student C
You work at Canada Import Co, a company which imports goods from all over the world to North America. Compose and send business email 1 below, using appropriate style. When you receive an email from another student, read it, then answer it following the instructions in 2. Continue in this way until you have written and sent four emails.

1 You have worked with Red Sea Products Inc (Student A) for more than two years and you are one of their best customers. Until now you have paid by Bill of Exchange at 60 days, but you would prefer to trade on open account in order to have more flexibility. Write to Red Sea Products requesting this change.

2 You have received an email from Beefeater Shipping Corp (Student B) offering to ship your containers from New York to Canada. Your current forwarding company charges $1.10 per mile per container and allows you to pay at 60 days. Write to Beefeater enquiring if they can improve their offer.

3 You have received a reply from Red Sea Products to your request in 1. Send a cheque and an apology, or ask for more time, explaining why you can't pay for the moment.

4 You have received a reply from Beefeater to your enquiry in 2. If their terms are now satisfactory, write an email confirming the order for shipping your containers to Canada. If the terms are not satisfactory, write an email rejecting their offer, apologizing for the delay in collecting your containers and promising to have them collected by next week.

3.3 Grammar

Definitions game (page 37, exercise 8)

Bs

Help the other team guess the noun combinations below by giving definitions using a relative clause. If you want to make it more difficult, use synonyms instead of the exact terms in the noun combinations.

1. a dead-end job
2. brand-building packaging
3. material-saving carton
4. call centre wages
5. newly empowered advisers
6. email risk policy

5.4 Speaking

Negotiating (page 65, exercise 9)

Student B

Harry Petersen's application service provider, Holman Multimedia, has gone out of business, taking with it Harry's site which was turning over a thousand dollars per day.

Harry needs to hire a new provider. This time he is determined to negotiate a contract which will protect his business if there are problems. You represent Easytail, a new supplier. Your boss has given you a list of points to negotiate below. You win if you obtain more 'Ideals' than 'Unacceptables'.

	Ideal	Acceptable	Unacceptable
Set-up time	> 2 weeks	2 weeks	< 2 weeks
Cost	15% more than Holman	same as Holman	less than Holman
Payment terms	< 30 days	30 days	> 30 days
Contract	> 18 months	12–18 months	< 12 months
Penalties if site is offline	no penalties	20–30% of average turnover	> 30% of average turnover
Penalties if contract is broken	no penalties	20% of turnover for 1 month	> 20% of turnover for 1 month

6.6 Case study

Reading and discussion (page 81, exercise 4)

Group C – Phoenix

Read the email from Head Office in Sydney and answer the questions.

Hi,
Just a few words about the meeting in Port Katherine. We want you to represent Phoenix in the best possible light – 'Operation Charm and Diplomacy', remember? We need to make friends and to sell the benefits of having a Phoenix recycling centre in their town: protect the environment, new jobs, investment, growth, higher profile for the town, taxes, involvement in community projects, etc. By the way, on the subject of community projects, find out what they're interested in, but try not to make any expensive commitments, OK?
Port Katherine will be our centre for most of Western Australia. In the long term, it could become the largest recycling centre on the continent, so it's pretty important for us. It's a good site for us, but they need us more than we need them. If things get difficult, we can go somewhere else.
Site A has the best access, but there's the problem of the school. Site B is expensive, and it's not flat, which means that limiting the risk of contamination by fluids is more difficult. Site C has poor access, unless the town builds a new access road. And I don't think they've really understood what having a recycling centre in the middle of the town would mean. Obviously, as we have our own trucking division, transport by sea is not an option for us.
Anyway, I know you'll do a good job. Let me know how the meeting goes.
Justin

1. What are your objectives at the meeting?
2. What sort of community projects do you think Phoenix could support?
3. What are Phoenix's plans for Port Katherine's future?
4. Which is the best site for Phoenix?
5. What arguments can you use against choosing the other sites?

7.4 Speaking

Presentation (page 91, exercise 7)

Student C

Present the three slides on Yarax Sports and explain why this company would be a good acquisition.

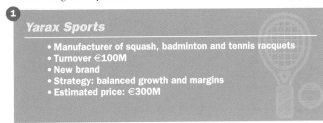

1

Yarax Sports

- Manufacturer of squash, badminton and tennis racquets
- Turnover €100M
- New brand
- Strategy: balanced growth and margins
- Estimated price: €300M

2

Yarax Sports

Sales & Earnings (M€)

3

Yarax Sports

Benefits
- synergy
- economies of scale

Disadvantages
- diversification might weaken our brand
- could lose market share overall

8.2 Vocabulary

Defining words (page 99, exercise 7)

Student B

Student A will give you definitions for 1, 2, 4, 6, 7 and 9 across to help you complete the crossword. Give Student A definitions for 1, 3, 5 and 8 down and 10 and 11 across.

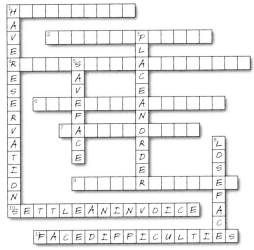

8.3 Grammar

Speaking (page 101, exercise 7)

Student C

Choose six words from the list below and write them on separate small pieces of paper. Hold a conversation with Students A and B on one of the topics listed on page 101. The goal is to use all six words in the conversation. The first person to use all their words (with the correct preposition) is the winner.

succeed (v)   consent (v)   wait (v)   sympathise (v)   tax (n)
solution (n)   comment (v)   damage (n)   invest (v)   consist (v)

Grammar and practice

Past tenses

1 Read a diary entry written by Joelle, a student on a work placement. Of the verbs in **bold**, identify which are examples of the:

- past simple
- past continuous
- past perfect.

I **was doing** my work placement in a large bank near to where I live. I **was working** in the back office (I **had asked** to do something where I could deal directly with clients, but they **said** no). Anyway, one day something really awful **happened**. My supervisor **had given** me some client information to enter into a database, and I **was filling in** the various fields on the screen. While I **was entering** the information, I suddenly **saw** a name I **recognized** – it **was** a friend from school called Sylvie. It seems that she **had applied for** a loan to have some cosmetic surgery! Of course, the bank **had** strict confidentiality rules and the next time I **saw** Sylvie I **didn't mention** anything. But, even so, I wish that I **hadn't found out** about it.

2 Complete the summaries of the main use of each tense in 1 by writing the correct tense name in each gap.

- You use the _____ to show that one event happened before another.
- You use the _____ to describe an activity in progress that gives the background to the main events.
- You use the _____ to describe the main events of the story.

3 Put one verb into the past simple and one into the past continuous in each sentence.

1 I _____ (revise) for my Economics exam when you _____ (call).
2 I'm sorry, I _____ (not / hear) what you said. I _____ (read) this article about Johnny Depp.
3 I _____ (see) Eva yesterday. She _____ (talk) to some friends outside the library.
4 While I _____ (work) in the bar last summer I _____ (meet) this guy called Fabio.

4 Look at the sentences in 3 again. In general, does the activity in progress (past continuous):

1 stop when the main event happens? *or*
2 continue after the main event happens? *or*
3 either 1 or 2 – we only know by the context.

5 Put one verb into the past simple and one into the past perfect in each sentence.

1 Before I _____ (get) my full-time job at the bank, I _____ (already / work) there for several months as an intern.
2 It's OK, don't worry, I _____ (just / finish) revising for my exam when you _____ (call).
3 It _____ (be) so nice to talk to Eva yesterday. I _____ (not / see) her for ages.
4 I _____ (not / meet) a man like Fabio before. He really _____ (listen) to me.

6 It may not be necessary to use the past perfect if you use *before* or *after* to make the time sequence clear. Both underlined forms are correct:

Before *I arranged the doctor's appointment, I* **spoke / had spoken** *to my supervisor.*

Underline the correct forms in **bold**. Sometimes both are correct, sometimes only one.

1 I understood the marketing part of the course much better after my internship **finished / had finished**.
2 The traffic was terrible, and when I got there the meeting **already started / had already started**.
3 Before I was promoted to Sales Director, I **was / had been** a sales consultant in our main city-centre branch.
4 By the end of the course I realized that I **bought / had bought** over a dozen books.

7 Match the time expressions on the left with the tense they are often used with on the right.

1 while   a) past simple
2 already, by the end of   b) past continuous
3 last year, two months ago   c) past perfect

Telling a story

8 When you tell a story, you can use the word *anyway* to:

1 change the subject *or*
2 return to a previous subject

Find the word *anyway* in 1 and say how it is used.

9 When you tell a story, you can use the words in the box. Find pairs with the same meaning.

actually	after that	apparently	eventually
in fact	in the end	it seems that	obviously
of course	the next thing that happened was		

10 Read a story written by Janek, a student who had a holiday job. Put the verbs into the correct form: past simple (x7), past continuous (x3) and past perfect (x4).

One day last summer I (1) _____ (work) in a bar on the beach. I (2) _____ (just / leave) school and I was young and naive. Anyway, on that day I (3) _____ (serve) the drinks by myself – my other colleagues (4) _____ (not / arrive) for work yet. A man (5) _____ (come) up to the counter and (6) _____ (ask for) 'a whisky on the rocks'. I (7) _____ (want) to be helpful, so I filled a glass with whisky, (8) _____ (take) it over to where he (9) _____ (sit) with his friends and (10) _____ (place) it on the rocks next to him. The next thing that happened was they all started laughing and laughing. I (11) _____ (never / be) so embarrassed in my life. Of course, when I realized my mistake I (12) _____ (see) the funny side as well, and in the end everything (13) _____ (be) OK. In fact, by the end of the evening, I (14) _____ (become) friends with them all. But, even today, when I hear the phrase 'on the rocks' it reminds me of that day.

11 A story is often told in four stages:

1 Background situation
2 Problem
3 Solution / resolution
4 Comment

In Joelle's diary entry in 1, the four stages are:

1 from *I was doing …* to *… said no.*
2 from *Anyway, …* to *… surgery!*
3 from *Of course …* to *… anything.*
4 from *But even so …* to *… about it.*

Identify the four stages in Janek's story in 10.

1 from _____ to _____
2 from _____ to _____
3 from _____ to _____
4 from _____ to _____

12 Write a short story about something that happened to you while you were at work, for example:

- while you were doing a holiday job
- while you were doing an internship
- while you were helping a family member.

Before you begin, look again at the diary entry in 1 and the story in 10. Also, use the vocabulary in 7 and 9 to help you.

Advice structures

13 Correct the mistake in each sentence.

1 You should to do it today.
2 You ought do it today.
3 He shoulds do it today.
4 Do I should do it today?

14 You can give advice using both *must* and *should*:

You **must** speak to your supervisor.
You **should** speak to your supervisor.

1 Which sentence means: 'It's a good idea to speak to your supervisor'?
2 Which sentence means: 'It's necessary to speak to your supervisor'?

15 Complete the sentences by using the verb *apply* in its correct form (*apply*, *to apply* or *applying*).

1 Why don't you _____ for that job?
2 How about _____ for that job?
3 You ought _____ for that job.
4 You should _____ for that job.

16 Grade these replies from 1 (agreement) to 4 (disagreement).

☐ No, that's not a good idea.
☐ That might be worth trying.
☐ I'm not sure about that because …
☐ That sounds like a good idea.

Should and *must* are examples of **modal verbs**. Other modal verbs are: *can, could, will, would, may, might* and *shall*. Modal verbs have special characteristics:

- They are 'auxiliary verbs'. This means they are used with another main verb.
  You should learn to set goals.
- Two modal verbs cannot be used together.
  NOT *I can will meet you.*
- They are followed by the infinitive without *to*.
  NOT *I must to meet him.*
- They only have one form, so there is no third person *-s*, no *-ing* form and no *-ed* form.
- To make a question you put the modal verb in front of the subject.
  Should I…?   Can I…?
- To make a negative you put *not* after the modal verb (often shortened to *-n't*)
  You shouldn't…   You can't…

Modal verbs are used to express ideas such as advice, ability, obligation, probability. The same modal verb can have different meanings.

Yes / no questions

1 Complete the table with these auxiliary verbs: *are, did, did, do, does, had, had, has, have, is, was, were, would.*

Present simple	_____ you work there? _____ she work there?
Present continuous	_____ you working there now? _____ he working there now?
Past simple	_____ you work there before? _____ she work there before?
Past continuous	_____ you working there then? _____ he working there then?
Present perfect	_____ you ever worked there? _____ she ever worked there?
Past perfect	_____ you already worked there? _____ she already worked there?
Modals	_____ you work here next year?

Now complete the rule using these words: *subject, main verb, auxiliary verb.*

You form *yes / no* questions using:

_____ + _____ + _____.

2 Read Frank's answers in the telephone conversation, then write Geeta's questions using the same tense.

Geeta: (1) _____ this software from us?
Frank: Yes, I bought it from you.
Geeta: (2) _____ a guarantee?
Frank: Yes, I have a two-year guarantee.
Geeta: (3) _____ restarting the computer?
Frank: Yes, I've tried doing that.
Geeta: (4) _____ at your computer right now?
Frank: Yes, I'm sitting at my desk.
Geeta: (5) _____ the software again, please?
Frank: No, I won't reinstall it again! I thought you were a helpline, but you're not being very helpful.

3 Underline the correct short answers.

1 Do you work in customer support?
 Yes, I work. / Yes, I am. / Yes, I do.
2 Are you working in customer support now?
 Yes, I work. / Yes, I am. / Yes, I do.
3 Did you work in customer support before?
 No, I didn't work. / No, I didn't.
4 Have you ever worked in customer support?
 No, I never worked. / No, I haven't.

Wh- questions

4 You make questions beginning with *Wh-* or *How* to ask for more information. Complete the text using *two* of the following items in *each* gap.

How	how far	How much	What	Why
are	do	does	will	will

Providing back office functions for global business is vital for India's economy. (1) _____ India earn from this per year? About $2 billion. (2) _____ so many companies outsourcing to India? The answer is simple: it's cheaper. But (3) _____ this process go? Surprisingly, not much further, at least as far as India is concerned. The problems are poor infrastructure, labour shortages and, in particular, wage inflation. (4) _____ we know there will be a problem? Because the same thing happened before: to Ireland in the 90s. So (5) _____ companies do? They will simply outsource their business processes to other countries, such as the Philippines, Malaysia, Vietnam and Eastern European nations.

5 Compare how *What* and *Which* are used. Then complete the sentences below using *What* or *Which*.

What + noun	Which + noun
• things • wide choice	• people and organizations • limited choice

1 _____ type of car do you drive?
2 _____ university do you go to?
3 _____ day would be best for you: Saturday or Sunday?
4 _____ time shall we meet? I'm free all day.

Sometimes *who, what* or *which* is the subject of the sentence. In this case, you don't use an auxiliary verb.

Who told you? NOT ~~Who did tell you?~~
What happened? NOT ~~What did happen?~~

6 Match the questions to the answers.

1 Who called?   a) The one he wanted.
2 Who did you call?   b) Pete got it.
3 Who got the job?   c) I called Mary.
4 Which job did he get? d) Alice called.

7 Write the questions for the answers given.

1 _____ at the station?
 I met Sue.
2 _____ at the station?
 Sue met me.
3 _____ at the training day?
 Thierry spoke. It was really interesting.
4 _____ about?
 He spoke about how to set up a small business.

Making requests

8 Saying *Help me with my bags!* or even *Help me with my bags, please!* can sound too direct. Instead, use:

> **Polite request forms**
> **Can / Could** you help me with my bags?
> **Will / Would** you help me with my bags?
> **Do you think you could** help me with my bags?
> **I wonder if you could** help me with my bags.
> **I was wondering if you could** help me with my bags.

1 Add the word *possibly* in the correct place in this sentence:
I wonder if I could leave a few minutes early today?
2 Fill in the missing letters to make two more polite request forms.
a) I'd be really g_ _ _ _ _ _ l if you could help me.
b) I'd really a_ _ _ _ _ _ _ _ e it if you could help me.

9 Read the contexts 1– 4 then match each one with an appropriate request form a)–d).

1 asking for help from a friend who should be helping you, but isn't ☐
2 asking a small favour of your brother / sister ☐
3 asking a small favour of a colleague who is doing something else ☐
4 asking a big favour of a senior colleague who is doing something else ☐

a) Can you give me a hand?
b) Come on, give me a hand here!
c) I was wondering if you could possibly give me a hand.
d) Do you think you could give me a hand?

10 When you agree to a request, 'OK' can sound too relaxed and informal. There are other more customer-friendly alternatives. Fill in the missing letters.

Can you give me a hand?

1 Yes, _ _ c_ _ _ _ _.
2 Yes, c_ _ _ _ _ _ _ y.
3 Yes, s_ _ _.

11 Match the first part of the phrase with the last part to make requests using *mind*.

1 Do you mind if I …   a) closed the window?
2 Would you mind if I …   b) closing the window?
3 Would you mind …   c) close the window?

> Requests with *mind* mean: 'Is it a problem for you?'
> So answering 'no' means: 'no problem'.
> *Would you mind helping me with this software?*
> **No**, not at all. / **No**, of course not.

12 If you want to refuse any kind of request, you can say:

A_ _ _ _ _ _ _ / To be h_ _ _ _ _, it's a bit inconvenient right now.

Giving instructions

13 Match 1–5 to a definition a)–e).

1 You can do it.   ☐
2 You might have to do it. ☐
3 You don't have to do it. ☐
4 You mustn't do it.   ☐
5 You have to do it.   ☐

a) It's necessary to do it.
b) It's OK – you're allowed to do it.
c) It's not necessary to do it.
d) I'm telling you not to do it.
e) It's possible that some action is necessary.

14 Choose the three phrases from the first group in 13 that mean the same as:

1 Don't do it!
2 You need to do it.
3 You needn't do it.

> • To say it is **necessary** to do something, use:
> *You **have to** do it. / You'**ll have to** do it.*
> *You **need to** do it. / You'**ll need to** do it.*
> (The forms with *'ll* are more informal.)
> • To say it is **not necessary to do** something (i.e. there is a choice), use:
> *You **don't have to** do it.*
> *You **needn't** do it.*
> • To say it is **necessary *not* to do** something, use:
> *You **mustn't** do it!*
> ***Don't** do it!*

15 In the affirmative, *you have to* and *you must* are very similar. But notice from the box above that, in the negative, *you don't have to* and *you mustn't* are different.

Complete the text below using *have to, don't have to* or *mustn't*.

You (1) _____ work in customer support but, if you do, then you will sometimes be faced with very angry callers. Luckily, there are some techniques to help you. First, you (2) _____ interrupt while the other person is speaking. They need to be able to express what they are feeling. Of course, if they're angry, then the message may get confused, so when they finish, you (3) _____ ask short, simple questions to establish the facts. Most companies insist that during this first call you (4) _____ accept any legal responsibility for the problems, but that's OK – you (5) _____. You can, however, still be sympathetic and try to help. Above all, your attitude is important – you (6) _____ be calm and patient at all times.

Articles

1 Complete the sentences using *the*, *an* or no article.

1 I have ___ idea. Let's develop ___ completely new model with extra features – we could call it 'Premia'. Of course, it would sell at ___ much higher price.
2 When we launch ___ new 'Premia' model, we will have to redesign ___ packaging. We want to differentiate it from ___ standard model we sell now.
3 Anyone who works in ___ marketing will tell you – ___ packaging is very important – ___ products don't just sell themselves.

2 Complete the grammar rules using *the*, *a/an* or *no article*.

1 You use _____ when the listener doesn't know which person or thing you are talking about because:
 • you are mentioning it for the first time or
 • it is not specific.
2 You use _____ when it is clear which person or thing you are talking about because:
 • it's clear from the context or
 • there is only one or
 • you have already mentioned it.
3 You use _____ when you are talking generally.

3 Fill in the gaps using *the* or *a/an*.

1 I've brought with me ___ mockup of our latest GPS device – ___ mockup shows how compact the new product will be.
2 I'd like to finish ___ presentation by telling you ___ story.
3 Have you heard about ___ MP-bunny? It's ___ electronic rabbit that dances and talks.
4 We've developed ___ great new product – ___ idea came from our R&D department.

4 Fill in the gaps using *the* where necessary.

1 People say that ___ money makes ___ world go round.
2 ___ money we spend on ___ market research is only a small part of our whole budget.
3 ___ football these days is much more commercialized than ___ football they played twenty years ago.
4 ___ plastic is often used as a packaging material, and ___ plastic we use is 100% biodegradable.

Defining relative clauses

5 Read how to join two short sentences.

> Here is the package. We designed it last week.
> → *Here is the package* **which / that** *we designed last week*.
> (NOT *Here is the package which we designed it last week*.)
> Here is the CV of the Portuguese candidate. She got the job.
> → *Here is the CV of the Portuguese candidate* **who / that** *got the job*.
> (NOT *Here is the CV of the Portuguese candidate who she got the job*.)
> The underlined phrases are relative clauses.
> The words in **bold** are relative pronouns. You use *which* for things, *who* for people and *that* for both things and people.
> (In speech, *that* is more common for things, and *who* is more common for people.)

Join the sentences below. Write both relative pronouns.

1 FedEx is an international company. It operates in the transportation business.

 _____

2 Charlie Wang is a dynamic man. He runs the New China Packaging Company.

 _____

Relative clauses without the relative pronoun

6 Look at the two joined sentences (after the arrows) in the box above.

In <u>one</u> of the sentences you can leave out the relative pronoun. Write the whole sentence again, without any relative pronoun.

 _____

7 Underline the correct words in **bold** to make a rule. Think about your last answer and look again at the box above to help you.

 • You can leave out *who*, *which* or *that* in a defining relative clause if they are followed immediately by **a verb / a pronoun / a noun**.
 • You must keep *who*, *which* or *that* if they are followed immediately by **a verb / a pronoun / a noun**.

Relative clauses with *whose*

8 The relative pronoun *whose* shows possession. Read the examples in the box.

> FedEx is an international company. Its reputation is very good.
> → *FedEx is an international company* **whose** *reputation is very good.*
> Charlie Wang is a dynamic man. His ideas about business are very interesting.
> → *Charlie Wang is a dynamic man* **whose** *ideas about business are very interesting.*

Combine these sentences using *whose.*

1 These are the views of the consultants. Their report was used by the government.

_____

2 Look at this article about that German manufacturing company. Their production was outsourced to Slovakia.

_____

Prepositions in relative clauses

9 Tick (✓) the two sentences that are in modern spoken English.

1 Microsoft is a company about which I know quite a lot.
2 Microsoft is a company which I know quite a lot about.
3 The person to whom I spoke was called Sandra.
4 The person I spoke to was called Sandra.

> Normally you put a preposition at the end of the relative clause (although this may not be the end of the sentence).
> The word *whom* following a preposition is rare in modern English. It sounds very formal.

Non-defining relative clauses

10 Read the examples of non-defining relative clauses in the box.

> *FedEx,* **which is one of America's largest companies,** *has its head office in Memphis.*
> *Charlie Wang,* **who is President of New China Packaging,** *has some interesting ideas about cross-functional teams.*

Underline the correct words in **bold** to make rules.

- A non-defining relative clause **identifies exactly which person or thing we mean / simply adds extra information.**
- In a non-defining relative clause you **use / do not use** commas around the clause.
- In a non-defining relative clause you **can / cannot** leave out *who* or *which*.
- In a non-defining relative clause you **can / cannot** use *that.*

Noun combinations

11 Read the information about noun combinations in the box.

> A **credit card** is a card used for getting credit.
> A **company credit card** is a card used for getting credit that has been provided by a company.
> An **insurance document** is a document that shows you have insurance.
> A **travel insurance document** is a document that shows you have insurance for travel.
>
> So, the main noun comes at the end, and any others describe it.
>
> An adjective can come at the beginning. The examples below are all two-part adjectives.
> a **long-lasting printer cartridge**
> a **high-quality water treatment system**
> a **six-month government training course**

Make two-word noun combinations from the words in each group.

1 rate   features   inflation   product
  inflation rate, product features

2 force   focus   task   group
  _____

3 forecast   aid   hearing   sales
  _____

4 leader   stock   market   control
  _____

5 price   feedback   customer   range
  _____

12 Make three-word noun combinations by putting the words in the correct order.

1 product   team   design   _____
2 hero   film   action   _____
3 development   strategy   staff   _____
4 engineer   computer   software   _____
5 feedback   program   customer   _____
6 construction   bridge   project   _____

13 Choose the best adjective to put at the beginning of each noun combination in 12. Find a solution that uses each adjective once only.

> ~~hard-working~~   long-term   nice-looking
> over-budget   self-employed   web-based

1 a *hard-working product design team*
2 a _____
3 a _____
4 a _____
5 a _____
6 an _____

Present simple and present continuous

1 Match the verb forms in **bold** in the sentences below with their uses a)– d) below.

1   I **speak** English mainly in my English lessons, and sometimes when I'm on holiday.
2   I'm bilingual – I **speak** French and German, like many Swiss people.
3   Don't ask me now – can't you see I'**m speaking** on the phone?
4   I've had a terrible argument with another team member, although we'**re** still **speaking**.

a)   Present continuous used for an action happening around now, but not at this exact moment. ☐
b)   Present continuous used for an action happening right now. ☐
c)   Present simple used for a fact or permanent situation. ☐
d)   Present simple used for a habit or routine. ☐

2 In these mini-dialogues the tenses are correct, but there are four mistakes of form. Find and correct the mistakes.

1   A: You work on Saturdays?
    B: No, luckily I not work on Saturdays.
2   C: You are going for an interview today?
    D: No, I not going today – the interview is tomorrow.

3 Put one verb into the present simple and one into the present continuous in each sentence.

1   Have you met Freda? She _____ (come) from Berlin. Oh, there she is. She _____ (come) over here now.
2   Usually we _____ (have) just two hours of English a week. But this month I _____ (have) some private lessons to help me get a better grade in the exam.

4 The time expression can give a clue about which verb tense to use. Look at the time expression in **bold** then put the verb into the correct form.

1   **Right now** I _____ (do) two assignments, one for Economics and one for Quantitative Analysis.
2   **Every semester** we _____ (have) an exam on all the material we've studied.
3   **Once a day** I _____ (check) all my emails.
4   **This week** a friend from Ireland _____ (stay) with me.
5   **At the moment** I _____ (wait) to hear from an IT company who I sent my CV to.
6   **From time to time** I _____ (do) a bit of work in my father's company – usually during the summer.

5 Some verbs (called 'state' verbs) are not usually used in a continuous form. Tick (✓) the verb forms that are correct. Change the incorrect forms in **bold** into the present simple.

1   The soup **is tasting** delicious!
2   The soup **is boiling**.
3   Sorry, I'**m not following** you.
4   Sorry, I'**m not understanding** you.
5   What **are you saying**?
6   What **are you meaning**?
7   This book **is belonging** to me.
8   This book **is selling** for €15 on Amazon.
9   Please don't interrupt me – I'**m doing** a grammar exercise.
10 This grammar exercise is easy – I'**m knowing** all of the answers.

Common state verbs

be   believe   belong   cost   depend   know
like   mean   measure   need   see   seem   taste
think   understand   want   weigh

Present perfect

6 Match the verb forms in **bold** in the sentences below with their uses a)–c).

1   I'**ve worked** here for nearly a year.
2   I'**ve worked** in several different bars and restaurants since leaving university.
3   I put my old camera for sale on eBay and I'**ve sold it**! With the money I'll be able to buy a better one.

a)   Present situation caused by a past event. ☐
b)   People's experiences up to now (*when* they happened is not important). ☐
c)   Something that started in the past and continues up to the present. ☐

7 Complete the grammar explanations in the box with these words: *present simple, present continuous, present perfect*.

- The _____ has several uses, but it shows that the speaker is looking back from the present to the past.
- The _____ has several uses, but it shows that a present action or situation is temporary.
- The _____ has several uses, but it shows that a present action or situation is permanent.

Now look back at all the example sentences on this page and compare with the explanations.

8 Underline the correct words in **bold**.

1 I've been a student at this university **for / since** I was 19.
2 I've been a student at this university **for / since** three years.
3 I had a great time **for / during** my university days.
4 I had a great time **for / during** the first two years at university, but after that there was a lot of work.
5 I was a student at that university **since many years / many years ago.**

9 Complete the rules in the box using these words: *ago, during, for, since.*

- _____: used with periods of time; used with the past simple and present perfect; answers the question 'how long'?
- _____: used with periods of time; used with the past simple; answers the question 'when'?
- _____: identifies the point an event began; used with the present perfect.
- _____: used to say how far back in the past something happened; used with the past simple.

10 Complete the sentences with these words associated with the present perfect: *ever, never, already, just, yet.*

1 Erica? She's _____ left. If you go out to the car park, you'll catch her.
2 Erica? She's _____ left. In fact, she left several hours ago.
3 Erica? She hasn't left _____. If you go up to the second floor, you'll catch her.
4 Have you _____ been really late for an interview? What happened?
5 We've _____ received so many application forms for one job. It's amazing!

Present perfect and present perfect continuous

11 Read sentences 1–8. A tick (✓) means correct, and a cross (✗) means incorrect.

1 **I've lived** here since last summer. ✓
2 **I've been living** here since last summer. ✓
3 **She's been interviewing** since 8am – she must be tired. ✓
4 **She's interviewed** since 8am – she must be tired. ✗
5 **She's interviewed** James Matthews and **has offered** him the job. ✓
6 **She's been interviewing** James Matthews and **has been offering** him the job. ✗
7 **I've written** two assignments this week. ✓
8 **I've been writing** two assignments this week. ✗

Refer to the examples above to complete the grammar rules in the box. Write *present perfect, present perfect continuous, present perfect* or *present perfect continuous.*

- When you talk about people's experiences up to now, you use the _____ or _____.
- When you focus on the action itself, not the result, you use the _____.
- When you focus on the result, not the action, you use the _____.
- When you say 'how many' you use the _____.

12 Put each verb into the correct form: present perfect simple or present perfect continuous. Some sentences may use the same form twice.

1 I _____ (send off) job applications all summer but I still _____ (not / have) any luck.
2 I _____ (send off) about 20 job applications this summer – perhaps I _____ (apply) for the wrong kind of job.
3 Joanna looks really disappointed – she _____ (just / receive) her exam results and I'm sure she _____ (fail).

Choosing forms: more practice

13 Put each verb into the correct form: present simple, present perfect or past simple.

1 Sales _____ (go up) by 5% last year.
2 Sales _____ (go up) by 5% so far this year.
3 Sales _____ (go up) by 5% every time we have an advertising campaign.
4 I _____ (work) for Johnson & Johnson for two years. It's a good company, but now I think it's time for a change.
5 After university I _____ (work) for Johnson & Johnson for two years. Then I was invited to join Novartis.
6 I _____ (work) for Johnson & Johnson. There's a great atmosphere in my department.

14 Complete the text by using each of these forms once: present simple, present continuous, present perfect, present perfect continuous, past simple.

'I really (1) _____ (want) that job I (2) _____ (apply) for a few weeks ago. I (3) _____ (wait) for ages – I wonder if they (4) _____ (decide) anything? I (5) _____ (sleep) so badly at the moment.'

Types of conditionals

1 Read sentences a)–c) below.

a) If I use Amazon, I buy more books than I really want, and then I don't have the time to read them afterwards!

b) If I use Amazon to find that book about marketing, it'll arrive within a week, and I won't need to go round all the bookshops looking for it.

c) If I used Amazon to find that book about marketing, it'd be cheaper, but of course I wouldn't be able to look at it first.

Now answer these questions by writing *a*), *b*) or *c*).

1 Which sentence shows there is a high probability of one event happening? ☐
2 Which sentence shows I'm just imagining one event that is unlikely to happen? ☐
3 Which sentence is not about one specific event? ☐
4 In which sentence could *If* ... be replaced with *Whenever* ... or *Every time* ...? ☐

2 Refer to sentences a)–c) in 1. Complete these statements by underlining the correct words in **bold**.

1 Sentence a) is called the **zero / first / second** conditional and the time reference is **past / present / future / general**.
2 Sentence b) is called the **zero / first / second** conditional and the time reference is **past / present / future / general**.
3 Sentence c) is called the **zero / first / second** conditional and the time reference is **past / present / future / general**.

First conditional

3 Correct the mistakes in these sentences. Think carefully about the word *will*.

1 If we will continue talking, I'm sure we find a compromise.
2 If I will agree to that price, can you sign today?

4 Match an *if* clause 1–3 with a main clause a)–c).

1 If you bring down the price, ☐
2 If they're asking for a discount, ☐
3 If we've discussed all the details, ☐

a) can we finish the meeting?
b) we'll place an order.
c) tell them it's impossible.

5 Underline the correct words in **bold** to make a rule. Refer to exercises 1–4 above to help you.

> The first conditional refers to a **likely / unlikely** event in the future. In the *if* clause you use the **present simple / any present tense** (simple, continuous or perfect) and in the main clause you use *will or other modals or the imperative*.

6 Read the whole sentence then underline the phrase in **bold** that is best in the context.

1 If I get lost, **I'll / I might** call you on my mobile – there's nothing else I can do.
2 If you sign the contract today, **we'll be able to / we might be able to** deliver by the end of the month, but I can't promise anything because our factory is very busy at the moment.
3 If you give us a 5% discount, **I'll be able to / I should be able to** place an order, but I just need to check with my boss first.

> Modals in conditionals have their normal meanings. So:
> • *will* means 'the result is certain'.
> • *should* means 'the result is probable'.
> • *might / could* mean 'the result is possible'.

7 Compare these sentences with the similar ones in 3 and 4.

I'm sure we'll find a compromise if we continue talking. We'll place an order if you bring down the price.

Now complete the rule:

> When the *if* clause comes at the end, you leave out the _____ in writing.

if and *when*

8 In the sentences below you can use either *if* or *when*. Compare the two alternatives. If the meaning is the same, write S. If the meaning is different, write D.

1 **If / When** I use Amazon, I buy more books than I really want. ☐
2 **If / When** I use Amazon to find that book about Marketing, it'll arrive within a week. ☐

Now underline the correct answers in **bold**.

a) In sentence 1, the word *if* suggests **certainty / uncertainty** about using Amazon.
b) In sentence 2, the word *when* suggests **certainty / uncertainty** about using Amazon.

> • In zero conditional sentences, *if* and *when* have the same meaning.
> • In first conditional sentences, *if* and *when* do not have the same meaning. *If* shows uncertainty and *when* shows certainty.

if and *unless*

9 Underline the correct word in **bold**.

1 **If / Unless** business improves, I'll lose my job.
2 **If / Unless** business improves, we'll all get a pay rise.
3 **If / Unless** you put down a 10% deposit, we can accept your order.
4 **If / Unless** you put down a 10% deposit, we can't accept your order.

unless = if not
Unless business improves, I'll lose my job.
= **If** business doesn't improve, I'll lose my job.

10 Rewrite these sentences using *unless*.

1 If we don't leave now, we'll miss the start of the film.
_____, we'll miss the start of the film.
2 If he doesn't agree to our terms, we should walk away from the negotiation.
_____, we should walk away from the negotiation.

Second conditional

11 Read sentences 1–4 then match the forms in **bold** to their best explanations a)–d) below.

1 If we **increase** our order, **will** you give us a discount?
2 If we **increased** our order, **would** you give us a discount?
3 If we **increased** our order it **would** be very risky. We might never resell all the items to our customers.
4 If we **increased** our order it **would** be too risky. We would never resell all the items to our customers.

a) First conditional: there is a high probability of the event happening. ☐
b) Second conditional: there is no probability at all of the event happening – it is purely imaginary. ☐
c) Second conditional: there is a low probability of the event happening, but it is not out of the question. ☐
d) Second conditional: there is no reference to probability, instead the speaker is using the past form to be indirect / tentative / diplomatic. It is easier for the other person to say 'no' without losing face. ☐

12 Correct the mistakes in these sentences. They should both be second conditionals.

1 If I would be the boss of this company, I will improve communications by having regular meetings.
2 If we would paid a 50% deposit now, you reduce the price to €25,000?

The second conditional refers to an unlikely, impossible or imaginary event in the future. In the *if* clause you use the past simple and in the main clause you use *would / might / could*.
The second conditional can also be used to make the speaker sound indirect / tentative.

providing (that) / *as long as*, etc.

13 Read the example sentence then underline the correct words in **bold** in the box to make a rule.

*I might consider working abroad, **providing (that) / provided (that) / as long as / so long as** the money was good.*

The expressions *providing*, *provided*, *as long as* and *so long as* all mean *if and only if*. They emphasize the condition. They have a **first / second** conditional form, so they are followed by a verb in the **present / past** simple.

Verbs patterns with *recommend / suggest / advise*

14 Read the verb patterns in the box.

recommend / suggest something
recommend / suggest something *to* someone
recommend / suggest (not) doing something
recommend / suggest (that) someone *do* something
advise (not) doing something
advise someone *(not) to do* something
advise (not) doing something

NOT I recommend ~~you~~ this.
NOT I recommend ~~you~~ doing this.
NOT I recommend ~~it~~ that you do this.
NOT I advise ~~you~~ doing this.
NOT I advise ~~that~~ you to do this.

Now correct these sentences by deleting one word from each.

1 I suggest we to buy the cheaper model.
2 I recommend it that we have a short break.
3 I advise that you to look again at the figures.
4 What do you suggest me?
5 I recommend you not parking here.

The passive

1 Compare sentences a) and b) then answer the questions below.

a) Our subcontractors **employed** a lot of illegal immigrants last year.
b) A lot of illegal immigrants **were employed** by our subcontractors last year.

1 Which sentence are you more likely to hear in a spoken conversation? ☐
2 Which sentence are you more likely to read in a written report? ☐
3 Which sentence uses a passive verb? ☐
4 Rewrite sentence b) so that the person or thing that did the action (the agent) is not mentioned.

_____

2 Read the sentences a)–d) then answer the questions below.

a) A lot of production **has been moved** overseas to countries where labour is cheap.
b) New laws **have been introduced** to protect health and safety at work.
c) The company admitted that mistakes **had been made**.
d) It **was agreed** that compensation would be paid to the employees who lost their jobs.

1 Which sentence uses the passive because the agent is obvious (it is clearly 'the government')? ☐
2 Which sentence uses the passive because the agent is unknown? ☐
3 Which sentence uses the passive because we are not interested in the agent (it is a group of people, but exactly who is irrelevant)? ☐
4 Which sentence uses the passive because the writer does not want us to identify the agent? ☐

3 Compare two ways to end this sentence.

Many tourists enjoy taking a cruise along the Danube, but over recent years …

1 … **the river has been polluted** by raw sewage, agricultural chemicals and industrial waste.
2 … raw sewage, agricultural chemicals and industrial waste **have polluted the river**.

Which ending makes a better link to the topic of the first part of the sentence ('the Danube')? ☐

- The passive is used when the agent (the person who does the action) is obvious, unknown or uninteresting.
- The passive is also used to bring a topic to the front of a phrase so that it links to the same topic just mentioned.
- The passive is more common in writing, and gives a formal, impersonal style.

4 Complete the table. Do not mention the agent.

Active form	Passive form
1 We make car parts here.	Car parts _____.
2 They're polluting the river.	The river _____.
3 We obeyed the law.	The law _____.
4 They've offered me the job.	I _____.
5 They were selling fake goods.	Fake goods _____.
6 We can change this policy.	This policy _____.
7 They might fine us.	We _____.
8 I will decide this later.	This _____.

5 Rewrite the sentences using a passive form. Decide whether or not to mention the agent.

1 We have put the environment at the centre of our future planning.
The environment _____.
2 Johnson & Johnson introduced the idea of corporate social responsibility.
The idea of corporate social responsibility _____ _____.
3 Someone services the elevator every week.
The elevator _____.
4 That guy with the crazy look in his eyes serviced the elevator last week.
The elevator _____.
5 The company is hiring 100 new employees this month.
A hundred new employees _____.
6 A problem delayed my flight.
My flight _____.
7 A major security alert involving 80 Chechnian terrorists delayed my flight.
My flight _____.
8 We must protect the environment.
The environment _____.

6 Rewrite the phrase in **bold** so that there is a better link to the first part of the sentence.

A terrible gas leak occurred in Bhopal in 1984 – it seems that **an act of sabotage caused the disaster**.

Reported speech

7 Match reported speech 1–7 with the quotations a)–h). One reported version is used twice.

Telling a friend about the conversation later:

She said (that) …
1 … she did that. ☐
2 … she would do that. ☐
3 … she had done that. ☐
4 … she was doing that. ☐
5 … she might do that. ☐
6 … she could do that. ☐
7 … she must do that. ☐

The actual words she spoke:

a) 'I'm doing that.'
b) 'I'll do that.'
c) 'I've done that.'
d) 'I did that.'
e) 'I do that.'
f) 'I can do that.'
g) 'I may do that.'
h) 'I must do that.'

8 Put a tick (✓) if the sentence is possible, and a cross (✗) if it is impossible. Think about if you are reporting something which is still true.

1 He said he would be here this afternoon. I need to speak to him. ☐
2 He said he will be here this afternoon. I need to speak to him. ☐
3 He said he would be here this afternoon. But his secretary has just called to say that he can't make it. ☐
4 He said he will be here this afternoon. But his secretary has just called to say that he can't make it. ☐

9 Read the actual words spoken then underline the correct words in **bold** in the reported version.

Actual words spoken on Monday:
'We'll give you our answer tomorrow.'
Reporting to a colleague on Tuesday:
She said that **we'd / they'd** give **you / me our / their** answer **tomorrow / today.**

> When you report what someone said earlier, the original verb tense moves back in time:
> • present simple ➔ past simple, etc. (see 7 above)
> • will ➔ would
> Both the past simple and present perfect change to the past perfect. There is no change for *must, should, might, could, would.*
> You don't have to change the verb tense if the statement is still true.
> Sometimes a pronoun or time expression changes as well.

Reporting verbs: *say / tell / ask*

10 Underline the correct form in **bold**.

1 She **said / told** that she would do that.
2 She **said me / told me** that she would do that.
3 She **said to me / told to me** that she would do that.
4 She asked me **that / what** I would do.
5 She asked me **that / if** I would do that.
6 She asked me what **I was doing / was I doing.**
7 She asked me when **I would arrive / would I arrive.**

> You *say* something.
> You *tell* somebody.
> You *say* something *to* somebody.
> To report a question you use *ask* + a question word
> (*what, when,* etc.) or *if.*
> The word order of a reported question is like a normal statement, not like a question.

Other reporting verbs

There are many other verbs to report what people say. Study the table.

> • Verbs like *say*, followed by 'something':
>   *admit, announce, claim, explain, imply, reply, state.*
>   NOT *She explained us the situation.*
> • Verbs like *tell*, followed by 'somebody':
>   *assure, inform, persuade, reassure, remind.*
>   NOT *She informed that the situation was under control.*
>   (Correct: *informed me that*)
> • A few verbs can be followed by 'something' or 'somebody': *guarantee, promise.*
>   *She guaranteed (us) that the goods would be here.*

11 Report the phrases in **bold** using the verbs in brackets. Include the word *me* where possible.

1 '**It's a really good deal** – you won't find this price anywhere on the market.'
   (persuade)
   He *persuaded me that it was a really good deal.*
2 '**We're stopping all production** until we discover the cause of the pollution in the river.'
   (announce)
   She _____.
3 'Don't worry, **we have fitted new filters** to make sure that the system is clean and safe.'
   (reassure)
   He _____.
4 'Do you want to know what we can do about this situation? We **can do absolutely nothing**.'
   (reply)
   She _____.

will

1 Match the forms of *will* in sentences 1–5 with their best explanations a)–e) below.

a) The merger **will** take place next January.
b) I think the merger **will** probably take place sometime early next year.
c) I**'ll** open the window – it's a bit hot in here.
d) I**'ll** carry your suitcase to the car.
e) I**'ll** call you next week. Bye!

1 a prediction about the future based on an opinion or belief ☐
2 a future fact ☐
3 a promise about the future ☐
4 an instant decision – sometimes referring to something immediate, not in the future ☐
5 an offer of help – sometimes referring to something immediate, not in the future ☐

> *will* has two main uses:
> 1 predictions and facts about the future.
> 2 decisions, promises and offers of help that we make at the moment of speaking.
> The second use is informal, and in this use *will* is usually contracted to *'ll*.
> Decisions, promises and offers of help are often combined:
> *OK, I'll email the information to you this afternoon.*
> (instant decision + promise)
> *I'll speak to my boss and see if we can do that.*
> (instant decision + offer of help)

2 Read the extract from a presentation then add the word *will* in three places and *won't* in two places.

'Good morning, ladies and gentlemen. I've called this press conference because of the rumours circulating in the media about our M&A strategy. Over the next few years our bank become a major player in Central Europe, and naturally we look at strong local banks as possible targets for acquisition. But we make any decisions until we have studied the market carefully. There has been much comment about possible job cuts, but I want to reassure you that the staff of a bank are amongst its most valuable assets. When we do make a move, there be significant job losses at the bank we acquire. In any case, we deal with this issue at the time, and I have no further comment to add now.'

3 Read these two sentences.

1 There will be significant job losses.
2 There won't be significant job losses.

Now add the word *probably* in the correct place to both sentences (but not at the beginning).

4 Match comments 1–5 with responses a)–e) below.

1 Bye! ☐
2 Are you ready to order now? ☐
3 Can you send me a copy of your new brochure? ☐
4 I only have an hour to get to the airport. ☐
5 Are you going for a drink with your colleagues? ☐

a) Of course, I'll put one in the mail this afternoon.
b) Bye! I'll see you tomorrow.
c) Don't worry, I'll call a taxi.
d) Yes, but I don't think I'll be back late.
e) Yes, I'll have the roast lamb.

5 Look at the use of *'ll* in responses a)–e) in 4. Which one is the *best* example of:

1 a prediction?
2 a future fact?
3 an instant decision?
4 a promise?
5 an offer of help?

be going to

6 Read the information about *be going to* in the box.

> *Be going to* has two main uses:
> 1 predictions, especially where there is strong evidence in the present situation.
> *Look out! It's going to fall.*
> 2 plans and decisions we have already made.
> *We're going to cut forty jobs next month.*

Now decide how *be going to* is used in each sentence. Write *prediction* or *plan*.

1 It says in this article that there are going to be job cuts in our banking sector because of all the foreign acquisitions. _____
2 I'm going to see my bank manager about the loan next week. _____
3 You want delivery by the end of the month? That's going to be difficult. _____
4 We're going to launch the new model at the Frankfurt Motor Show. _____

7 Read the evidence in the first sentence. Then use the words in brackets to make a prediction with *be going to*.

1 American banks want to expand in Slovakia.
(Citibank / make a bid for Tatra Banka.)
_____

2 There's too much to do before the deadline.
(We / not have enough time.)
_____

Present continuous

8 Read the information about the present continuous in the box.

> The present continuous has a present time reference (see *Grammar and practice* 4) page 124.
> It also has a future time reference: to talk about fixed arrangements.
> The fixed arrangements are often social arrangements and appointments.
> There is usually a time phrase.
> *I'm seeing my bank manager at 11:30 next Tuesday.*

Now complete the text by putting the verbs into the correct form of the present continuous.

'I _____ (fly) to Paris on Thursday morning. Louis and Isabelle _____ (come) from Lyons to join us. We _____ (give) a presentation about the merger to institutional investors on Friday morning, at the offices of BNP Paribas.'

will or *going to*?

9 Read the information in the box.

> Often either *will* or *going to* are possible, and you could use both in the same situation. However there are some small differences that can influence your choice.
> **Predictions:**
> • *will* is more likely if the prediction is based on the speaker's thoughts and opinions.
> • *going to* is more likely if the prediction is based on evidence in the present situation.
> **Decisions:**
> • *will* is more likely if the decision is spontaneous, made at the moment of speaking.
> • *going to* is more likely if the decision has been made previously, and so now it is a plan.

Now underline the form in **bold** that is more likely (but remember that both are possible).

1 Have you heard the news? Citibank **will make / are going to make** a bid for Tatra Banka.
2 The UK **will probably start / is probably going to start** using the euro eventually.
3 If you're busy, **I'll come back / I'm going to come back** later.
4 I was talking with my friends yesterday - **we'll go / we're going to go** skiing in the Alps.

going to or present continuous?

Read the information in the box.

> *Going to* and the present continuous are both used for plans and arrangements. Nearly always both are possible in the same situation.
> *Going to* is slightly more likely if it's just a plan.
> The present continuous is slightly more likely if the

arrangement is fixed, with a time and a place.
I'm going to see my bank manager next week.
I'm seeing my bank manager at 11:30 next Tuesday.

Expressing likelihood

10 Use these expressions to complete the sentences below. Match the expression to the degree of probability in brackets.

> it's almost certain to   it's likely to   it might
> it might just   it will definitely
> there's no way it will   there's not much chance it will

1 (100%) _____ be a success.
2 (90%) _____ be a success.
3 (70%) _____ be a success.
4 (50%) _____ be a success.
5 (20%) _____ be a success.
6 (10%) _____ be a success.
7 (0%) _____ be a success.

11 Rewrite each sentence with one of these words so that the probability changes as shown in brackets.

> almost   definitely   definitely   fully
> good   highly   just

1 There's a chance the merger will go ahead. (50%→70%)
  There's a good chance the merger will go ahead.
2 The merger will go ahead. (100%→100% with emphasis)
  _____
3 The merger won't go ahead. (0%→0% with emphasis)
  _____
4 The merger might go ahead. (50%→20%)
  _____
5 The merger is certain to go ahead. (100%→90%)
  _____
6 It's likely the merger will go ahead. (70%→90%)
  _____
7 We expect the merger to go ahead. (70%→90%)
  _____

12 Write *T* (true) or *F* (false) after each statement.

1 The three alternatives in **bold** below all have approximately the same meaning. ☐
  *The merger **may / might / could** go ahead.*
2 The three alternatives in italics below all have approximately the same meaning. ☐
  *The merger **may not / might not / could not** go ahead.*
3 The two alternatives in italics below have approximately the same meaning. ☐
  *The merger **should / is likely to** go ahead.*

Prepositions of time

1 Complete the sentences with these prepositions.

after	at	by	during	for
from	on	until	within	

1 My flight gets in _____ 20:15, a few hours _____ yours.
2 I'll be away _____ Monday, 11 June, and I won't be back _____ Wednesday, 20 June.
3 My holidays begin _____ Monday, 11 June.
4 The meeting should have finished _____ 4.30pm at the latest.
5 I'll be away _____ about ten days _____ the month of June.
6 When I get back there are a few things I need to sort out, but you'll hear from me _____ a few days.

2 Cross out the <u>one</u> incorrect word in **bold** in each sentence.

1 I'm away from Monday **by / to / until** Wednesday.
2 What did you do **at / during / in / over** the holidays?
3 How long was his presentation? Oh, it lasted **during / for** about an hour.
4 **During / While** my time at university I learned a lot about economic theory.
5 **During / While** I was at university I learned a lot about economic theory.
6 **Last year / In the last year** sales were slightly better than this year.
7 **Last year / In the last year** sales have been improving; by the end of the year we predict growth of around 2%.

3 Cross out the <u>one</u> word or expression that is not used with the preposition at the beginning.

1 *in*   April / 2006 / the 90s / lunch / the morning / the summer / the third quarter / the 21st century
2 *on*   Friday / Friday morning / 2 April / Christmas Day / the summer / my birthday
3 *at*   half past ten / the weekend / lunch / Christmas / the end of the week / the morning / night

4 Write at the beginning of each time expression either *in*, *on*, *at* or Ø if no preposition is used.

1 _____ this morning
2 _____ yesterday afternoon
3 _____ last night
4 _____ the day before yesterday
5 _____ a few days ago
6 _____ last week

5 Complete each sentence with *by* or *until*.

1 I need your report _____ Friday.
2 I'll be away _____ Friday lunchtime, but I'm free all Friday afternoon.
3 I waited _____ ten and then left.
4 _____ ten I had dealt with all my emails.

Now complete the explanation in the box by writing *by* or *until*.

_____ means 'up to'.
_____ means 'on' or 'before'.

6 Complete each sentence with *in time* or *on time*.

1 I got to the airport _____ – but another few minutes and I would have missed my flight.
2 I got to the airport _____ , and had a chance to look at the stores.
3 If you order today, you'll get the goods _____ for Christmas.
4 You can trust us to deliver your goods _____ every time.

Now complete the explanation in the box by writing *in time* or *on time*.

_____ means 'with enough time' (usually: to do something else).
_____ means 'at the right time'.

7 Complete the explanation in the box by writing these phrases: *at the end, by the end, in the end, towards the end, at last*.

• _____ means 'eventually' or 'finally'.
  The negotiation was going nowhere, and _____ we just walked away.
• _____ refers to the last part of something.
  _____ of the negotiation their line manager will have to sign the contract.
• _____ means 'at' or 'before the end'.
  _____ of the negotiation we had explored every possible option.
• _____ means 'near the end'.
  _____ of the negotiation our legal team will have to start preparing the contract.
• _____ shows pleasure because something happens that you have been waiting for.
  _____ the negotiations are finished! Let's all go out for a meal to celebrate.

8 Look at the alternatives in **bold** and write *S* (same meaning) or *D* (different meaning).

1 We appointed a sales agent in October, and **the following month / the month after that** we started to get our first orders. ☐
2 We appointed a sales agent in October, and **soon after / shortly after** we started to get our first orders. ☐

Verb + preposition

9 Match the verbs on the left in each group of five with a construction on the right.

1	apologize	a)	to something
2	succeed	b)	somebody to do something
3	rely	c)	in doing something
4	conform	d)	on somebody to do something
5	convince	e)	for (not) doing something
6	hear	f)	to doing something
7	insist	g)	about something from somebody
8	look forward	h)	to somebody about something
9	complain	i)	for something
10	wait	j)	on doing something

10 Use a verb + preposition from 9 to complete these sentences.

1 My soup was cold, so I _____ _____ the waiter. He _____ _____ the poor service, and said he would bring some hot soup immediately.
2 While I'm away on business I _____ _____ my secretary to do everything. If anything important happens, she calls me or sends an email so that I _____ _____ it straight away.
3 The salaries in our company should _____ _____ those in other similar companies. I've been saying that for ages, and I've now _____ _____ convincing senior management. We all get a 10% pay rise next month!
4 I'll ask the waiter to bring the bill, and I _____ _____ paying. You can pay when I visit you in your country, and I _____ _____ to doing that very soon.

11 Use a verb from A and a preposition from B to complete the sentences. Sometimes it is necessary to add a third person –s to the verb.

> **A**
> agree   apply   comply   consist   depend
> insure   invest   suffer
> **B**
> against   for   from   in   of   on   with   with

1 As well as owning stocks and bonds, a good way to diversify your portfolio is to _____ _____ property.
2 The shipping cost _____ _____ two figures: the transport itself, and the insurance.
3 Health and safety is a big issue these days, and the company has to _____ _____ all the regulations in this area.
4 It all _____ _____ what you mean by 'profit'. Are you talking about gross profit, or net profit?
5 If there was a fire in the factory, or a serious accident, it would be a disaster – we must _____ _____ these kinds of risks.
6 Ruth persuaded me to _____ _____ the sales job, but I'm not sure that I want my career to go in that direction.
7 Don't worry, I'm quite OK. I _____ _____ an allergy to dairy products, but it's nothing serious.
8 I _____ _____ you up to a point, but I think there are some important issues that you haven't considered.

Noun + preposition

12 Complete the sentences using these prepositions.

> for   for   for   for   in   on   on   to   to   with

1 A company's image can be seriously damaged by involvement ____ illegal trading practices.
2 Bills of exchange are no substitute ____ careful credit checks.
3 Credit insurance can eliminate the need ____ letters of credit.
4 Credit ratings are a solution ____ the problem of evaluating risk.
5 It's important to be transparent in dealings ____ foreign governments.
6 Late payment can have a damaging effect ____ a company's cash-flow.
7 Negotiators should show respect ____ other cultures.
8 Some countries levy a special tax ____ imports.
9 The seller's bank may have access ____ information about the buyer's credit-worthiness.
10 The seller's bank takes responsibility ____ obtaining payment.

13 Find a word in 12 that means:

1 the act of taking part in an activity or event: _____
2 something that is used instead of something else: _____
3 measurements of how good something is: _____
4 the business relationship that you have with another person or organization (plural): _____
5 harmful _____
6 to officially request payment, especially of a tax _____
7 an amount of money that you have to pay to the government _____
8 the degree to which an organization is likely to pay back money that they borrow _____

Recordings

1 Corporate culture

1.1 About business Work culture and placements

 1:01

I got my first placement in a PR firm in Paris, which I was pleased about, 'cos I'm really interested in communication and image management. We'd been well prepared, and our teachers had warned us about dress code, being on time, respecting our commitments ... you know, all the usual things. But I had a problem I really wasn't expecting.

The first day, I arrived at 8.30 and I was a bit surprised because I had to wait an hour and a half for my supervisor to turn up. In fact, most people seemed to get in at about 11 o'clock – and by the time they'd had their coffee and read their mail, and so on, they didn't really start work much before twelve. But everybody was very relaxed and very friendly. My supervisor gave me a project to work on and told me to be autonomous and take initiative, you know, which I enjoy. So, I thought, great, I can really do a good job here and, you know, make a really good impression.

Anyway, for the first two weeks I worked from nine in the morning to about seven in the evening. I didn't really talk to other people very much, because when they arrived I was already working, and when I stopped for lunch, they were all busy. My boyfriend wasn't very happy about me getting home late, but, like I said, I wanted to impress the company, and I've never been afraid of hard work. But then, after the first couple of weeks, people seemed to be less friendly than when I started. I couldn't understand why they were giving me these funny looks, especially when I went home in the evening.

Anyway, in the end, I went and asked my supervisor what I'd done wrong. And it turned out that it wasn't the done thing to go home until eleven or midnight – and, because I left at about seven, I was breaking the unwritten rules. They all thought I was just some lazy student skiving off work! I mean, I knew I was the first to leave, but I'd been there since 9am, and I was working really hard, you know?! But as far as they were concerned, you couldn't do any work before twelve, so being in the office from nine in the morning didn't count!

 1:02

I'm a department manager in the civil service. My office is just a few minutes' walk from the Houses of Parliament. Contrary to what you might think, we're actually very informal and friendly in the department – we're all quite young and everyone's on first name terms. We all have lunch together in the canteen and we'll often go to the pub for a drink together after work. We have one or two interns per year and we try to make them feel at home and part of the team, and usually it's fine.

But, a year or two ago, I had a problem with a student I was supervising. At first, everything was fine. She was very bright and friendly, and immediately got on well with everybody. For example, the whole department was invited to her birthday party. But then, one day we had a bit of a crisis in the office. We'd got behind schedule on one particular project, which Monica, the intern, was working on, and my manager wanted a report for a meeting at 10am. Of course, Monica was the only person who knew where the file was – only that day she didn't arrive at the office until 10.15. In fact, she'd been to the dentist's, but she hadn't told me that she'd be late. Well, as you can imagine, I was pretty stressed out and I made it very clear that this was unacceptable. I suppose I sounded angrier than I really was. And Monica just burst into tears, so I had to tell her that, you know, that was unprofessional too.

Anyway, after that, things were never the same. She became very quiet and reserved and stopped socializing with the rest of the team. She wouldn't say anything in meetings and she didn't even eat in the canteen with us any more. Obviously, her work suffered and I don't think she enjoyed the placement. I tried to explain that I was her boss and that it was my job to tell her when there was a problem, but that it wasn't personal and it didn't mean we couldn't be friendly. But she didn't seem able to accept that. For her, a boss was a boss, and a friend was a friend, and you couldn't be a boss and a friend.

1.2 Vocabulary Work organization and responsibility

 1:03

A: All right, Samantha, welcome to San Antonio. Now, I just want to give you an overview of the company and who does what, so you know who to ask when you need information, OK?

B: OK, Mr Newman.

A: And please call me Bertram, Samantha – we're very informal here in Texas.

B: All right, Mr New- er, Bertram. And, er, everyone calls me Sam.

A: Right, Sam. Now, as you know, my role is to manage Marketing and Sales; you'll be working with Jake, our Art Director, and Saidah, who's our PR Officer, but you're going to report directly to me. I'll introduce you to Saidah and Jake in a few minutes.

B: All right.

A: As I told you, we're a small company, so the organization is simple for the moment, but we're growing fast, so that's going to change as we hire new staff. For example, right now we don't have an HR department as such – Monica Overstreet, our Office Manager, takes care of personnel, so she's the person to see if you have any administrative questions.

B: Yes, I met Ms Overstreet last time I was here.

A: That's right. She also looks after finance, and she has two accountants working under her. Now then, as you probably know, Warndar Technologies was founded by Merilyn Warner, our CEO, and David Darren, who's now COO.

B: COO?

A: Yuh. Chief Operating Officer. Basically, David runs the business on a day-to-day basis. Merilyn deals with strategy, and she's on the board of our parent company, so she's often away in Houston.

B: Uh-huh – and Warndar is a subsidiary of the Irysis group, right?

A: That's right. They took us over a couple of years ago. Anyway, as well as Monica and myself, there are three other department heads who all report to David. The woman we met just now in the corridor is Roxane Pawle. Roxane is in charge of IT and Technical Support. She's new – she joined six months ago when our old IT Manager resigned. He was appointed Head of IT at one of the big consultancy firms up in Washington. Nice job, but too much stress. They fired him after three months. He's working as a bar tender now!

B: Wow!

A: Yeah. Glad you chose marketing, eh? It's dog eat dog in IT. Anyway, Roxane has a web developer and two support engineers reporting to her. OK? Now, the biggest department here is R&D. We have seven research scientists in the lab, plus Doug Pearson who coordinates our development programmes. He liaises with me in Marketing and with our Program Manager, Herb Monroe. Herb manages the Engineering Department, and he's responsible for building our product package – CD-ROMs, user manuals, and so on. Herb has a team of three: two software engineers and a technical writer.

B: OK.

A: All right, I think that's everyone. Unless you have any questions, we'll go and meet Saidah and Jake. Oh, and I think David wants to see you in his office ... don't look so worried ... he's not going to fire you on your first day!

1.3 Grammar Past tenses and advice structures

 1:04

Do you know the one about the CFO and the crocodiles? Well, there was this CEO, who was giving a party for his executive team. Over the years, the boss had done very well for himself, so he was proudly showing the executives around his luxurious country house. Anyway, at the back of the house, he had built the largest swimming pool any of them had ever seen. Absolutely huge, you know? But the pool was full of very hungry crocodiles. So, the CEO said to his executives, 'The most important quality for an executive is courage. Without it, you will never become a CEO like me. So, this is my challenge to each of you: if anyone can dive into the pool, swim through those crocodiles and reach the other side, I will give them anything they want. My job, my money, my house, anything!'

Well, of course, everyone laughed at the challenge and nobody took it very seriously. Anyway, they had just started to follow the CEO towards the barbecue when suddenly there was a loud splash. Everyone turned around and ran back to the pool where the Chief Financial Officer was swimming for his life. The crocodiles had almost caught him when he reached the edge of the pool. He'd just managed to climb out of the pool when he heard the mouth of the biggest crocodile close shut – snap – behind him.

Well, the CEO shook the CFO's hand and said, 'I'm really impressed. Until you dived into that pool, I never imagined you had such courage. You accepted my challenge and now anything I own is yours. Tell me what I can do for you.' The CFO was still recovering from the swim. He looked up at the CEO and said, 'You can start by telling me who the hell pushed me into the pool!'

1.4 Speaking Meetings – one to one

 1:05

Version 1

A: Morning, Tifany. Good weekend?

B: Oh, yes, it was cool. And you?

A: No, not really. Listen, Tifany, come into my office, I need to talk to you.

B: Oh no, what now?

A: Look, I hear you had a problem with Maureen on Friday.

B: Oh that. Yeah. That idiot refused to help me! Who does she think she is?!

A: You mustn't talk about your colleagues like that. Maureen is a very experienced assistant and a valuable member of the team.

B: Maybe, but she still refused to help me.

A: Yes, but she had a good reason to refuse. Maureen was very busy on Friday and you didn't ask for help: you demanded her immediate attention. As a future manager, you should show respect to all the staff.

B: But I was just trying to finish the job.

A: Well, you won't get results from people like Maureen if you're rude.

B: Look, I was tired. I had a difficult week, OK?

A: Tifany, everyone gets tired, and I'm getting tired of your attitude. You apologize, or there'll be trouble. Do you understand?

B: Me? Apologize to some stupid little secretary? No way!

 1:06

Version 2

A: Morning, Tifany. Good weekend?

B: Oh yes, it was cool and you?

A: Yeah I had a good weekend too – apart from having to finish off this report. How about you? What did you do?

B: I went to the swimming pool yesterday. Gorgeous weather.

A: Sounds good. Er, Tifany, have you got a minute?

B: Sure.

DVD-ROM The recordings are available as MP3 files on the DVD-ROM, to be downloaded or played back with interactive script.

Recordings

A: Come in. I just wanted to have a quick word. Erm, I hear you had a problem with Maureen on Friday.
B: Oh that. Yeah. That idiot refused to help me! Who does she think she is?!
A: Well, Tifany, I think perhaps you should be more careful about how you talk about your colleagues. Maureen is a very experienced assistant and a valuable member of the team.
B: OK, but she still refused to help me.
A: Well, you might want to think about why she couldn't help you. Maureen was very busy on Friday, and I understand you didn't really ask for help so much as demand her immediate attention. We try hard to respect all our staff here. As a future manager, I think you ought to do the same.
B: But I was just trying to finish the job.
A: Well, I understand that, and I appreciate that you work hard and that you expect other people to show the same commitment. But, don't you think you might get better results from people like Maureen by being a little more diplomatic?
B: Yeah, OK. I'm sorry, you're right. I was tired. I didn't mean to be rude.
A: OK. It can happen to anyone. Why don't you ask Maureen to have a coffee with you, and just clear the air? OK?
B: OK. Thanks, Simon.

1:07

1 I hear you had a problem.
2 Perhaps you should be more careful.
3 You ought to do the same.
4 I appreciate that you work hard.
5 I didn't mean to be rude.
6 It can happen to anyone.

1.5 Writing **A placement report**

1:08

A: Hi, Jason!
B: Oh hi, Alex.
A: Do you fancy going out tonight? They're showing the new Will Smith movie at the Astoria.
B: Oh yeah. Look, I'd love to, but I've got this essay to finish, and then I've got to write my placement report.
A: Placement? Oh, that's interesting, I didn't know you did a placement. What did you do?
B: I spent three months near Birmingham at a place called Diftco. They export construction equipment.
A: Oh yeah, good job was it?
B: It was all right. They're a bit crazy there. People worked really hard, sometimes from eight in the morning to nine or ten in the evening.
A: Hm. Sounds like school!
B: Yeah! Anyway, I was in charge of preparing shipping documents. Good job we did international trade last semester. It really helped me understand what was going on.
A: Preparing shipping documents, eh? Sounds boring. Didn't like international trade much myself. Did you get on well with your boss?
B: Oh, she was very strict. But, OK, I suppose. She didn't scream at me or anything when I did something wrong.
A: Why, did you mess up a lot?
B: No. Only once when I sent a container to Austria instead of Australia.
A: You're joking!
B: Well, it wasn't my fault. This guy on the phone had a really strong accent. I didn't understand half of what he said.
A: So you sent a container to Austria? What an idiot!
B: Well, I bet you wouldn't do any better. Anyway, it was interesting, 'cos they had this really sophisticated automatic system, but you can't ever completely eliminate human error.
A: Yeah, Jason, the guys at IBM didn't expect you to be using their systems, otherwise they would've spent another ten years making it completely idiot-proof!
B: OK, OK ... Now, if you've finished taking the

mickey, I've got an essay to write.
A: No, come on. I'm just joking. I'm really interested in Diftco. I need to find a placement for next summer.
B: Well, it's a good placement for first-years, but I think second-years should have more management responsibility. I was hoping to get some management experience but I mostly worked alone, so it wasn't that great.
A: You wouldn't recommend it, then?
B: No. I learned quite a lot in three months, but I certainly wouldn't like to work there.
A: Mm, I see what you mean.
B: Listen, now I've told you all about it, you couldn't help me with the report, could you? If we finish by nine, we can still make it in time for the movie. Look, I've already made these notes. You just have to write them up for me ...

1.6 Case study **Counselling**

1:09

Does that answer your question? Now, before we go on, I'll just summarize the three points we've already discussed. Firstly, the goal of counselling is to help another person manage a personal problem using their own resources. Secondly, counselling is about listening, not about telling. It's about talking to someone and helping, not about persuading or manipulating. And, counselling is about assisting and exploring problems. It's not about reassuring someone or solving their problems for them. Thirdly, the three phases of counselling. Phase one, talk. This is where you encourage the problem holder to talk about the problem, and to start to understand how they feel about the problem and why they feel that way. Phase two, think. This is where you encourage them to think about the problem and reassess it. You help them to see their situation from a new perspective, so that they can consider the different options for dealing with the situation. And phase three, act. This is where you help them to choose their own solution and to establish an action plan to manage the problem. OK, are there any questions? OK, I now want to say a few words about some of the skills that counsellors need. I'm going to pass out another handout. As you can see, there are a number of
...

2 Customer support

2.1 About business **Call centres**

1:10

Host: Good evening, and welcome back to *Career Choices*. Tonight's programme looks at one of the fastest growing businesses in India today – customer care.
Call Delta Airlines, American Express, Citibank or IBM from almost anywhere in the world, and there's a good chance you'll be talking to an Indian. With more than a million English-speaking college graduates entering the job market each year, India is the ideal location for American call centres: low labour costs for highly competent staff mean savings of around 50% over the equivalent operation in the States. Attracted by good money, comfortable working conditions and genuine promotion prospects, Indian graduates are queuing up for jobs in call centres. Only five applicants out of every 100 are accepted. Nevertheless, staff turnover in many call centres is high and critics talk about dead-end jobs in sweatshops where staff are routinely monitored and humiliated. So before you rush out to join the queues for jobs in customer care, *Career Choices* has invited two experts to give us the facts about call centres.
With me in the studio are Lavanya Fernandes, who is a customer relationship management expert with a New Delhi consultancy, and Tashar Mahendra, a call centre manager from Mumbai. Lavanya, call centres have had a lot

of bad publicity recently: how much truth is there in the sweatshop stories?
Lavanya: Well, first of all, I think it's important to say that call centres have now largely been replaced by contact centres. Customers' problems and queries are no longer handled just by telephone, but also by email, SMS, online chat and even browser sharing – this is where the operator actually takes control of the customer's computer and shows them how to resolve their problem. This means that the operator's job has become more complex and, at the same time, more satisfying. Now, it is certainly true that in the past there were cases of abuse, you know, where employees were closely monitored, and so on ...
H: Yes, only three seconds between each call and being timed when they went to the toilets!
L: Yes. Of course this kind of intimidation can still happen. But, on the whole, contact centres now realize that forcing operators to deal with customers as quickly as possible is not in their interest. One long conversation which solves the customer's problem is obviously much better than several short calls which leave the customer feeling dissatisfied. So in fact most centres are trying very hard to respect their staff and make their lives more pleasant.
H: Yes, I see. Tashar, I've heard that you pay for taxis to bring your staff to work.
Tashar: Yes that's right. More than 60% of our customer care executives are young women between 20 and 35 years old, many of them working part-time. As in Mumbai we are almost 11 hours ahead of New York, most of the work is at night. Taking a taxi to and from work means their husbands or their families don't have to worry about them.
H: Yes, I see. Tell us about some of the other ways you look after your staff. I believe you also supply drinks and cakes?
T: Yes, that's right. Our customer care executives spend about 80% of their time communicating with customers. We want them to be energetic and happy because we know that happy staff make satisfied customers. So, for the rest of the time, they can enjoy fresh fruit, drinks, cakes, subsidized meals, on-site massage, air-conditioning, competitions, meetings at the beach ...
H: At the beach?!
T: Yes, that's right. We have a meeting area with real sand, deckchairs, parasols and the sounds of the seaside. It feels just like being on the beach!
H: Wow, that sounds great! Lavanya, we know that salaries are six to ten times the average wage, so it's not surprising that these jobs are so popular. But what sort of profile are the call centres, sorry, the contact centres, looking for?
L: Well, the most important thing is very good English. And then computer literacy, good typing speed, marketing skills ... these are all a plus. But, basically, good communication and listening skills are essential. You need to be patient, polite, good-natured and reasonably intelligent. In some jobs, persuasion skills are needed when you have to collect debts from customers or encourage them to use your client's products.
H: And Tashar, I suppose you give your new staff special training?
T: Yes, that's right. Usually between two weeks and three months, depending on the project. This training includes accent training and neutralization, listening skills, slang training, telephone etiquette, telesales etiquette and customer relationship management skills, and call centre terminology.
H: And I believe your staff all have American names, Tashar, is that right?
T: Yes, that's right. For our customers it's easier to talk to Sharon, Julia or Alison than to Jayashree, Suhaila or Kanjri, and it helps our customer care executives to slip into an American identity.
H: And what about promotion prospects?

T: Yes, that's r... Oh, yes, after about three or four years, depending on your skills and results, you can become a supervisor, and then eventually a manager. And, if you decide to work in another sector, experience in a contact centre is very valuable, especially in sales, insurance or other customer relations jobs.

2.2 Vocabulary Customer service and telephoning

 1:11–1:20

1 Operator: Now, don't worry, madam. This is just a minor problem that a few customers experience at first. It will only take a few minutes to resolve.
2 ... or if you would like more information about our products, please press four.
Customer: All I want is to speak to a human being, not a stupid, condescending, brainless piece of ... silicon!
3 Operator: All right sir. Yes, it is an unusual problem, and it's a little complicated, but you'll be pleased to know there is a solution.
4 Customer: Oh, that's wonderful. You're so clever! Thank you so much!
5 Customer: It's just so annoying. I thought your product would solve all my problems, but it just seems to be creating new ones!
6 Operator: I fully understand your position, sir, and I would feel exactly the same way myself.
7 Operator: Alternatively, the simplest solution is to upgrade to the professional version of the software. The extra cost is only around one euro per month. I think you'd agree that that's excellent value, wouldn't you?
8 Customer: Oh, thank you so much. You're so patient. I bet nobody else has these problems. I just feel so stupid!
9 Operator: A very good morning to you, and thank you for calling the helpline. How I can help you today?
10 Customer: Well, that's all very well. You say you've sorted out the problem and it's working now, but how can I be sure it won't break down again tomorrow?

 1:21

Interviewer: Excuse me, madam, I see you've just been to the bank. We're doing a survey about customer service, and ...
Old Lady: Oh, don't talk to me about service! Now, in the old days, the customer was always right! You could telephone the bank and there was always a pleasant young man or woman, you know, who would listen to your problems, and they used to provide a solution in no time. Nowadays, you're lucky if you even get to speak to a human being, let alone get your problems sorted out.
I: Yes, now, could I just ask you ...
OL: And if you want to actually see someone, you can't just walk in, oh no, you have to phone the bank to make an appointment. And they have these machines now, you know, if you want this, please press one, if you want that, please press two, if it's the second Thursday in January, please press three ... dear, oh dear. I just get so annoyed!
I: Yes, of course, but ...
OL: So, then you have to wait for ages and when you do finally speak to someone, either they say they'll call you back and then you never hear from them again, or they tell you they'll have to escalate the problem to their supervisor. Huh! 'Escalate the problem!' They're supposed to be so competent and knowledgeable and all that, but really they just don't want to take any responsibility these days.
I: Yes, but could I ...
OL: So, then they tell you to hold on again and you get another machine playing the same twenty seconds of Vivaldi again and again, and then finally you go back to the beginning again ... 'If you would like to speak to an adviser, please press four.' What is the world

coming to, I ask you?
I: Well, yes, I see what you ...
OL: And now they want me to use that interweb thingy with all those viruses, as if we didn't have enough trouble already! Anyway, I haven't got time to stand here and talk. I must be getting on. Goodbye!

2.3 Grammar Asking questions and giving instructions

 1:22

A: Welcome back to *Guess the Product*. Our next mystery product is a very clever and very practical piece of technology. Panel, you've just *ten* questions to help you 'guess the product'!
B: OK. Is it advertised on TV?
A: No, it isn't.
C: Do you use it for work?
A: Yes, you do.
D: Would you find one in every office?
A: Yes, you would.
C: Can you put it in your pocket?
A: Yes, you can.
D: Did it exist ten years ago?
A: No, it didn't.
C: Does it use electricity?
A: Yes, it does.
B: Do you use it to speak to people?
A: No, you don't.
C: Is there a connection with computers?
A: Yes, there is.
B: Does it cost more than $30?
A: No, it doesn't.
D: Has it replaced the floppy disk?
A: Yes it has. All right, that's ten questions. Now, have you 'guessed the product'?
D: We think it's a USB memory stick.
A: Yes! Well done! You have correctly 'guessed the product'!

 1:23

Steve: OK, Pete. First of all, you open the printer. No, wait a minute, don't just open it, select 'change cartridge' from the menu.
Pete: From the menu? Do I have to switch the printer on?
S: Er, yes, of course you have to switch it on, otherwise you can't use the menu!
P: Oh, right. What about the computer?
S: No, that's all right, you needn't switch the PC on, just the printer.
P: All right. So, the printer's on, select 'change cartridge', OK, and open the printer. What now?
S: So now you gently remove the old cartridge. Don't force it. If it's difficult, you might have to pull it back first, then upwards.
P: Backwards, then upwards. All right, I've got it.
S: OK. So now you can install the new cartridge. You'll need to remove the adhesive tape first, but be careful you don't touch the printed circuits – they're very fragile.
P: You needn't worry. I'm being very careful. OK, that's it.
S: Right. It'll ask you if you want to align the new cartridge, but you needn't bother. Usually it's fine as it is.
P: OK. What about the old one? Can I just throw it in the bin?
S: Oh no, don't throw the old cartridge away. You can recycle them.
P: Oh yes, right. Listen, that's great. I really appreciate your help. Is there anything I can do for you?
S: No, that's all right, Pete. You needn't worry. Just buy me a beer some time!

2.4 Speaking Dealing with problems by telephone

 1:24

Helpline: Thank you for calling the Superword helpline. Please hold the line.
Dean: Good morning. Dean speaking. How can I help you?
Customer: Oh, good morning. Yes, I'm afraid your program isn't working properly.
D: Oh, I'm sorry to hear that. What exactly seems to be the problem?
C: Well, the thing is, I can't put those automatic table thingies in my documents.
D: I'm sorry, it's not a very good line. Could you speak up a little?
C: Yes, sorry. I'm on my mobile. Is that better?
D: Yes, that's much better, thank you.
C: All right. Anyway, I was just saying, I can't insert those tables.
D: Oh, I see. You're having trouble importing spreadsheets into a Superword document?
C: Yes, that's right.
D: All right, I'll put you through to our spreadsheet specialist.
C: Thank you.
D: Hello?
C: Yes?
D: I'm sorry, the number's busy. Could I ask her to get back to you in a few minutes?
C: Yes, that's fine.
D: OK, then. So, you're on 0680 425232?
C: That's right.
D: And could I have your name please?
C: Wyndham. Delia Wyndham.
D: Is that Wyndham with a 'y'?
C: That's right. W-Y-N-D-H-A-M.
D: Thank you, Ms Wyndham. I'm sure we'll be able to sort it out.
C: Thank you very much.
D: Not at all. Goodbye.

 1:25

Operator: Customer support. May I help you?
Customer: Yes, well, I'm having trouble with WordPerfect.
O: Well, let me sort that out for you. What exactly seems to be the problem?
C: It doesn't work. It won't accept anything when I type.
O: I see. How long have you been having this problem?
C: Well, about ten minutes.
O: And was it working properly before that?
C: Sure. I was just typing away, and all of a sudden the words went away.
O: You mean they just disappeared?
C: Yes. Just like that.
O: So what does your screen look like now?
C: Nothing.
O: Nothing?
C: It's a blank. Like I said, it won't accept anything when I type.
O: Uh-huh. Have you tried hitting 'Escape'?
C: Yes. Nothing happens.
O: OK. Did you quit WordPerfect?
C: I don't know. How do I tell if I quit?
O: Can you see the toolbar on the screen?
C: What's a toolbar?
O: OK, never mind. Can you move the cursor around on the screen?
C: There isn't any cursor. I told you, I can't type anything.
O: I see. Does your monitor have a power indicator?
C: What's a monitor?
O: It's the thing with the screen on it that looks like a TV. Does it have a little light that tells you when it's on?
C: I don't know.
O: Well, could you look on the back of the monitor and find where the power cord goes into it? Can you see that?
C: Yes, I think so.

O: Great. Now you just have to follow the cord to the plug, and tell me if it's plugged into the wall.

C: Er, yes, it is.

O: All right. Now, when you were behind the monitor, did you notice that there were two cables plugged into the back of it, not just one?

C: No.

O: Well, there are. I need you to look back there again and find the other cable.

C: ... OK, here it is.

O: Good. Could you tell me if it's plugged securely into the back of your computer?

C: I can't reach.

O: Uh-huh. Well, you don't have to touch it. Can you just see if it's plugged in?

C: No. It's too dark.

O: So, you mean the lights are off?

C: Yes.

O: Well, couldn't you just turn on the light?

C: I can't.

O: No? Why not?

C: Because there's a power outage.

O: A power ... A power outage? Ah, OK. I can handle this now. Listen, for the power outage, I'll have someone call the electricity company. For your WordPerfect problem, do you still have the boxes and manuals and packing stuff your computer came in?

C: Well, yes. I keep them in the closet.

O: Good. I'd like you to go and get them, to unplug your system and to pack it up just like it was when you got it. Then I want you to take it back to the store you bought it from.

C: Really? Is it that bad?

O: Yes, I'm afraid it is.

C: Well, all right then, I suppose. What do I tell them?

O: Tell them you're too stupid to own a computer.

1:26

a) What does your screen look like now?
b) What's a toolbar?
c) Did you quit WordPerfect?
d) Does your monitor have a power indicator?
e) Can you see the toolbar on the screen?
f) What do I tell them?

2.6 Case study **Cybertartan Software**

1:27

Interviewer: So, Laurie, these recruitment and turnover problems we're having — is it just a question of money?

Laurie McAllister: Well of course salaries are not terribly attractive these days. They were quite good a few years ago when the centre opened, but they haven't really increased with the cost of living, especially now house prices are so expensive here, so we're finding it more difficult to attract people from outside the area. But, actually, salaries are not the biggest problem. Basically there are two reasons why our turnover is high: working conditions and job satisfaction.

I: I see. What's the matter with working conditions? We give them free coffee, don't we?

LM: Well, things are very different now from when we started. In the past, the volume of calls was much lower, so things were more relaxed. Advisers had time to chat or have a cigarette between two calls. Now, the workload is much heavier, and the supervisors have to be very strict about breaks. Two bathroom breaks per day, and twenty minutes for lunch. There's a lot of unhappiness about that. And punctuality, well, the bus service here is totally inadequate. A lot of advisers can't afford a car, so transport is a real problem, especially at night.

I: Yes, I can see why that's a problem.

LM: And there are little things, you know, like having your own personal space. When you share your desk with your colleagues on the other shifts, you can't really personalize anything.

I: Hm. Maybe there are things that can be improved there. What's the problem with job satisfaction?

LM: Time, mostly. Our software products have become so complex that customers need more and more help. There are more calls than we can answer, so advisers have to keep them as short as possible. That's frustrating because there isn't time to build a relationship with the customer; sometimes there isn't even time to explain the solution properly. And then of course they say if they can't spend longer on the phone, they would like to send out instructions by email.

I: Yes, well, the customers would like that too, but we can't charge them for it like we can phone calls!

LM: Exactly. And we really need to give the advisers more training, especially the new people, but there just isn't time. They often have to read out instructions from the manual; it's not much fun answering questions when you don't really understand the answers yourself!

I: No. I can see that.

LM: Of course the thing they really don't like is the shift system. They work one week in the morning, from 6am to 2pm, one week in the afternoon from 2pm to 10pm, and one week nights, 10pm to 6am. I mean, it's OK for young, single people, but it's impossible for women with children, so that's a whole category of the population we have virtually no chance of employing. And some people actually like working nights, so they would happily swap their day shifts with other colleagues who don't want to work nights — but the company won't let them. It's company policy, but it's too rigid, it's just not realistic ... Anyway, perhaps you should talk to the advisers themselves — get it straight from the horse's mouth, as they say.

3 Products and packaging

3.1 About business **Packaging**

1:28

Interviewer: Mr. Wang, you often say that packaging is the manufacturer's last chance to seduce the customer. Why is that?

Wang: Yes. Today's marketplace is highly competitive; many products are almost identical, at least from the consumer's point of view. Branding is not enough: unless you are the number one brand on the market, you start from the same level as everyone else. That's especially true here in Asia where there may be literally hundreds of competitors making the same product in the same city. In order to persuade the customer to buy your product rather than your competitor's, you have to differentiate, that is to say, to create and, above all, to communicate the difference which makes your product the better choice. In his book *Differentiate or Die*, the American business guru Jack Trout says, 'Every aspect of your communications should reflect your difference. The bottom line is: You can't overcommunicate your difference.'

I: So, packaging is the best way to communicate your difference?

W: Exactly. Seventy-five per cent of purchasing decisions are made at the point of sale. Today, nine times out of ten that purchase will be made in a self-service context. Your product is alone on the shelf, surrounded by its competitors. According to Wal-Mart, the world's largest retailer, your product has to pitch its promise to the customer in three seconds or less, from up to fifteen feet away. If your packaging is not attractive, effective and distinctive, how are you going to communicate its difference? That's why I say that packaging is the last chance to seduce the customer.

I: Yes, I see. Now, if packaging is so critical, with millions of dollars poured into design, graphics and efficient use of limited shelf space, why is it that there are so many failures?

W: The principal problem is a lack of communication between the different partners involved in the design and development process. Typically there'll be several different groups of experts, all working in their own specialized field: market research people who know nothing about design, designers who know nothing about manufacturing, and production people who know nothing about consumer needs. Traditionally, the design team has always been kept well away from business and manufacturing constraints so as not to limit their creativity. The result is inevitably a compromise. What starts out as an original, creative idea turns out to be impractical, for reasons of cost or technical limitations. So, it gets watered down, simplified, adapted – until, in the end, you are left with a package which is easy to make, easy to transport and within budget, so production, logistics and finance are happy, but it's no longer what the consumer wanted! So, you get focus groups where consumers don't really like any of the concepts that are presented. That means, in the best case, you go back to the drawing-board and start all over again or, in the worst case, you have to choose the least unpopular option.

I: So, how do you avoid this problem at New China Packaging?

W: Well, basically, what we do is to build what we call a 'task force'. This is a cross-functional team with players from all the stakeholders in the project. We literally lock them up in a hotel together, we provide all the tools they need to produce mockups and prototypes, and we don't let them out until they produce something that everybody is enthusiastic about.

I: And do you include consumers in the task force?

W: Yes, indeed. We need the end user's input right from the beginning. Everything is consumer-led. And, because we know that what consumers say they need and what they really need are frequently two different things, we also observe them using the product. Frequently, we can detect behaviours and needs that the consumer is not even conscious of.

I: Really? Uh-huh. So, who else is involved?

W: Corporate marketing, because we need to work within the constraints of brand strategy, funding and schedules; manufacturing, so that we deal with technical issues as and when they arise; and, of course, our own designers and consultants, who contribute creative ideas, technical know-how and marketing expertise.

I: And how long does the process take?

W: Traditionally, months or sometimes years. Today, our task forces can usually deliver an optimal solution in one week, sometimes less. And remember, when they deliver, it means that every aspect of the package is consumer-validated, is realistic and practically feasible, and respects business limitations. So, this extremely short turn-around means that the manufacturer can react very, very quickly to changes in the market, almost in real time.

I: Yes, I see, and ...

3.2 Vocabulary Specifications and features

🎧 1:29–1:34

1
A: I want to listen to English while I go jogging. Is that possible?
B: Oh, yeah. Jogging, cycling, skiing … whatever you like. Nothing can stop it. I even dropped mine down two flights of stairs, and when I picked it up, it was still working.

2
C: I hear you bought one of those new robots. What do you think of it?
D: It's fantastic! I used to spend hours cleaning the flat. Now I can just program the robot and sit back and watch it work.
C: That's incredible! I must get one …

3
E: I really like the colour. It's a beautiful car!
F: Yes, and it's an interesting shape too. Quite unusual. Very different from other cars in this category, isn't it?

4
G: Mum, what's in this bottle? I can't open it!
H: Give that to me, dear. You mustn't touch that. It's for cleaning the kitchen, and it's dangerous. Fortunately, they put it in a special bottle that children can't open …

5
I: Quick, it's starting to rain and there's a pallet of those electronic toys outside!
J: OK, I'll move it straight away. But don't worry – the boxes are made of special paperboard. A little rain won't do any damage.

6
K: Are you sure I'll be able to record TV programmes? I mean, I'm not very good at anything technical.
L: Oh, yes. No worries. My five-year-old can operate this model. It's dead easy.

🎧 1:35

Good afternoon everybody. Imagine you're on a fishing trip. It's the middle of the night. It's dark, it's foggy, you can't see a thing, and you're sailing your boat between small islands and dangerous rocks. Are you afraid? Not at all. You are supremely confident, checking and adjusting your route with just a touch of a finger on a screen. How do you do it?

Well, I'm here today to tell you about the Maptech i3, an extraordinary, integrated nautical information system, where a touch-controlled screen enables you to enjoy single finger operation of several different navigation functions.

Let's start with Touch Screen Command. 'Let your finger do the navigation' is our slogan. Just by touching the screen, you can view and change charts, calculate distances, create a route and a lot more. The large colour display screen automatically shows you a bird's-eye view of where you are and where you're heading. Let me show you an example of what I mean. As you can see, it's a little like floating about 1,000 feet above the boat and watching as you progress up the channel.

Moving on to what's below the water, thanks to the radar overlay, you see exactly what the fish are seeing. Some of you here today may think fishing is boring, but I can assure you that it's a lot more exciting when you know where the fish are – and with the Touch Screen 3D Fishfinder, that's exactly what you can do!

Now, can I just turn to communications? The Maptech i3 can send fax, email and voice messages. You can even send a message showing your boat's location on a real chart. You can request and receive weather reports based on your actual GPS position. And you can even automatically monitor vital onboard systems when you're away from your boat.

So, I'll just sum up the Maptech i3's main features. Let's just go back to our midnight fishing trip. First, Touch Screen Command lets you navigate between the rocks with just one finger and a bird's-eye view. Secondly, the

underwater radar and fishfinder shows you where the rocks are, and where the fish are hiding. Finally, the communications functions mean you can receive and send important data on the weather, your location and your boat at any moment.

I'd like to finish by inviting you to try the Maptech i3 for yourself. Our website has an incredibly realistic simulation that you can try out without ever getting your feet wet. Thank you very much.

3.3 Grammar Articles, relative clauses and noun combinations

🎧 1:36

Synth voice: Please record your product review and your rating out of five after the beep. Thank you for your feedback.
Customer: This is easily the best phone I've had so far. It's the perfect phone for the basic user. I have already bumped it and dropped it a few times but it's still going strong. The battery life is incredible. Overall, it's a real workhorse – there are no frills, but it does what a cellphone needs to do. I rate it five out of five.

🎧 1:37–1:38

1
Synth voice: Please record your product review and your rating out of five after the beep. Thank you for your feedback.
Customer: I hate this phone. It's too small – I can't open the flip cover with one hand. There's no screen on the outside to see the caller identity. The reception is horrible. It drops calls probably 30% of the time. There is a very long key delay, which is incredibly annoying. I am anxiously awaiting the day I can upgrade and get rid of this monstrosity. I rate it zero out of five.

2
Synth voice: Please record your product review and your rating out of five after the beep. Thank you for your feedback.
Customer: I've had the phone for about three weeks. I like the size and the design. The features are good too. It's easy enough to use, and it has survived a couple of drops. However, the alarm clock won't work anymore. I'm not too sure about the internal antenna. I hate having a full signal when making a call, only to have a dramatic drop when I put the phone to my head. Everybody says it's the telecom company's fault, not the phone, or maybe I just got a bad one. We'll see. I'm going to try the 9200 next. I would give it a rating of three out of five.

3.4 Speaking Presentations – structure

🎧 1:39
Version 1
A: Um, shall I start then? OK, I know, erm, I know you're going to be very excited by the Pingman, like me! So, I'm sure you'll have lots of questions. And, perhaps we'll take questions after the demonstration.

OK, er, we've done lots of tests, which have all been very positive, and, er, there are lots of different markets for the Pingman, children, adults, dogs, businesses, and so on. We think there's an enormous potential for this product. Until now, GPS tracking systems have been too bulky, too heavy and too unreliable indoors to be used as personal tracking devices. Our Pingman weighs only 75g; and, well, we'll show you how it works in a few minutes … on the, er, the Internet. So, you know, you connect to the Internet from anywhere in the world, and just ping your user to know exactly where they are. Within one metre… er. Nobody else has a product like this on the market, so we want you to approve the investment, because there's a huge market.
B: What do you mean by 'ping'?

A: Oh, yes, on the Internet, you tell a satellite to send a signal to the device, and the device answers the signal, and then the satellite can calculate the device's exact location.

Anyway, it only weighs 75g, did I say that already? Yes, er, 75g, it's five centimetres in length and about three point five centimetres wide, so, about half the size of a cellphone, and there are different models for children or adults. Tests were really positive, and our sales forecasts are excellent. There's also a model for animals; it's built in to a collar so, if you lose your dog, for example, you just ping it from the Internet to know where it is.

So, er, unless you want to ask questions, I think we'd better have the demonstration. Um. Oh, I forgot to mention profitability. We think it will, er, will be profitable. Very profitable. OK, are there any questions? No? No questions? Um, OK then, let's have the demonstration. It's, er, at the back of the room. Yes. Er, …

🎧 1:40
Version 2
Good morning everybody.

How would you like to know at all times exactly where your young child or teenager is? How comforting would it be to know that your elderly mother is safely back home from the shops? Did you know that, on average, sales representatives spend less than 20% of their time actually with customers? How much would it be worth to know precisely where your sales reps or technicians were? And how much time would you save if you knew where, to the nearest metre, your dog was hiding?

Well, now you can. I'm here this morning to present the Pingman, a revolutionary new personal GPS tracking device – an eye in the sky which will bring peace of mind to parents, carers, businesses, animal lovers and many, many other potential customers. As you know, the reason I'm here today is to demonstrate our prototype and to ask you, members of the Board, to approve the investment needed to start production.

Now, I know you're going to be very excited by the Pingman, so I'm going to give you a quick overview of the product and the market in about fifteen minutes. After that, there'll be a hands-on demonstration, and I've allowed about forty-five minutes for questions and discussion after that. But if you have questions that can't wait, feel free to interrupt me. OK?

I've divided my presentation into three sections. First of all, I'm going to remind you of the background to this project and the current offer on the market. After that, I'll be talking about the prototype, the specifications and the data we've collected from tests, focus groups and market studies. Finally, I'd like to present a business plan; this will show you why we expect a return on investment that is without precedent for our company. Is everybody happy with that agenda?

OK, so, let's start with the background. Now, GPS tracking systems are not new. We've been able to install them in vehicles and containers for some time, but until now they've been too bulky, too heavy, and too unreliable indoors to be used as a personal tracking device. What's new about the Pingman is that for the first time we can build it into a wrist strap or collar small and light enough to be worn comfortably by a small child or a dog. For the first time, it will be possible to locate the wearer via the Internet, anywhere in the world, indoors or out, 24 hours a day and up to every ten seconds …

… does that answer your question?
OK, so, I'd like to wrap up the presentation and move on to the demonstration. Let me just summarize what I've already told you. Firstly, I explained why there is a huge market just waiting for this product, and why the competition are still months behind us. Secondly, I presented the different specifications for the child, adult and animal versions we intend to launch, and the overwhelmingly positive reactions we've had

during trials. Last, but not least, I have given you the strongest possible reasons why you should approve this investment: extraordinary sales forecasts, strong cash flow and unprecedented profitability.

So, ladies and gentlemen, these are the reasons why I am asking you to give this project the green light. I believe we cannot afford to miss this opportunity.

Now, if you'd like to move to the back of the room, our R&D staff are ready to start the demonstration and to answer your questions. Thank you very much for your attention.

 1:41

I've divided my presentation into three sections. First of all, I'm going to remind you of the background to this project and the current offer on the market. After that, I'll be talking about the prototype, the specifications and the data we've collected from tests, focus groups and market studies. Finally, I'd like to present a business plan; this will show you why we expect a return on investment that is without precedent for our company. Is everybody happy with that agenda?

3.6 Case study Big Jack's Pizza

 1:42

Jack Jr: OK, so, we all agree on that then? A completely new range of pizzas for the twenty-first century, featuring fusion cuisine with the best of contemporary Chinese and Western influences? Great. We'll need at least five really new recipes, so see what you can come up with.

Mick: We'll need new names for each new pizza, then, Jack …

J: Of course, but we can come back to that later. OK, so, can we move on to point two – new promotional ideas? What suggestions do we have? Billie?

Billie: Well, obviously with the new pizza range we should do a relaunch. And what about doing specials at different times in the year? You know, New Year, National Day, Dragon Boat Festival …

J: Well, Billie, it's been done before, but I guess we could do that. Why not? Mick?

M: What about a BOGOF?

J: I'm sorry?

M: You know, B-O-G-O-F – buy one, get one free. Two pizzas for the price of one. And another idea would be to have a two-pizza box. The pizzas stay hotter when you have two in a box.

J: Hm. I'm not sure that's a direction we really want to go in. The franchisees won't like it, and we want to get away from the idea that Big Jack's is just good for filling your stomach.

M: Well, what about a gourmet club? Customers get special privileges if they become members. Or feature different national cuisines each month – Indian in the first month, Thai in the second, and so on?

B: Yes, that's good, Mick. And don't forget the Internet – what if you could build your own pizza and order your take-out or delivery online?

J: Sounds like it might be expensive, Billie, but yeah, that's more the kind of thing I had in mind. Anyway, let's go on to points three and four on the agenda. I think we can take them together, because the box depends very much on the logo and the colour scheme. Billie, I think you feel strongly about this?

B: Yes, Jack, I do. We've had our current logo ever since your dad started the business. The Big Jack logo was perfect thirty years ago, but a lot of things have changed since Big Jack's time. Apart from anything else, the symbolism is all wrong, and remember, people are very sensitive to that kind of thing here.

J: What do you mean, the symbolism is all wrong? Green and red are the colours of Italy, it's what pizza is all about!

B: Maybe, but the green chequered table-cloth on the round table – it symbolizes old-world values that people in Hong Kong just don't

identify with. And it's well-known that green isn't a good colour for packaging for Chinese people.

M: Oh, really? Why's that?

B: Oh, you know, it's that thing about green hats – it means your wife is, you know, seeing another man …

J: Billie, this is all very interesting, but …

M: No, hang on, Jack. I think Billie's right. We have to take this kind of thing into account. And the box; the box is really important. It's easily the best way we have to communicate with our customers. Couldn't we have a more exciting box, as well as new colours and graphics? I mean, every baker in the city sells pizza in the same standard box as us. We need to differentiate! An octagonal box would be good, maybe with a window so you can see the delicious hot pizza you're carrying?

J: Well, as long as it doesn't complicate storage or delivery, I don't see why not. But it seems to me we need to get more advice on this. I trust you'll agree that we need to have some brand-building and packaging consultants work on this … we'll consider their proposals at our next meeting.

4 Careers

4.1 About business Career choices

 2:01

Part 1

Interviewer: Most people sense that choices in business today are different. When it comes to people and careers, what actually has changed?

James Waldroop: People in business simply have many more choices today than ever before. Just a decade ago, when you took a job, the company dictated the moves you made. When it came to your career, you had one area that you specialized in. That was all you did, and you more or less did it for your whole work life.

Ten or twenty years ago, you'd join a company, put down roots, and stay put, like a tree. Today the image of the tree has been replaced by a surfer on a surfboard: you're always moving. You can expect to fall into the water any number of times, and you have to get back up to catch that next wave.

But the biggest change is in who is responsible for your career. Ten or fifteen years ago, a social contract went along with a job. Companies accepted certain responsibilities for their people. Today that contract is completely different. You are responsible for creating your own career within an organization – and even more important, between organizations.

I: It's frequently said that careers are over. Instead, you should expect to hold a series of jobs and to participate in a succession of projects. Timothy Butler, how do you see the evolution of the career?

Timothy Butler: There are three words that tend to be used interchangeably – and shouldn't be. They are 'vocation', 'career', and 'job'. Vocation is the most profound of the three, and it has to do with your calling. It's what you're doing in life that makes a difference for you, that builds meaning for you, that you can look back on in your later years to see the impact you've made on the world. A calling is something you have to listen for. You don't hear it once and then immediately recognize it. You've got to attune yourself to the message.

Career is the term you hear most often today. A career is a line of work. You can say that your career is to be a lawyer or a securities analyst – but usually it's not the same as your calling. You can have different careers at different points in your life.

A job is the most specific and immediate of the three terms. It has to do with who's employing you at the moment and what your

job description is for the next six months or so. These days, trying to describe what your job will be beyond 12 to 18 months from now is very dicey.

 2:02

Part 2

I: What advice do you have for people facing a tough career choice, one that could permanently change the direction of their work life?

Butler: Everyone tries to do something that seems like the wise thing to do – but that you shouldn't do: compromise. You've got two competing needs or desires – say, independence and security – and you try to find the position that's halfway between them. Typically that doesn't work.

An equally bad approach is to jump radically from one pole to the other, to pretend that you can forget entirely about one need and recognize only the other. When you do that, the genuine need you're trying to deny simply goes underground and becomes stronger.

Waldroop: We have exercises where we ask people to choose among 13 different business reward values. An obvious one is financial gain. How important is it to you to make a lot of money? Another one is lifestyle. How important is it to you to work in a way where you're networking all the time? A third is power and influence. How important is it to you to be a player?

It's not uncommon for an individual to have a high score on financial gain, a high score on lifestyle, and a high score on power and influence. You can try to jump from one to the other, but when you choose one, the other two don't go away.

So, what's the answer? To be aware of and live with this tension. It's a dynamic part of your personality. And if you try to come up with an easy solution, you're only going to get into trouble. At different times in your life, you're going to shift more toward one pull than toward the others. But the tension is never going to go away. You can't balance them out, you can't take an average of them, you can't somehow live in the middle. Ultimately, what's required is to live with the tension – and to know that you have to live with it.

I: The biggest decision that people face in the world of work is which career to choose. What advice do you have for people who aren't sure what their career – or their vocation – should be?

Waldroop: Good career decisions have to be based not just on your aptitudes, but also on your 'deep' interests. The most common mistake that people make in their career decisions is to do something because they're 'good at it'. It's a story I hear all the time. Someone will say to me, 'I'm an engineer, but I don't like it.' Why did you become an engineer? 'I was good at science and math, so people told me I should be an engineer.' Did you ever like engineering? 'No, but it was easy.'

The real question is: Where are your deep interests? Think of your interests as a deep geothermal pool. Once you tap your interests, you can express them in any number of ways. You may have a particular aptitude – science and math, for instance – but without a deep interest in expressing that aptitude, you'll fail.

Butler: Identifying those deep interests has been the focus of our research for the past ten years. Once you recognize that those deep interests are the best predictor of job satisfaction, the next step is to get in touch with your interest patterns and connect them with the activities that go on in business. Human interests are quite difficult to measure until we reach our early twenties. At that point, they gel – we can measure and describe them. We each develop a unique signature of life interests. And that signature remains virtually constant over time. The pattern won't change.

Our research tries to tap into this deep structure of interests and translate them into the kinds of work that go on in business. There are eight core business functions – not functions like marketing, sales, and finance, but basic activities such as managing people, enterprise control, and influencing through language and ideas. If you look at your deep interests and think about how your interests can be expressed in specific business behaviours, then you'll have the elements of a good career decision.

4.2 Vocabulary Careers, personal skills and qualities

 2:03

B: All right. So that brings us to Rachel Ratcliff. You've flagged her as a high-flier. She's certainly very committed to her work.
A: Absolutely. Rachel is doing a terrific job for us. She's an excellent team-player, and she really enjoys taking initiative.
B: Great, so what's the problem?
A: Well, she's a very talented lady, but she's also very ambitious.
B: Nothing wrong with being ambitious, is there?
A: No, except we don't really have any way to satisfy her ambition for the moment. We planned to make her a department manager in a couple of years' time, but there are no openings right now. She's obviously had other offers, perhaps from a headhunter, and she's thinking about resigning.
B: Hm. It would be a shame to lose her. Solutions?
A: Well, we could offer her a two-year assignment in Germany. I know there's a vacancy over there for someone with her profile, and she'd certainly be able to make a valuable contribution. But I don't know whether she'd agree. She has a fiancé, so it may be difficult.
B: Hm. A two-year assignment in Germany? I'm not sure. But go on, I can see you have another idea.
A: Well, yes. I'd like to put her on the fast track. Send her on an MBA course, and start preparing her for senior management.
B: You really think she's that good? A potential MBA? Well, let me think about that one. I'll come back to you in a couple of days.
A: OK.
B: By the way, how is young Paul Stevens getting on? I believe he had a problem with his manager?
A: Yes, that's right. He was working to very strict deadlines, and just needed a break. I'm working closely with him now, and everything's fine. He's back on the high-fliers' list. He has strong negotiating skills, and I think he'll be an excellent engineer.
B: Good. OK, then, let's move on to Michael Diegel. He's a new hire too, isn't he?
A: Yes. Michael's been with us almost a year now, and we've marked him as a concern because he's not really delivering the goods. He arrived with a fantastic resumé, lots of skills and some good experience. We thought he'd be a real asset, but he's consistently underperformed, he just isn't able to manage the workload.
B: Hm. Any idea why?
A: Well, I'm not too sure. There are two views of Michael in the department. Some people feel that it's a problem of motivation; he doesn't like Seattle, and he wants to move east just as soon as he can. On the other hand, some of us feel that perhaps he just doesn't have the strengths that his resumé claimed. He looked good in the interview process, but he isn't taking on ownership of his projects in the way we hoped he would. Maybe he has more weaknesses than strengths.
B: So, what do we do, give him an official warning? Tell him we'll fire him if he doesn't deliver?

A: Maybe. But we've already invested too much time and money to just dismiss him. Perhaps we should think about moving him east, if that's what will motivate him.
B: And pass the problem on to our colleagues in Chicago or Boston? I'm not sure they'll thank us for that.
A: Hm. How about offering him an easier position in Chicago? Something that won't be so difficult. If he realizes that the job here in Seattle is too much for him, perhaps he'd be more motivated to perform at his real level. Moving to Chicago would be a good way to save face.
B: Yes, that's not a bad idea. Could you liaise with his manager, and see what's available in Chicago or Boston, then come back to me?
A: OK.
B: Good. Now then, we come to our old friend Shane Garney, Mr Wannabe himself. Is he still on the high-fliers list?
A: Not really. He's more of a concern now. He certainly has the skills, but he's getting greedy. We gave him a big raise six months ago when he was promoted, but now he says it's not enough. He says he's had a much better offer from the competition.
B: Well, I think it's time we had a serious talk with Mr Garney. He needs to understand that, although we appreciate ambition, our corporate policy is to reward achievement, not potential.
A: The problem is, of course, that he's very well-connected. You remember that his father's a senator. Wouldn't it be easier to give Shane a small raise to keep him happy?
B: Yes, I'm fully aware of that, and I'm aware that government contracts are very important to this company. But if Shane is only interested in money, he should join his father in Washington. The answer is 'no'. If he thinks he can get a better deal somewhere else, then fine, he can resign. We have a lot of good people like Rachel Ratcliff who would be happy to take his place.

4.3 Grammar Present tenses

 2:04–2:13

1
A: Well, the job's yours if you want it.
B: Well, thank you very much, I'm delighted to accept.
2
C: Congratulations! Don't forget, the degree ceremony's next Friday!
D: Thank you, sir!
E: Thank you very much!
3
F: Nearly finished now.
G: Wow! Seventeen candidates in one day! And it's almost dinner time. What time did you start?
F: Eight o'clock this morning!
4
H: Ten kilometres! Phew! When they said 'recruitment tests', I thought they meant IQ and graphology, not an army assault course!
5
I: Have you seen the results, Jon?
J: Yeah.
I: Oh. Oh, I'm so sorry.
J: It's all right. It's not the end of the world.
6
K: I still think Ms Brown has more relevant experience than the others.
L: Look, we're not getting anywhere like this. Why don't we meet again tomorrow? And, remember, we can always ask all four candidates back for a second interview if we still can't decide.
7
M: Nick? Are you coming out for a drink?
N: Nah. Gotta finish my CV.
M: You still working on that CV?! I mean, how long can it take to say you've got no skills, no qualifications, and you've never done an honest day's work in your life?!
N: Very funny.

8
O: Hey, Paula, how did the interview go today?
P: Oh, so-so. Pretty much the same as the last 26.
O: Ah. Well, I've got to hand it to you Paula, you certainly don't give up easily.
9
Q: Look out!
R: Oops, too late. Oh dear, it's all over your papers. Sorry about that, these cups are very easy to knock over, aren't they?
Q: Never mind.
R: Hope it wasn't anything important. Er, are you here for the interviews, then?
Q: Yes, as a matter of fact I am. I'm conducting the interviews, actually. It's Mr Singh, isn't it?
R: Oops!
10
S: … 98, 99, 100! There we are! Finished!
T: Finished what, Sally? You don't mean …?
S: Yep. Job applications. Started this morning.
T: One hundred job applications?! You're kidding!

4.4 Speaking Job interviews

 2:14–2:18

A
Interviewer: Where do you see yourself in five years' time?
A: Well, that's a difficult question to answer; let's just say that I see myself as a top performing employee in a leading company, like this one. I plan to gain experience and learn new skills. Hopefully, in five years' time, I would be ready to move up to a position with more responsibility.

B
Interviewer: How do you cope with people who resent your success?
B: Do you mean how do I manage working with someone who doesn't like me? Well, fortunately that hasn't happened very often. But, yes, I'm able to cope with being unpopular. I remember doing a summer job in a food processing factory. The person I was working with had been there for twenty years, and didn't much like the idea of working with a business student, especially a woman. On the first day, I made the mistake of finishing more pieces than him, and he took it really badly. Of course, I soon realized that he was just feeling insecure, so over the next few days, I made sure I asked him for advice about different aspects of the job; you know, made it clear I wasn't there to teach him any lessons. Well, gradually he came round, and in the end we got on really well.

C
Interviewer: How do you motivate people to do their best?
C: Well, I think there are two important aspects to this question. The first is to create a positive atmosphere. If people feel happy about what they're doing, they're much more motivated to work towards a common goal. So making sure they understand the objectives and the process, and that the atmosphere is pleasant and relaxed – those are really important. The second thing is to give feedback, especially when somebody does a good job, not just when they get something wrong. When I worked in a restaurant a couple of years ago, I realized that knowing how well you're doing is essential to staying motivated.

D
Interviewer: What are your weaknesses?
D: Well, of course, I'm aware that there are areas that I can improve on, but I have to say, as far as this job is concerned, I don't feel that I have any significant weaknesses. And if I do identify a problem, I take action to resolve it. Take time management, for instance. A couple of years ago, I realized I wasn't the most organized person in the world, so I followed a time management course. I applied

what I learned, and now I would say that organization is one of my strengths.

E

Interviewer: Can you give an example of a situation you found stressful, and how you coped with the stress?

E: Yes. Last term, for example, I was on a work placement where my supervisor had to go off sick for three weeks, so the company asked me to take over responsibility for the project. It meant a huge workload, which was pretty stressful. Anyway, I sat down and planned out exactly what I had to do each day for those three weeks. I also planned an hour each evening in the gym. That really helped to ease the stress. I managed to finish the project on time, and in much better shape than when I started! Does that answer your question?

4.6 Case study Gap years and career breaks

 2:19–2:24

1
My gap year? Oh yes, it was a fantastic experience. It was between my second and third years at university. I went to Nepal to teach English. I think I learned more in that year than in three years at university. It was incredible. Everybody should do it.

2
I went to live with a family in Dublin for a year before starting my degree course. Of course, it was really good for my English, and interesting from a cultural point of view. But it was pretty boring going back to school for another year, even if it was in English.

3
I've had a great year. I've been around the world, working for two or three weeks, then moving on to the next place. I've just gone back to my job, and now I have a much clearer idea of where I'm going and what I want to achieve. My only regret is not doing something to help people. If I could do it again, I'd definitely volunteer for charity work, probably in Africa.

4
Yeah, I took a gap year before starting business school. I needed to earn some money, so I worked in a car factory. It was hell. I've never been so bored in my life. I suppose I learned some valuable lessons, but now I wish I'd done something more exciting, gone somewhere exotic. I feel I wasted a year of my life.

5
I'd been in the same job for about twenty years, and I decided I needed to step back and think about what I wanted to do with the rest of my life. So I took a sabbatical. Fortunately my company was very understanding. I travelled in India for six months, then wrote a book about my experiences. It completely changed my outlook on life. I'd recommend it to anybody.

6
I've just started studying medicine. I wanted to get away from my parents and see the world, so I've just come back from nine months in East Africa. It was really hard. I almost came home after the first week. I'm glad I stayed, because I felt I made a difference to people's lives – a very small difference, but a difference all the same. But if I'd known what it would be like, I'm sure I wouldn't have gone.

5 Making deals

5.1 About business E-tailing

 2:25

Johnny: Now, ladies and gentlemen, tonight we're going to talk to Hermelinda Ray, who is an e-tailing consultant, and who's going to tell us what's new in the world of Internet shopping. Hermelinda, welcome to the show!

Hermelinda: Thank you, Johnny. It's my pleasure to be here.

J: Now, tell me, Hermelinda, what exactly does

an e-tailing consultant do?

H: Well, basically, my job is to help e-tailers to grow their businesses by improving their websites, their products and services, and increasing their sales.

J: I see. I guess a lot of people, like me, do a lot of window-shopping on the Internet, but we don't often buy anything.

H: That's right Johnny. And that's one of the main challenges for e-tailers today, especially because they have to pay to advertise their sites to increase traffic. But only a small percentage of that traffic results in sales, and so when you visit a site without buying anything, your visit is actually costing the e-tailer money!

J: OK, now you're going to tell us about a new way to increase sales: conversational agents?

H: Uh-huh.

J: So, what exactly is a conversational agent?

H: A conversational agent, or virtual host, is what computer specialists call an avatar. It's an animated character that appears on the customer's screen, and can answer questions and chat with the customer, just like you would chat with a sales rep in a store.

J: But it's not a real person, right?

H: No. Having real people to chat with customers online is too expensive for small e-businesses. A conversational agent is a computer program which uses artificial intelligence to interact with customers.

J: OK. But does it work? Do people really want to chat to a machine?

H: Oh, yeah. Of course, some people are happier with the idea than others, but depending on the product and the type of customer, conversational agents can increase sales by as much as 50%.

J: Really! 50%?

H: Yeah. The longer customers spend on the site, hearing and asking questions about a product, the more chance there is they'll buy it. It builds their confidence in the product. And research has shown that people trust what they hear from a conversational agent much more than what they simply read on a website.

J: Well, we thought you should judge for yourselves, so Hermelinda has very kindly brought along a sample for us.

Female Synth voice: Hi, I'm Laurie! I'm here to help you find your way around the site. I'll answer all your questions about our products. Click on a question on the left. Would you like to tell a friend about us? Click on the referral zone so your friends can experience our site for themselves.

J: Well, ladies and gentlemen, would you buy a used car from that lady? All right, let's have a big round of applause for Hermelinda Ray, and for Laurie, the conversational agent!

5.2 Vocabulary Negotiating and e-tailing

 2:26–2:33

1 So that's five hundred at 12 euros a box, then. And you need them by Wednesday, you say?

2 Considering this would be a regular order, I think two and a half thousand is still a bit expensive.

3 How about if we paid cash? Could you give us an extra 2%?

4 No, I'm sorry, that's my final offer. I can't go any lower than that.

5 And then we'd need you to be available five or six weeks a year. Or maybe a bit less. Anyway, we can talk about it. Nothing's decided yet.

6 Yes, we usually ask for 20% now, and the balance on delivery.

7 Look, this just isn't good enough! If you don't deliver until tomorrow morning, it'll be too late!

8 Well, there's not much between us now. What do you say we split the difference?

 2:34–2:38

1 five hundred at 12 euros a box
2 two and a half thousand
3 an extra 2%
4 five or six weeks a year
5 We usually ask for 20% now.

 2:39

Ben: OK then, Jacky. Let's get to work. You've pointed out the benefits of your policy, but there are still one or two issues I'm not happy with.

Jacky: All right, then. What exactly are the issues you'd like to discuss?

B: First of all, I'd like to clarify your remarks about returns.

J: OK. To summarize the situation, our policy insures you against any damage caused during shipping. It does not cover any problems resulting from incorrect assembly or operation by the customer.

B: I see. So, basically, if it's the customer's fault, you don't pay?

J: Right.

B: And are you prepared to extend your cover to include installation difficulties?

J: Well now, Ben. We could certainly make an offer, but there'll be extra costs.

B: Well, considering the size of the contract we're talking about here, I was hoping we could work out a compromise. If not, I might have to consider alternative solutions.

J: I'm sure that won't be necessary, Ben. Why don't we break for lunch, and I'll have my team do a simulation? I'm sure we'll find common ground.

5.3 Grammar Conditionals and recommendations

2:40

Petra: OK, we have to decide how to divide this list of responsibilities between us. What are your priorities?

Jan: Well, I'd really like to go the conference in Madagascar. Could I suggest that you go to Siberia? If you agreed, I'd be willing to take my holidays in January and let you take yours in August.

P: I'm sorry, but I'd really like to go to Madagascar too. Um, I couldn't agree to your proposal, unless you were prepared to take your holidays in January and go to the exhibition in Kazakhstan.

J: Hm. Well, I might consider going to Kazakhstan. I've got an uncle who lives there …

P: Great!

J: … providing you looked after the foreign customer at the tennis tournament – I know nothing about tennis.

P: OK, we're making progress. So, can I just summarize the position so far? You can go to Madagascar, as long as you also go to Kazakhstan, and you let me take my holidays in August. OK?

J: OK. But only if you do the tennis weekend.

P: All right, no problem, I'll handle the tennis, if you take your holiday in January.

J: And you go to Siberia.

P: Oh, now wait a minute, I never agreed to that! I couldn't possibly go to Siberia unless you were able to …

5.4 Speaking Negotiations – bargaining

2:41

Part 1

Ingrid: So, Mr Petersen, you want to set up an e-business to sell music – MP3s and so on?

Harry: Oh, please call me Harry, everybody does. No, not MP3s – sheet music. You know, printed music for musicians to play, like song books, orchestral parts, and so on. At the moment we sell through our network of shops in Denmark, but I'm getting more and more enquiries from other countries, and I'd like to set up an e-business to reach customers worldwide.

I: I see. You want to compete in a global market?

H: Exactly. But the problem is, we don't have the skills, the staff, or the money to do it ourselves.

I: Well, Harry, that needn't be a problem. My company, Holman Multimedia, is used to working with small businesses, and we have a complete e-tailing package solution. You don't have to worry about anything at all. We will design, build and manage your website, and process your sales. We deal with the payments, and we can even handle the logistics for you if you want. Although I suppose most of the sheet music will be sent electronically as PDF files, right?

H: That's right – it's much easier for us, and the customer gets immediate delivery.

I: Exactly. So all you have to do is make sure you have the product in stock, and count your profits!

H: And pay you a monthly fee, is that right?

I: That's right, Harry. No capital investment for you, no new staff, and no overheads. And once you start selling music all over the world, that monthly fee is going to look insignificant compared to the money coming in.

H: OK, Ingrid, er, can I call you Ingrid?

I: Yes, of course.

H: All right, I think we're in business. So what's next?

I: That's terrific, Harry! OK, well, would you mind telling me exactly what you want the site to do? You see, it all depends just what you …

2:42

Part 2, Version 1

H: All right, Ingrid, I think we agree on what we need. Now let's get down to the nitty-gritty – how soon can you deliver, and how much is it going to cost?

I: OK, look. I'm going to write down a figure per month here, just so it's clear, then you can tell me what you think.
There, how do you feel about that?

H: Wow, as much as that! There's no way I could pay that.

I: Well, that figure is based on what you say you need, Harry. I might possibly be able to bring it down a little, but only if we had a three-year contract.

H: A three-year contract! No, I couldn't agree to that.

I: Well, in that case, I can't bring the monthly fee down, I'm afraid.

H: Hm. And what about lead time? Could you have the site up and running by next month?

I: No. I'm afraid development time is around three months.

H: Isn't there any way you could have the site online in two months?

I: Well, I don't think there's much point in talking about lead time unless we can agree on the monthly fee. You're sure you won't consider a three-year contract?

H: No. I can't commit myself to three years.

I: OK, Harry, you have my phone number. If you change your mind, you know where to find me.

2:43

Part 2, Version 2

H: All right, Ingrid, I think we agree on what we need. Now let's get down to the nitty-gritty – how soon can you deliver, and how much is it going to cost?

I: OK, look. I'm going to write down a figure per month here, just so it's clear, then you can tell me what you think.
There, how do you feel about that?

H: Wow, as much as that! Is there any way we could bring it down a little?

I: Well, that figure is based on what you say you need, Harry. I might possibly be able to bring

it down a little, but only if we had a three-year contract.

H: Well, I'd be reluctant to agree to a three-year contract unless you could guarantee a maximum down time of 24 hours per month. Could you do that?

I: Let me reassure you on that point, Harry. Our sites and servers are very, very stable, and average down time is less than 24 hours per year – and so we're happy to guarantee less than 24 hours per month, as long as you choose our platinum service level – but of course, it's more expensive.

H: Well, I don't really want to increase the budget. Hm. What about lead time? Can you have the site up and running by next month?

I: Not unless we hire another developer. I suppose we could do it, providing you paid a year's fees in advance.

H: Hm.

I: Normally, development time is around three months.

H: Look, let's split the difference. I can pay six months in advance on condition that you have the site online in two months. And if you can bring the monthly fee down 5% and include the platinum service, I'll agree to the three-year contract.

I: You're a tough negotiator, Harry. But, OK, I think we can agree to that.

H: It's a deal. Oh, but wait a minute, what about penalties – you know, if you can't deliver for any reason, or if the site is offline for more than 48 hours, for example?

I: Oh, you don't need to worry about that, Harry. It never happens. In fact, nobody in the industry has penalty clauses these days. Now, I just happen to have a bottle of champagne in my bag here – if you can just sign – here, here and here – I'll open the champagne and we can celebrate your new e-business!

2:44–2:46

1 I might possibly be able to bring it down a little, but only if we had a three-year contract.

2 I might consider reducing the price, if you increased your order.

3 I'd be reluctant to agree to a three-year contract, unless you could guarantee a maximum down time of 24 hours per month.

5.6 Case study St John's Beach Club

2:47

Loretta: Oh, Malcolm, there you are. I just wanted a quick word.

Malcolm: Sure. Shall we use my office?

L: No, here is fine. I think I'll have a coffee too.

M: Black, no sugar?

L: Yes. Thanks, Malcolm. I saw your memo about the incentive trip – it sounds great. I wish I was going!

M: Well, why don't you? It would be an excellent opportunity to get to know the sales team better.

L: Yes, it would, wouldn't it? But I just don't have the time, I'm afraid. Anyway, the reason I wanted to catch you was to confirm the budget.

M: Ah, yes.

L: Mm. I spoke to Charles. I've asked him to allocate a global budget of $28,000. That's for everything except travel, which is a separate budget. That's up about 5% on last year. How does that sound?

M: That sounds great. Thanks, Loretta. I'm going to get one of our best negotiators to talk to a couple of travel agents, see what sort of deal we can get. The hotels usually work with several agents, and some of them are prepared to negotiate better terms than others.

L: Uh-huh. Try to persuade them to throw in some extra benefits too. After all, if we use the full budget, we're giving them a lot of business. Sometimes you can get a free upgrade to an executive suite, that kind of thing. How many people are you taking?

M: Well, the top ten sales people, plus myself,

and partners – that makes 22. But if we can negotiate a really good package, I'd like to take one or two more sales reps along. They've all worked fantastically hard this year.

L: Yes, I agree. It would encourage the reps who almost made it into the top ten. I always think it's hard on number eleven! It'll be about a week, like last year, I suppose?

M: Well, again, if we can squeeze a couple more nights out of the budget, that would be great. But we'll see.

L: OK, Malcolm. Let me know what you decide.

M: Sure. Thanks, Loretta.

6 Company and community

6.1 About business Corporate social responsibility

2:48–2:50

Part 1

Interviewer: Despite all the scandals of recent years, Mark Gunther thinks that corporate behavior is improving. He's a senior writer at *Fortune* magazine and author of a book contending that companies are becoming more socially responsible. Gunther is tracking companies that treat employees well, look after the environment and avoid exploiting developing countries.

Mark Gunther: If you just think back 15 or 20 years ago, the workforces were much less diverse than they are now; now you see businesses working very closely with environmental groups in a whole lot of areas. Employees have become company owners in a way they never had been before. You have a company like Starbucks that gave away what it calls 'bean stocks' to everyone who works there, including part-timers, and that aligns the interests of the company with its employees.

I: I wonder if part of the question here is which company you focus on, because you just said businesses are getting along better with environmentalists, there are certainly examples of that; there is also an administration in office that has battled with environmentalists over business questions, and there are businesses that are doing things that dismay environmentalists across the country right now.

MG: Right and of course it is hard to generalize, but even on the environment, I mean the Bush administration has not even acknowledged really global warming as a serious man-made problem. If you look at the US utility industry, you have utilities that are out there planting trees to offset their emissions, you have companies like UPS and FedEx which have huge transportation costs looking for ways to drive hybrid vehicles and get off the gasoline powered cars; I'd argue that the big companies in America are much more green than the Bush administration at the moment.

Part 2

I: What is motivating companies to do that?

MG: Purely bottom-line considerations, this is not about altruism. It's about, predominantly I think, attracting and engaging the best employees, no one really wants to go to work every day to enhance shareholder value, we really want to go to work and be in a place where we feel aligned with the company's goals, where we feel there's some meaning to what we do, and where we feel we can make the world a little bit of a better place every day.

I: Somewhere you've written that, er, Southwest Airlines will favour its employees in some cases over its customers?

MG: Southwest is very explicit about the hierarchy. They put the employee first, the customer second, and then the shareholder third, and the theory is if you have happy, engaged, motivated employees, they're gonna attract customers and therefore your business is going to work, and shareholders are going to benefit, and by the way, if you go to a Southwest gate, get into an argument with someone there, the presumption when word gets back to Southwest headquarters in Dallas is that you were wrong, the customer was wrong and the employee was right because they hire people very carefully and train them and they trust their people 100%.

Part 3

I: Well, let's talk about a long-term trend that's been tracked by some business writers who will say that in the nineteen-fifties and sixties American corporations believed that they should take care of their employees, believed that they should take care of their customers as well as their shareholders, but that from the seventies, eighties onward, they've been pressured to just take care of the stock price, just take care of the share-holder, and in fact they get sued when they don't do that, or they get taken over when they don't do that.

MG: My argument is we are now correcting back from that. That we are not as short-term driven, that we are starting to think more long-term about building sustainable businesses and this short-term model not only doesn't work for businesses in the long run, it doesn't work for our society in the long run.

6.2 Vocabulary **Ethical behaviour and social performance**

 2:51

Rhonda Abrams: Thank you. Thank you very much.

Every entrepreneur hopes to do well. We'd all like to make a lot of money and have a big, profitable customer base. But over the years, I've realized that most entrepreneurs want to do more. They'd not only like to do well; they'd like to do good. They'd like their business to contribute to their community, respect the environment, play a positive role in the lives of their employees and customers.

I'm not naïve or simplistic. I strongly believe that building an honest, responsible business, with a healthy bottom line, in and of itself makes a valuable contribution to our economy and society. Such businesses buy supplies and materials, often employ others, and obviously meet a need of their customers.

Over the years, however, I learned that companies with a sense of integrity and purpose actually have a competitive edge over companies that are solely focused on the bottom line. I want to tell you about four ways they achieve this.

First of all, being socially responsible helps you attract and retain employees. Having a strong corporate culture committed to good corporate citizenship enables employees to feel that they are part of something important. Company programmes allowing employees to use job time to be involved in community causes are viewed as a valuable benefit. Prospective employees look at a company's values and social commitment when comparing job offers.

Secondly, being socially responsible helps you attract and retain customers. People like to do business with companies they respect. Some customers will be attracted by specific company policies, such as looking to buy products that aren't tested on animals or are recycled. But all customers are attracted to companies that consistently deal with them honestly and fairly.

Thirdly, being socially responsible helps you reduce employee misbehaviour. Businesses that act with integrity and honesty toward their employees, customers, and suppliers are more likely to have their employees also act with integrity and honesty toward the company and their fellow workers. An atmosphere of honesty helps keep everyone honest.

And, finally, being socially responsible helps keep you out of trouble. Being a good corporate citizen – whether in your advertising, employee treatment, or environmental policies – makes it less likely that your company will get in trouble with regulatory agencies, taxing authorities, or face lawsuits or fines.

When your company does good – treats employees, customers, and suppliers fairly, as well as participating in community and social activities – you'll find you also do well. Good companies can become great companies.

6.3 Grammar **The passive and reported speech**

 2:52–2:57

1
Leila Belabed: Mr. Bullard, the mayor is very upset. You've just dismissed 100 people from the factory! Have you forgotten that when your company arrived, you promised to create jobs for our town?

2
Geoffrey Bullard: Well, of course I understand that you are upset, Ms Belabed. Unfortunately, new technologies have revolutionized our industry. You must understand that with new automated machinery, we will no longer need so many operators.

3
LB: I know that it is difficult to remain competitive, but what about these people and their families? It's a disaster for them. What are you intending to do to help them, Mr Bullard?

4
GB: Please call me Geoffrey. Of course we share your concerns. We are setting up an outplacement service to help people find new jobs, and I'm confident that most of them will find work very quickly.

5
LB: But what about those who don't, Mr Bullard? How will they survive? These people don't have a lot of savings, you know! Are you offering them financial help?

6
GB: Yes, of course, Ms Belabed, you don't need to worry about that. Each person has already received a generous redundancy payment. And we're also making interest-free loans and advice available for those who want to start their own businesses.

6.4 Speaking **Meetings – teamwork**

2:58

Version 1

Anna: Do we all agree on that then? All right. That brings us to the next point on the agenda – company policy on gifts from suppliers. Now, in the past we used to turn a blind eye, but now I tend to think that we need …

Stan: Well, it's stupid!

A: I'm sorry, Stanislas. Did you want to say something?

S: Yes. It's stupid. Really, really stupid. Well, it is, isn't it, Anna?

A: Well, I'm not quite sure why Stanislas feels so strongly about this issue, but the fact is, we had a major problem with our packaging supplier recently. It seems they had been sending regular 'goodwill packages' to our buyer's home.

S: What?!

Jon: Gifts, Stan. Cases of vodka, I believe.

S: Vodka?! Oh, I see.

A: Yes. Well, apparently, the suppliers thought the contract was guaranteed for life, and unfortunately Mr Vieri, from our purchasing department, 'forgot' to mention our policy of calling for new tenders every three years.

S: So, we should sack Vieri, that's what I think!

J: Stan, I see your point, but you can't just sack someone for making one mistake after twenty years with the company!

S: No, you're wrong, Jon! It's not right, and he has to go.

J: But Stan, don't you think that everyone should have a second chance? I mean …

A: Jon, Stan, I think we're getting side-tracked here. The question today is not how we deal with Mr Vieri, but what our company policy should be in future.

S: Yes, but his behaviour was unethical, do you understand? Unethical! So he must be fired!

Magali: Could I just come in here?

A: Yes, Magali, do you have any views on this issue?

M: I'm sorry, Anna. But when you say this issue, do you mean our policy, or Mr Vieri's vodka?

A: Listen, perhaps we should break for coffee. I think we're all getting a bit tired. Could we come back to this later?

2:59

Version 2

Anna: Do we all agree on that, then? All right. That brings us to the next point on the agenda – company policy on gifts from suppliers. Now, in the past we used to turn a blind eye, but now I tend to think that we need …

Stan: Sorry to interrupt, but …

A: Yes, Stan. Go on.

S: Well, I must say, I think accepting gifts from suppliers is unwise. Would you agree, Anna?

A: Well, Stanislas, on the whole, yes, I would. Now, recently we had a major problem with our packaging supplier. It seems they had been sending regular 'goodwill packages' to our buyer's home.

S: Sorry, Anna. I don't see what you mean.

Jon: Gifts, Stan. Cases of vodka, I believe.

S: Vodka? Oh, I see.

A: Yes. Well, apparently, the suppliers thought the contract was guaranteed for life, and unfortunately Mr Vieri, from our purchasing department, 'forgot' to mention our policy of calling for new tenders every three years.

S: Well, I feel strongly that we should dismiss Mr Vieri!

J: Stan, I see your point, but you can't just dismiss someone for making one mistake after twenty years with the company!

S: I'm afraid I can't agree, Jon! It's not right, and he should leave the company.

J: But Stan, don't you think that everyone should have a second chance? I mean …

A: Jon, Stan, I think we're getting side-tracked here. The question today is not how we deal with Mr Vieri, but what our company policy should be in future.

S: Yes, but wouldn't you agree that his behaviour was unethical? So he should be dismissed.

Magali: Could I just come in here?

A: Yes, Magali, do you have any views on this issue?

M: I'm sorry, Anna. When you say this issue, do you mean our policy on gifts, or the wider issue of corporate ethics? You see, it seems to me that we need some kind of global charter or code of conduct which would cover all possible …

6.5 Writing **Reports and minutes**

2:60

Jan: All right, then. Let's move on to point two on the agenda: diversity. As you know, our workforce is still 80% male. What's more, we have very few employees from ethnic minorities. The general feeling within the group is that we need to take measures in order to reflect the increasing diversity …

Ines: Sorry to interrupt, Jan, but when you say 'measures', do you mean positive discrimination? Hiring women in preference to men, for instance? Because that's all very well in sales and admin, but I really, really can't see women doing the heavy jobs in production. And anyway, I'm not sure that positive discrimination is the right way to approach the problem.

Christopher: No, I don't think it is either. It seems to me that we would just go from one extreme to another – you know, all our employees would be middle-aged female immigrants with disabilities!

J: Point taken, Christopher. But, seriously, that's what we want to avoid – extremes. In fact, what we need are measures to ensure that we don't discriminate against anyone on whatever criteria, whether it's their age, their race, their gender, their religion, or anything else.

C: But Jan, don't you think that's just an HR problem? I mean, they're the people who interview the candidates, not us. Nine times out of ten, we only see a short-list of people they've already approved. It's even worse when we recruit from the agencies. And that's another problem, by the way: half of the people they send us are absolutely hopeless. I don't know how they select them, but honestly …

J: Yes, Christopher. I know the agencies are a problem, but I think we're getting side-tracked here. Could we agree that we'll talk about the agencies next Monday?

C: OK.

J: Good. So, getting back to diversity. Ines, what can we do to attract more applications from women?

I: Well, for a start, we should offer more part-time positions. Flexible hours, longer holidays when the schools are closed, a four-day week. You know, jobs that women with families can manage. That's really obvious. I've been saying this for years! I mean, why don't we start by allowing our present staff to go part-time if they want to? I can think of at least four women who'd be delighted to work part-time! That would mean we could offer more part-time jobs to new candidates.

J: Yes, Ines, thank you. That's an excellent idea. Shall we get HR to work on it? Christopher?

C: That's fine by me.

J: All right, that's decided then. All right, shall we break for coffee now, or take point three first?

6.6 Case study **Phoenix**

 2:61

Justin: … so we all agree that we need to keep an eye on that one. All right, that just leaves point six on the agenda: the new site for the South West. Helen, can you bring us up to date?

Helen: Yes, Justin. There's good news: we've identified three possible sites in a place called Port Katherine.

Glenn: Never heard of it!

H: Well, it's a small town about 30 miles south of Perth. It's exactly what we were looking for: close to Perth, but far enough away not to attract too much attention from the environmentalists.

G: Well, that's good news! We don't want another disaster like Cairns. Those Greens have absolutely no idea what this country would look like if we didn't recycle cars!

J: Yes, all right, Glenn. Shall we let Helen finish?

G: Oh, yes. Sorry, mate.

J: Helen?

H: Thank you. Port Katherine's population is only about three and half thousand, so Glenn will be happy to know there shouldn't be too much local resistance. And the local authorities are desperate to attract new business and jobs to the area.

J: Sounds good. You said there were three possible sites?

H: Yes, that's right. I've put all the details in this handout. There you are, Glenn.

G: Oh, yeah. Thanks.

H: Now, Site A is a good one. It's a greenfield site just on the edge of town. There are several plus points. Firstly, it's close to the highway, so access for our trucks is easy. Secondly, the price of land is reasonable. And thirdly, it's a nice flat site to build on.

J: Any negatives?

H: Well, just one. It's right next to the local school.

G: Uh-oh!

H: But I don't think it's going to be a problem. I spoke to someone at the planning department, and they were very enthusiastic. Sites B and C are also possible, but they have other problems. Site B is on a business park, so no problems with residents, but it's a bit expensive and taxes will be higher. Site C is actually in the town centre.

G: Oh yeah, perfect! Twenty ton trucks in the high street!

H: Actually, Glenn, it's not that bad. It's on a big old factory site near the harbour. We'd have to demolish the old building, and access would be a bit of a problem, but they could build a new road. It's possible.

J: OK, thanks, Helen. Excellent work. I'll send somebody out there to start talking to the locals.

G: 'Operation Charm and Diplomacy', eh?

J: Yes.

H: Hm. Better not send Glenn, then!

7 Mergers and acquisitions

7.1 About business **Risks and opportunities in M&A**

 3:01

Interviewer: If mergers are so difficult to do well, why bother with external growth at all? Why not just grow internally?

Bernard Degoulange: Well, the most common reason, and probably the best reason for a merger, is that your customers are asking you for something you can't deliver. Let's say you sell champagne. If people are satisfied with your champagne, they're going to start asking you for whisky, simply because everybody would like to be able to get the solution to all of life's problems from the same place. Now, if you can't give your customers the whisky they're asking for, you have a problem. Because however satisfied they are with your champagne, they're going to go somewhere else for whisky, and that's when you risk losing those customers.

I: What advice would you give on finding the right company to acquire?

BD: Personally, I have five points that I want to examine when looking at a possible acquisition: the five Gs. If I don't get good answers to at least four of them, I don't do the deal. The first of the five Gs is Goals. Are our goals compatible? Are both companies trying to achieve something similar? If not, keep looking.
Secondly, Gains. I want to know if there will be real gains in terms of economies of scale. And will these gains compensate for perhaps not being able to react as quickly to new trends in the market because of the size of the organization? Being bigger is not always better.
The third point is Genes. That's genes with a G, not with a J! By genes, I mean company culture. There's no point in trying to merge a traditional, hierarchical family business with a fast-moving start-up with a laid-back management style. It just won't work, the cultural genes are too different. It's not enough to find a partner whose strengths compensate for your weaknesses, and vice versa; there has to be a real synergy in culture and personality.

I: Yes, if that synergy isn't present, there's a risk that neither company's customers recognize the firm that they used to trust.

BD: Exactly.

I: OK, so, Goals, Gains and Genes. What are the other two Gs?

BD: Geography and Growth. Are the companies based in the same city or geographical area? If not, communication between headquarters is much more difficult, and the Gains are harder to achieve.

I: And Growth?

BD: Will the merger provide technology or skills that you don't have now, which would take too long to develop yourself, and which will unquestionably allow your company to grow? If the merger will open new markets, which would otherwise be inaccessible, then it makes sense.

I: When you've identified the right partner, how can you make sure the merger goes smoothly?

BD: The most important thing is to look after your people: employees, management and of course customers, but especially employees. First of all, you have to keep them focused and productive. A merger is a wonderful opportunity for everybody to take their eye off the ball – and so it's a wonderful opportunity for the competition to jump in and take market share from both companies in the merger.
Secondly you have to help employees get over their feelings of loss and perhaps anger as quickly as possible, and accept the new situation. Whenever there is a merger, two companies die and a new company is born. It's essential to help people get through that traumatic period, to explain how things will change and what their new roles will be, and to get them to accept the new organization and their new identity. It's essentially about communication, sometimes counselling, and compensating those who leave the company, whether by choice or not.

7.2 Vocabulary **Business performance**

 3:02

Anchor: Oxter Holdings today confirmed that they have increased their bid for Fraxis Corp. to $98 per share. Nelson Brown has the details of the New York industrial designer's Wall Street success.

Nelson Brown: Fraxis Corp. was floated in 1988 at just $15 per share. After a sudden drop of $3 in 1989, the stock rose gradually over the next two years to reach $50 in early 1991, when Fraxis acquired one of their smaller competitors, Nimmco. The market was not enthusiastic about the takeover, and Fraxis fell sharply by over 40%. It then recovered slightly and levelled off around the $30 dollar mark for the next three years. In 1995, Fraxis CEO Alex Firman announced an alliance with the European market leader Haffmann; the reaction was immediate. The stock price soared to $65 as institutional investors rushed to share in the profits. The alliance has been a great success; with the exception of temporary dips to $50 in 2001 and $59 in 2006, Fraxis has climbed steadily to peak at $95, shortly after Oxter's first offer of $90 a share was rejected last week. Analysts believe that Fraxis are unlikely to accept anything less than $110, so expect to see the price jump to $100 plus when trading opens on Monday.

7.3 Grammar **Future forms and expressing likelihood**

 3:03

Ashley: Emma, Happy New Year!

Emma: Happy New Year!

A: What are you doing all alone over here? I haven't had a chance to talk to you all evening. Have some more champagne!

E: No, I shouldn't. I'm going to give up smoking and drinking this year. It's my New Year's resolution.

A: Really?! Well, you can start tomorrow. Come on, Em, it's New Year!

E: Oh, all right, just a drop. Thanks. Anyway, what about you, Ashley? What's the New Year going to be like for you? Have you made any resolutions?

A: No, not really. But I'm definitely going to find a new job. There's no way I'm staying at that company for another year.

E: Right. Have you got anything in mind?

A: No, but I'm going to read the job ads until I find something good. I'm bound to find something better than what I do now.

E: Oh, I'm sure you'll find something easily. Or you could go freelance, with the talent you've got …

A: Freelance?! Well, I suppose I could, but I think it's unlikely. It's far too complicated. No, I'm just going to choose about ten or twelve jobs to apply for, go along to the interviews, and we'll see what happens. I'm going to take my time, not rush into anything.

E: Right. I think that's very sensible.

A: So, what about you? Are you going to stay at Artip?

E: I doubt it.

A: Really?! Are you going to leave, or are they going to throw you out?

E: Well, both of those are quite likely, actually. The company's being taken over in February, so we don't know what will happen. I mean, they're bound to make redundancies, we just don't know how many. Anyway, I'm starting evening classes next week. I'm going to retrain as a marketing assistant.

A: Excellent! Well, here's to a successful New Year for both of us!

E: Yes, cheers! But, um, Ashley, isn't there another New Year's resolution you've forgotten to tell me about? Is that a real diamond? Who's the lucky man, then?

7.4 Speaking **Presentations – visuals**

 3:04–3:08

A
Now, my next slide shows how the number of takeovers is likely to increase over the next decade. This one gives a breakdown by sector. This next slide highlights the probable effect on company performance. And this one, this one and now this third slide show how share prices will fall.

B
Moving on to my next point, which is, er … yes, management buy-outs. No, sorry, just before that I'm going to show you another slide about corporate raiders. Ah, sorry, I can't seem to find it. Well, there's a hand-out which gives you the main points. I'll, er, make some copies when we finish. So, have a look at this slide which shows the confusion which resulted from … Ah, no, sorry, those are my holiday photos …

C
Now, then. Let's look at the next slide which shows some very interesting data. As you can see here – oh, or perhaps you can't see – yes, I'm sorry, the figures are rather small. Anyway, the sales forecasts are particularly good, in contrast to the data for the last three years, which is in the, ah, smaller table, over here on the right. Ah. You can't read that either?

D
If you look at the next slide, you'll see that we intend to collect data for the survey using a Grossman scheduled EMTI questionnaire modified from the standard CDF rapid assessment surveys procedure, and compensated for statistical significance using an unbiased reflex standard deviation algorithm.

E
OK, customer reactions to price and service levels after mergers: 30% of customers noticed an improvement; 49 said things had got worse. Erm, customer satisfaction by sector: almost 9% down in retail; stable in the service and financial sector; and 5% up for manufacturing companies.

 3:09

How will our customers react to a merger? My next slide shows two charts which illustrate the problem. Recently, customers of large Spanish companies that had been involved in mergers were asked if they felt that prices and service had improved, remained the same or deteriorated as a result of the merger. As you will notice in the pie-chart, only a third of customers noticed an improvement, compared to almost half who said

that things had got worse.

Let's look at the second chart, which shows customer satisfaction by sector. As you can see, after a merger, customer satisfaction falls by an average of almost 9% in the retail sector, whereas it remains about the same in the service and financial sector, and rises by 5% on average for manufacturing companies.

The figures seem to suggest that, on the whole, customers are always likely to react negatively to mergers. This is due to a perceived drop in levels of service after a merger. The results indicate that retailers, where service is crucial to customer satisfaction, are particularly affected, as opposed to manufacturers, who benefit from mergers. Of course, this is the result of improved product quality and design, which are the most important factors for their customers.

 3:10–3:13

1 Customers were asked if service had deteriorated as a result of the merger.

2 Only a third of customers noticed an improvement.

3 Customer satisfaction falls by an average of almost 9%.

4 This is essentially due to a drop in levels of service after a merger.

7.5 Writing **Presentation slides**

 3:14

Good morning everyone, and thank you for coming. Two months ago, you asked me to conduct a strategic analysis of the company's strengths, weaknesses, opportunities and threats. I'm here today to present my findings, and to make recommendations on the basis of those findings.

I intend first to give a short summary of the company's position, and then to invite you to ask questions and give your reactions to my proposals. If anything is not clear, please feel free to interrupt me.

First of all, I'd like to remind you of the company's main strengths. As you know, Galway Software has a reputation for innovation and quality in developing highly-specialized customer applications. We are able to provide excellent service thanks to our small team of expert engineers and developers. What's more, our finances have been carefully and cautiously managed: as you can see from the figures on this slide, today the company is in good financial health with practically no debt.

However, although there are many reasons for satisfaction with the company's position, there are also a number of weaknesses which must be considered. The first, small weakness is office space. We just don't have enough. The second, more significant weakness is costs. As this graph shows, our development costs have risen steadily, whereas market prices are falling. It is becoming increasingly difficult to maintain our profit margins. The principal explanation for these high costs is the high salaries we have to pay to attract experienced developers. A third, associated problem is recruitment: in spite of high salaries, we are finding it increasingly difficult to attract young engineers who prefer to join large international companies. This brings me to perhaps the most significant weakness, and a problem which I want to come back to in a few moments when I talk about threats, and that is our size. As a small company in a very specific niche market, we are vulnerable. If things went wrong with just a few of our big customers, we could have serious difficulties.

But before looking at the threats, let's move on to opportunities. In particular, new technologies and a changing world economy are opening up exciting ways of re-thinking our business activities. For example, the new member states of the European Union in Eastern Europe have excellent schools and universities: their young engineers are talented, well-trained and keen to acquire experience in companies like ours. Another possibility is to do part of our development work offshore, in countries

like India where labour costs are significantly lower than in Europe. Last, but certainly not least, we must look at opportunities in our own industry: competition is fierce, and a process of consolidation is under way. Many firms are forming alliances or launching takeover bids in order to exploit synergies, to make economies of scale and to diversify into new market segments. I believe these are opportunities we should not ignore, and I will be making a specific recommendation in the last part of my presentation.

So, I've talked about our strengths, our weaknesses and our opportunities. I want now to explain why one of the opportunities I have just described is also a serious threat. In the context of the consolidation I referred to earlier, Galway Software, as a small, successful, well-managed company with no debt, is a perfect target for a takeover. It is only a matter of time before a big international firm comes knocking at the door with its cheque book open. … Unless we move first.

In the last part of this presentation, I am going to recommend that Galway Software should itself launch a takeover bid. There are many good reasons for this. Firstly, external growth with a reasonable amount of debt will make us less vulnerable. Secondly, a takeover will allow us to diversify into new markets, to expand our customer base and spread our risks, and to make economies of scale. And thirdly, the ideal candidate, Oranmore Video Games, which is based just 20 miles away, currently has more developers than it needs, and has a lot of unused office space.

I'm going to give you a handout which gives more details of why I believe we should acquire Oranmore …

7.6 Case study **Calisto**

 3:15

President: As you know, this year Calisto has lost one point five million dollars. Obviously this situation cannot continue. Unless we take action now, we will go out of business next year. We have several options to consider.

Our first option is to adopt the same strategy as IMM. IMM have reduced their operating expenses by 20% over the last two years. However, they have achieved this by ruthlessly cutting jobs: one fifth of IMM's staff have been made redundant. Here at Calisto we have a long tradition of looking after our staff, and I do not wish to choose this option unless there is no other alternative.

Our second option is to follow the example of our friends at Reysonido, and buy European technology which would reduce our cost of sales by 10–15%. However, we estimate that this investment would increase our operating expenses by half a million dollars a year.

A third option is to cut our prices in order to increase sales. We estimate a price cut of 10% might increase next year's sales to $16.5 million – assuming, of course, that our competitors do not reduce their prices. However, our cost of sales would increase to just under 9 million dollars.

My friends, there are three more options which I have not yet discussed with you, but which I would like you to consider carefully. Option number four is a merger. IMM have offered us three million dollars, which, in view of our desperate situation, is a very reasonable offer. If we agreed to a merger with IMM, the new company would be the new market leader, and be in a far better position to compete with Dylan. However, there would no doubt be some redundancies in order to make economies of scale.

As I said at the beginning of my presentation, I will take questions at the end. Now, option five. This is a high-risk strategy, but we must consider all possible solutions. In order to compete with Dylan, we need to be bigger; one way to obtain that critical size is by acquisition. Our fifth option is to acquire Reysonido.

Reysonido are likely to accept a takeover bid of around four million dollars. As well as synergy and economies of scale, this acquisition would also give us another bonus: access to the technology which means Reysonido's cost of sales is 10% lower than our own. Of course, we would need to borrow the money, and the repayments would represent around half a million dollars per year over ten years: not so unrealistic with combined sales of 25 million, I believe.

The final option is one which I sincerely hope you will not choose. That is, to close the company, and sell off our assets to pay our debts. I have kept it until last in order to stress that it is a serious option.

All right, I'm sure you are anxious to ask questions. After that, I would like us to consider all the options in detail; everybody's contributions will be valuable. Thank you.

8 International trade

8.1 About business Export sales and payment

 3:16

Interviewer: Mr Sullivan, Daryl Vincenti of Eisenhart Games recommends using a credit agency like yours. But can you tell us first what exactly credit agencies do?

James Sullivan: Well, basically, we offer a range of services in two main areas: information and insurance. Some of our clients are interested in information to help them manage credit risk, and others come to us for insurance. But many companies, like Eisenhart, need both information and insurance.

I: What sort of information can you provide?

JS: We have details of over 50 million businesses in countries all over the world. So, for example, we can help Daryl by telling him how businesses and countries in the Middle East are doing financially; we can tell him if his prospective customers pay, and how quickly they pay; and, in particular, we can warn him if one of his customers gets into financial difficulty.

I: And you give each company a rating which indicates how reliable they are?

JS: Yes, companies – and also countries – are given a rating. This gives us a quick guide to how safely you can do business with a particular company or in a particular country. Actually, there's much more than just the rating. Clients like Daryl receive detailed credit reports which help them decide if and how to work with different companies.

I: I see. Now, what about credit insurance? Is that something new?

JS: Well, it's relatively new over here in the States, but not in Europe. European companies have been using it for a long time. Seventy per cent of European companies use credit insurance, whereas in the States the figure is below 5%.

I: Why is that?

JS: Essentially because European firms have to export, because their internal markets are too small. Until now, the majority of American firms have done most of their business in America, so they didn't need credit insurance unless the customer was very risky. Nowadays, companies like Eisenhart need to export, so they're discovering the advantages of credit insurance. For example, it means that in Saudi Arabia, Daryl can trade on open account, with no need for letters of credit, which take a lot of time and are relatively expensive.

I: I see. Talking of expense, what does credit insurance cost?

JS: Well, of course, it depends on the contract. The more risk the insurer takes on, the higher the premium will be. But, on average, I would say, for international credit insurance, between a quarter and 1% of sales.

8.2 Vocabulary International deals and payments

3:17–3:21

1
A: Bruno, have you seen this letter from those people in Slovakia?
B: No, what do they want?
A: Well, they say they're ready to place a large order now if they can pay next year.
B: Well, you'd better do some research on the company. Make sure they can pay! But be discrete. We don't want to upset them.

2
C: I'm still worried about sending these parts by sea. They're quite fragile, you know.
D: Well, don't worry. We're meeting the insurance people tomorrow. If anything goes wrong, we'll be covered.
C: But the insurance premium will be expensive, won't it?
D: Probably. But we have to do it anyway. It's one of the conditions in the contract. No insurance, no deal.

3
E: Francesca, have we received a payment from Kawasaki?
F: No. And I've already sent two reminders.
E: Two? Listen, could you give them a call? If we're not careful, they'll be late every month, and I don't want to have the same problems we had last year.

4
F: So, could you send the payment as soon as possible, Mr Takahashi?
G: Well, it's just that there seems to be a small problem with your invoice. It's more expensive than we expected.
F: I'm sorry, Mr Takahashi, but the invoice is for exactly the same amount as our quotation, which you accepted.
G: Ah, yes. Well, exceptionally, as we are regular customers, could you perhaps wait two or three weeks? We just have a small cash-flow problem at the moment. I'm sure you understand, Ms Trevi. It's nothing to worry about …

5
H: Well, we'll accept your terms providing you deliver direct to our factory.
I: Hm. Our customers normally collect the goods from the port of entry.
H: But you said yourself these parts are fragile, so surely it would be better for the same forwarder to deliver all the way to the door? That way there's less risk of damage.
I: Well, you have a point there, I suppose.
H: And this will be a regular order, so it means a lot of business for the forwarder. I'm sure you can negotiate good terms with them.
I: Yes. Yes, you're right. OK, then. It's a deal.

8.3 Grammar Prepositions

3:22

Paul: Oh, Jenny, did you pick up my tickets?
Jenny: No, I'm picking them up this evening. I have to be there before six, so I'll be able to drop them off here by 6.30.
P: That's great! What time's the flight?
J: It's at 23.10. But it's OK – check-in doesn't open until 21.15. You've got plenty of time.
P: Hm. I've got the finance committee tonight. That usually goes on until at least half seven. I'll only just have time to go home and pick up my suitcase. I probably won't see the kids for a week now. They'll be in bed by quarter to eight. When do I get back from the States again?
J: On Sunday morning. You've got six meetings between tomorrow morning and Friday. That leaves you a day to visit New York, and you fly back late on Saturday evening.
P: Well, I don't think I'll have much time to visit New York. I've got the Merosom pitch to prepare for next Monday. I'm going to be jet-lagged on Sunday, so I'll have to do it before flying back.

J: Oh, yes, that's right. When do you expect Merosom to announce their decision?
P: Well, they said within three weeks. By the way, have you got the files for the New York meetings?
J: Yes, they're all ready. Do want to look at them now?
P: No, I've got another meeting!
J: Well, you'll have to read them during the flight, then.
P: Hm. I suppose so.
J: OK. Well, I'll get on, then, unless you've got any other questions?
P: Er, yes, just one. When am I going to sleep?

3:23–3:32

1
A: It seems to me that with interest rates so low, property is still a better choice than the stock market.
B: Yes, you're right. I think a small flat in the town centre should give a good return.

2
C: I think you should talk to her. She's still upset.
D: OK, OK. I'll call her and tell her I'm sorry. I didn't mean what I said.

3
E: What state is it in after the accident?
F: Well, it could have been worse. Apart from a broken windscreen and headlights, there are only a few scratches on the paintwork. I was lucky.

4
G: It's amazing. She already speaks seven different languages, and she's picking up Chinese really fast!
H: Yeah, some people just have a gift, I guess.

5
I: You desperately need to get some more contracts. Relying on just one big firm is so dangerous.
J: Yes, I know. But we've always done most of our turnover with them.

6
K: The Americans are much more demanding. The Food and Drug Administration are terribly strict. But if you want to sell in the States, there's no other way.
L: Yes, there's no choice. We'll have to adapt the product to their norms.

7
M: What if we deliver the goods but they don't pay?
N: Well, we have a policy which covers that risk. For a small percentage of the value of the goods, we will guarantee to pay you if the customer defaults.

8
O: Well, sales are up 300%, we've reduced costs, our stock price has almost doubled and shareholders are delighted! Everything's worked out perfectly!
P: Yes. It doesn't get any better than this.

9
Q: Have you had any news from Taiwan?
R: No, not a word. It's strange. Usually they're in touch at least once a week.

10
S: Hey, Terry. Have you changed the passwords? I can't get into the database!
T: No, I'm having the same problem. I've tried everything but the system won't let me in.

8.4 Speaking Negotiations – diplomacy

🎧 3:33–3:35

1

A: I'm afraid I think we might need more time to explore all the implications, and perhaps to include some of our senior management in the discussions.

B: Look, Mr. Yamada, I've already been here a week, and I have a plane to catch this evening. If you don't want to do this deal, just say so!
   I mean, when I get back, I have to tell my boss we have a contract, or explain why I failed to get one!

2

C: We feel there are still quite a large number of difficulties to face in this project, and these will take a very considerable amount of time and money to resolve.

D: OK, Amal, let's sit down and work out a schedule.

C: I am not sure that at this stage a schedule is appropriate, in view of the considerable, er, cultural differences between our companies.

D: Well, we need to start work soon if we want to meet the deadlines.

C: Frau Meier, perhaps we should talk again in a few days, by telephone?

D: Are you saying you're quitting the project?!

C: If you insist on putting it in those terms, then, yes, I think probably that is best.

3

E: And you pay the shipping costs.

F: No, as I told you, our prices are ex works. You pay for shipping.

E: So you don't want to sell us your machine tools?

F: No, why do you say that? I never said that!

E: Your terms with Auckland Industries last year included shipping, I believe.

F: Yes, but that was a much larger contract.

E: So our order is not very important for you?

🎧 3:36–3:38

1

A: I'm afraid I think we might need more time to explore all the implications, and perhaps to include some of our senior management in the discussions.

B: Uh-huh. Yamada-san, correct me if I'm wrong, but you seem to be saying that you're not completely convinced by this deal.

A: I'm afraid there seems to be a slight misunderstanding, Mr Bryson. Let me put it another way. We are as enthusiastic about this deal as ever, but here in Japan, it is very important to take the time to consult everybody, and to be sure there is a consensus.

B: Ah, yes, I understand. It's important for me to keep my board informed too.

2

C: I'm afraid we feel there are still quite a large number of difficulties to face in this project, and these will take a very considerable amount of time and money to resolve.

D: OK, Amal, have I got this right? You're saying that you're not sure we have the time or the money to make this project a success?

C: That's right. Especially in view of the considerable, er, cultural differences between our companies.

D: So, would I be right in saying that you are considering withdrawing from the project?

C: No, I'm sorry, Sabine, that isn't quite what I meant. What I was trying to say was, we need to take our different approaches to these problems into account, but I'm sure we can find solutions.

D: Yes, I'm sure we can. Perhaps we should talk again in a few days, by telephone?

C: Yes, that would be fine.

3

E: And if I've understood correctly, you will pay the shipping costs.

F: I'm sorry, perhaps I haven't made myself clear. The price we quoted was ex works. But we can quote including shipping if you like.

E: But didn't you say you would give us the same terms as for Auckland Industries last year?

F: Ah, I see, yes. Well, allow me to rephrase that. What I meant was, we would be very happy to give you the same terms as Auckland, if you were in a position to order the same volume.

8.6 Case study Jeddah Royal Beach Resort

🎧 3:39

Frederick: Good evening, Riaz!

Riaz: Oh, hello Frederick. Everything OK?

F: Yes, fine, thanks. I just wanted to give you these applications, if you've got a moment?

R: Yes, of course. Have a seat.

F: Thanks.

R: OK, so what have we got here?

F: Well, first of all, there's Ms Koepple in room 406. She's with Cool Breeze. It's a record label based in Buenos Aires. Now, I know you don't like record companies, but …

R: Yes, Frederick, and you know very well why I don't like record companies and those vulgar rock groups they send us, always causing damage and disturbing the other guests: Argentina, you say?

F: Yes. But Ms Koepple says they want to organize a big conference for their executives. There won't be any rock groups or that kind of thing, just corporate executives. So, they're applying for our credit card.

R: Well, it's true we need to develop in the conference market. It's good business, and it often brings in more business by word of mouth. But Argentina … OK, leave it with me and I'll look into it. How big is Ms Koepple's bill?

F: Well, she's been here for four nights. Leaving on Saturday. She's spending a lot of money – maybe six thousand dollars so far. But she's very nice, very friendly. I'm sure she won't leave without paying.

R: Hm, she's applying for a credit limit of twenty thousand. Let's keep an eye on her, anyway. Let me know if her account goes over ten thousand dollars, OK?

F: Sure.

R: What else have you got there?

F: The next one is Mr Kobayashi from Tokyo. Remember him?

R: Oh, yes. The second-hand car salesman?

F: Yes. He's a really difficult customer. We've had to move him to a different room three times this week because he didn't like the view, or it was too far from the restaurant …

R: Well, he may be difficult but his credit's good. He seems to have built himself quite an empire over there. Kobayashi Auto Sales is doing very well. We've never had any problem with his people.

F: Well, I wouldn't buy a car from him. He never looks you in the eye, never smiles, never says 'thank you'. He wants us to raise his credit limit, but I don't trust him.

R: Let me see. From fifty up to a hundred thousand, eh? All right, I'll think about it.

F: Right. And this last one is our old friend Mrs Saman and her team from Egypt.

R: Oh, no. Are they still coming here? I thought we stopped their credit last year.

F: No, the company paid up in the end, remember?

R: Yes, I do now. Charming lady, of course, but that company – what's it called? Black Nile, that's it. They invented the concept of the slow payer! I think it took 18 months to get them to pay their last invoice. What does she want now?

F: Well, she wants us to raise their credit limit to a hundred thousand, too.

R: Oh, no way!

F: But there are ten of them this time, and she's such a wonderful little old lady!

R: I should really suspend their credit and insist on cash in advance. They're on, let's see … thirty thousand dollars. It's just too big a risk. Have you seen the latest cash-flow figures? Our customers are taking longer and longer to pay, and uncollectibles have gone over 3%! I'm getting a lot of pressure from management to take firm action.

F: Well, be careful: Mrs Saman told me yesterday that her brother is a very senior government official. And remember, we have a lot of guests from Egypt now. We don't want to upset them.

R: Yes, that's true. You never know who Mrs Saman might talk to. She's a very influential old lady. All right, leave it with me, Frederick. I'll let you know what I decide tomorrow.

Wordlist

1 Corporate culture

1.1 About business
Work culture and placements

assignment /əˈsaɪnmənt/ noun [count or uncount] task given as part of your studies or your job: *His first assignment as a reporter was to cover the local election.*

autonomy /ɔːˈtɒnəmi/ noun [uncount] the power to make your own decisions: *New regulations have severely restricted the autonomy of doctors.*

beating /ˈbiːtɪŋ/ noun [count] the act of hitting someone hard a number of times as a punishment: *The man had been given a severe beating.*

(be) the done thing /(biː) ðə ˌdʌn ˈθɪŋ/ phrase to be the correct thing to do or be the way that people think you should behave

burst into tears /ˌbɜːst ɪntə ˈtɪəz/ phrase to suddenly start crying

dress code /ˈdres ˌkəʊd/ noun [count] a set of rules about what you should wear in a particular place or at a particular event: *The dress code in our office is very formal – everybody wears a suit.*

etiquette /ˈetɪket/ noun [uncount] a set of rules for behaving correctly in a particular situation: *Office etiquette demands that you don't read other people's messages.*

get in (to the office) /ˌget ˈɪn(tə ðə ˌɒfɪs)/ phrasal verb [intransitive] to arrive at work: *Mark never gets in before 9.30.*

initiative /ɪˈnɪʃətɪv/ noun [uncount] the ability to think of ideas and take decisions independently: **take the initiative**: to take the first step or be the first to take action: *She would have to take the initiative in order to improve their relationship.*

intern /ˈɪntɜːn/ noun [count] a student or recently qualified person who works in a job in order to get experience: *Most employers prefer interns who already have some work experience.*

pick up /ˌpɪk ˈʌp/ phrasal verb [transitive] to learn information or a new skill without trying or without meaning to

skive off /ˌskaɪv ˈɒf/ phrasal verb [intransitive or transitive] BRITISH INFORMAL to stay away from school or work when you should be there

stressed out /ˌstrest ˈaʊt/ adjective suffering because of pressure at work or other problems

turn out /ˌtɜːn ˈaʊt/ phrasal verb [intransitive] to be discovered to be something, have something, etc: **it turns out (that)**: *It turns out that I was right all along.*

1.2 Vocabulary
Work organization and responsibility

as such /əz ˈsʌtʃ/ phrase [usually in negatives] used after a noun when you are referring to the usual meaning of the word

dog eat dog /ˌdɒg iːt ˈdɒg/ phrase a situation in which people compete very hard and will do anything to be successful

on a day-to-day basis /ɒn ə ˌdeɪ tə ˌdeɪ ˈbeɪsɪs/ phrase used for saying how often something happens: **on a daily / monthly / annual, etc. basis**: *Safety equipment was checked on a daily basis.*

organigram /ɔːˈgænɪˌgræm/ noun [count] a drawing or plan that gives the names and job titles of all the staff in an organization or department

overview /ˈəʊvəˌvjuː/ noun [count] a description of the main features of something: **overview of**: *The book gives an overview of management techniques.*

predecessor /ˈpriːdɪˌsesə/ noun [count] the person who had the job before: *Alexander seems to have learned nothing from the faults of his predecessors.*

take over /ˌteɪk ˈəʊvə/ phrasal verb [transitive] to take control of something: *IBM is taking over a much smaller company.*

1.3 Grammar
Past tenses and advice structures

blame /bleɪm/ verb [transitive] to say who or what is responsible for an accident or problem: *If it all goes wrong, don't blame me.*

dive /daɪv/ verb [intransitive] to jump into water head first: *He dived into the pool and swam off.*

neglect /nɪˈglekt/ verb [transitive] not to do something that you should do: **neglect to do something**: *She had neglected to inform me that the company was having financial problems.*

nickel /ˈnɪkl/ noun [count] a coin in the US and Canada worth five cents

polish /ˈpɒlɪʃ/ verb [transitive] to rub the surface of something in order to make it shine

successor /səkˈsesə/ noun [count] the person who has a job or position after someone else: **successor to**: *They haven't yet named a successor to the outgoing CEO.*

tactful /ˈtæktfl/ adjective careful in the way you speak and behave so you do not upset other people: **tactfully** adverb: *Speak tactfully if you want the boss to accept your criticism.*

1.4 Speaking
Meetings – one-to-one

authoritative /ɔːˈθɒrɪtətɪv/ adjective used for telling people what to do

clear the air /ˌklɪə ði ˈeə/ phrase to discuss a difficult situation which is creating a bad atmosphere.

commitment /kəˈmɪtmənt/ noun [singular or uncount] determination to work at something or intention to support something: **show commitment to**: *The government has failed to show its commitment to the railways.*

deadline /ˈdedlaɪn/ noun [count] a specific time or date by which you have to do something: *They've given us a five o'clock deadline.* **meet / miss a deadline** finish / not finish something in time: *If we can't meet the deadline, they won't give us another contract.*

dogmatic /dɒgˈmætɪk/ adjective so sure that your beliefs and ideas are right that you expect other people to accept them

threatening /ˈθretnɪŋ/ adjective showing or saying that someone is likely to do something that will harm you: **a threatening look**

1.5 Writing
A placement report

appendix /əˈpendɪks/ noun [count] a section giving extra details at the end of a book or document: *Technical specifications are included in the appendix to Chapter 9.*

conveyor belt /kənˈveɪə ˌbelt/ noun [count] a machine with a flat wide belt used for moving objects from one place to another, especially in a factory

fancy /ˈfænsi/ verb [transitive] INFORMAL to want to have or do something: *What do you fancy for your lunch?*

gearbox /ˈɡɪəbɒks/ noun [count] a metal box that contains the parts of a vehicle or a machine that change engine power into movement

it's a good job (that) phrase BRITISH used for saying it's lucky that something has happened because it prevents something bad from happening

mailshot /ˈmeɪlʃɒt/ noun [count] a letter or advertisement sent to many people at the same time

mess up /ˌmes ˈʌp/ phrasal verb [intransitive or transitive] to make a mistake or do something badly

rapport /ræˈpɔː/ noun [singular or uncount] a good relationship and understanding between people

take the mickey /teɪk ðə ˈmɪki/ phrase BRITISH INFORMAL to laugh at somebody, usually in a friendly way

waste /weɪst/ noun [count or uncount] useless materials that are left or thrown away: *A bill was introduced to clean up toxic waste from local factories.*

1.6 Case study
Counselling

body language /ˈbɒdi ˌlæŋɡwɪdʒ/ noun [uncount] the movements or positions of your body that show other people what you are thinking or feeling: *Their body language betrayed the tension between them.*

bounce back /ˌbaʊns ˈbæk/ phrasal verb [intransitive] to become healthy, happy, or successful again after something bad has happened to you

echo /ˈekəʊ/ verb [transitive] to express someone else's ideas or to say the same words that someone else has said: *Blake echoed the views of many employees.*

headache /ˈhedeɪk/ noun [count] a pain in your head: *I've got a splitting headache* (= an extremely bad headache).

open question /ˌəʊpən ˈkwestʃ(ə)n/ noun [count] a question with a *wh-* question word, as opposed to **a closed question** which has a *yes / no* answer

outlook /ˈaʊtlʊk/ noun [singular] your general attitude to things: **share an outlook**: *They shared the same kind of outlook on life.*

paraphrase /ˈpærəfreɪz/ verb [transitive] to express what someone else has said using different words: *It is particularly important when paraphrasing to be sure that you do not distort the meaning of the original statement.*

pass out /ˌpæs ˈaʊt/ phrasal verb [transitive] to give something to each member of a group: *The hall was silent as the examination papers were passed out.*

perspective /pəˈspektɪv/ noun 1 [count] a way of thinking about something: 2 [uncount] a sensible way of judging the importance of something in comparison with other things: **keep something in perspective**: *It's important to keep things in perspective and not dwell on one incident.*

reassess /ˌriːəˈses/ verb [transitive] to reconsider something in order to make a new judgment: *We tried to reassess his suitability for the job.*

2 Customer support

2.1 About business
Call centres

betray /bɪˈtreɪ/ verb [transitive] to harm someone who has trusted you: *They felt their assistant had betrayed their trust in publishing his diaries.*

browser /ˈbraʊzə(r)/ noun [count] a computer program that allows you to look at information on the Internet

bully /ˈbʊli/ verb [transitive] to threaten or frighten someone to get what you want

cause (an) uproar /kɔːz (ən) ˈʌprɔː/ verb [transitive] to provoke angry public criticism

cheery /ˈtʃɪəri/ adjective feeling or showing happiness

computer literacy /kəmpjuːtə ˈlɪt(ə)rəsi/ noun [uncount] being able to use a computer

counterpart /ˈkaʊntəpɑːt/ noun [count] someone that has the same job or purpose but in a different country or organization: *The Prime Minister is meeting his German counterpart.*

dead-end job /ˌdedˌend ˈdʒɒb/ noun [count] a job that gives no chance of promotion or improvement

East Enders /ˌiːst ˈendəz/ TRADEMARK a British TV soap opera about a group of people who live in an imaginary part of east London

emphasize /ˈemfəsaɪz/ verb [transitive] to give particular importance or attention to something: *At school they emphasize good manners.*

farm out /ˌfɑːm ˈaʊt/ phrasal verb [transitive] to send part of your work to be done by people outside your company

leak /liːk/ verb [intransitive or transitive] if an object leaks, liquid or gas comes out of it: *If the boiler is faulty, it may be leaking dangerous gas.*

overseas /ˌəʊvəˈsiːz/ adverb to or in a country across the sea

perk /pɜːk/ noun [count] a special benefit that you get in your job: *Free theatre tickets are one of the perks of this job.*

slap in the face /ˌslæp ɪn ðə ˈfeɪs/ noun [count] action or criticism that causes serious disappointment

slip into /ˌslɪp ˈɪntʊ/ phrasal verb [transitive] to quickly put on a piece of clothing or here, assume an identity

sweatshop /ˈswetʃɒp/ noun [count] INFORMAL a factory where people work very hard in bad conditions and earn very little money

UNISON, USDAW /ˈjuːnɪs(ə)n/, /ˈʌzdɔː/ large British trade unions

worlds apart /ˌwɜːldz əˈpɑːt/ completely different from each other

2.2 Vocabulary
Customer service and telephoning

brainless /ˈbreɪnləs/ adjective INFORMAL extremely stupid, without a brain

clip /klɪp/ noun [count] a small object that holds something in position

condescending /ˌkɒndɪˈsendɪŋ/ adjective showing that you think you are more important or more intelligent than other people

earth /ɜːθ/ verb [transitive] BRITISH to connect a piece of electrical equipment to the ground so that it is safe

retain /rɪˈteɪn/ verb [transitive] to keep someone or something

side panel /ˈsaɪd ˌpænl/ noun [count] a flat part of a box or other object that can be removed

slot /slɒt/ noun [count] a long narrow hole that you can fit something into

2.3 Grammar
Asking questions and giving instructions

broadband /ˈbrɔːdˌbænd/ adjective SCIENCE able to send different types of communication signals at the same time and in large volumes

ISP /ˌaɪ es ˈpiː/ noun [count] COMPUTING Internet service provider: a company that provides a connection to the Internet

laptop /ˈlæpˌtɒp/ noun [count] a small computer that you can carry with you

network /ˈnetˌwɜːk/ noun [count] a system of connections between different points: *a mobile phone network*

router /ˈruːtə/ noun [count] an electronic device which allows several computers to share information and an Internet connection

upgrade /ʌpˈgreɪd/ verb [intransitive or transitive] to make a machine more powerful or effective: *The system has been upgraded to meet customers' needs.*

2.4 Speaking
Dealing with problems by telephone

closet /ˈklɒzɪt/ noun [count] MAINLY AMERICAN a small room for storing things such as clothes or sheets

come again? /ˌkʌm əˈgen/ INFORMAL used for asking someone to repeat what they have just said

crash /ˈkræʃ/ verb [intransitive or transitive] COMPUTING if a computer or computer program crashes, it suddenly stops working

freeze /friːz/ verb [intransitive or transitive] COMPUTING if a computer screen freezes or is frozen you cannot move anything on it because there is something wrong with the computer

PDF /ˌpiː diː ˈef/ noun [count] COMPUTING Portable Document Format: a type of computer file that can contain words, images, etc. and can be sent on the Internet and read on any computer

plug /plʌg/ noun [count] the device on electric equipment which connects to the electricity supply by a socket in the wall

plug in /ˌplʌg ˈɪn/ phrasal verb [transitive] to connect a piece of equipment to an electricity supply

power outage /ˌpaʊwə ˈaʊtɪdʒ/ noun [count] AMERICAN a period when the electricity supply stops

quit /kwɪt/ verb [intransitive or transitive] INFORMAL to leave: COMPUTING to shut down a computer program

sort out /ˌsɔːt ˈaʊt/ phrasal verb [transitive] to solve a problem or deal with a difficult situation successfully: *This matter could be sorted out if they would just sit down and talk.*

toolbar /ˈtuːlˌbɑː/ noun [count] a row of icons on a computer screen that perform particular actions when you click on them

unplug /ʌnˈplʌg/ verb [transitive] to separate a piece of equipment from its power supply by taking its plug out of an electric socket

2.5 Writing
Formal and informal correspondence

accounts payable /əˌkaʊnts ˈpeɪəbl/ noun [plural] MAINLY AMERICAN a record of how much money a company owes other people or companies for goods and services

asap /ˌeɪ es eɪ ˈpiː/ as soon as possible: used especially for asking someone to do something quickly: *I want those files on my desk asap.*

crack /kræk/ verb [transitive] to damage something so that a line appears on its surface, but it does not break into pieces: *I dropped a plate and cracked it.*

duplicate /ˈduːplɪˌkeɪt/ adjective made as an exact copy of something else

inconsistency /ˌɪnkɒnˈsɪstənsi/ noun [count] something that does not match something else

patch /pætʃ/ noun [count] a piece of software that you add to a computer program to improve it or remove a fault

Trojan (horse) /ˈtrəʊdʒ(ə)n ˈhɔːs/ noun [count] COMPUTING a program that seems useful but is designed to cause damage, for example by destroying information

write-off /ˈraɪt ˌɒf/ noun [count] a vehicle or machine that is so badly damaged that it cannot be repaired

2.6 Case study
Cybertartan Software

bathroom break /ˈbɑːθruːm ˌbreɪk/ noun [count] a short time when you can stop work to go to the toilet

claim /kleɪm/ verb [transitive] to say that something is true: *He claims he is innocent.* or here, to say that a product can do something

come up with /ˌkʌm ʌp ˈwɪð/ phrasal verb [transitive] to think of something such as an idea or a plan

count on someone /ˈkaʊnt ɒn ˌsʌmwɒn/ phrasal verb [transitive] to depend on someone to do something for you

from the horse's mouth INFORMAL information from the horse's mouth comes from someone who is directly involved

meal break /ˈmiːl ˌbreɪk/ noun [count] a short time when you can stop work to eat

obsolescence /ˌɒbsəˈlesns/ noun [uncount] the state of something which is no longer used: **planned obsolescence** the practice of making products that will not last long, so that people will need to buy new ones

Q4 /ˌkjuːˈfɔː/ adjective / noun fourth quarter, also Q1 (first quarter) Q2 (second quarter), Q3 (third quarter) = four quarters of a business year

shift /ʃɪft/ noun [count] a period of work in a factory or business where some people work during the day and some work at night: *a three-shift system*

staff turnover /ˌstɑːf ˈtɜːnəʊvə/ noun [count or uncount] the rate at which people leave jobs and new people arrive: *a high turnover of staff / personnel*

swap /swɒp/ verb [intransitive or transitive] to give something to someone in exchange for something else: *Do you want to swap seats?*

triple /ˈtrɪpl/ verb [transitive] to increase something so that it is three times bigger than before: *He helped triple the value of the company.*

3 Products and packaging

3.1 About business
Packaging

arthritic /ɑːˈθrɪtɪk/ adjective suffering from **arthritis**, a medical condition affecting the joints (the place where two bones meet) making them very swollen and painful

blister pack /ˈblɪstə ˌpæk/ noun [count] packaging for small items like pills, consisting of a flat layer and a raised cover of plastic that protects the product: also **bubble pack**

branding /ˈbrændɪŋ/ noun [uncount] Business the use of advertising, design and other methods to make people recognize and remember a particular product

bruise /bruːz/ noun [count] a mark you get on your body if you are hit or knocked

drawing-board /ˈdrɔːɪŋ ˌbɔːd/ noun [count] a large board or table that designers use to work on: **(go) back to the drawing board**: to start again from the beginning, look for a new idea

focus group /ˈfəʊkəs ˌgruːp/ noun [count] a small group of people who are interviewed together and give their opinions to help a company make decisions

interface /ˈɪntəˌfeɪs/ verb [intransitive] interact and communicate with each other

know-how /ˈnəʊˌhaʊ/ noun [uncount] practical knowledge or experience

mockup /ˈmɒkʌp/ noun [count] a model of a future product that is the same size as the real thing

pilfer /ˈpɪlfə/ verb [intransitive or transitive] to steal things, especially from the place where you work: **pilfering** noun [uncount]

pitch /pɪtʃ/ verb [transitive] to try to sell something by saying how good it is

pliers /ˈplaɪəz/ noun [plural] a metal tool that looks like a strong pair of scissors, used for holding small objects or for bending or cutting wire

point of sale /ˌpɔɪnt əv ˈseɪl/ noun [count] the place where something is sold

premium /ˈpriːmiəm/ adjective more expensive or of higher quality

rag /ræg/ noun [count] a piece of old cloth: **a red rag to a bull** something that will make someone very angry

rage /reɪdʒ/ noun [count or uncount] a very strong feeling of anger: MAINLY JOURNALISM angry violent behaviour in a public situation: *It is clear that air rage is now on the increase.*

seduce /sɪˈdjuːs/ verb [transitive] to persuade someone to do something by making it seem easy or exciting

shape /ʃeɪp/ noun [count or uncount] the outer form of something

shrinkage /ˈʃrɪŋkɪdʒ/ noun [singular or uncount] a reduction in stock in a shop

slash /slæʃ/ verb [transitive] to cut something in a violent way

sprain /spreɪn/ noun [count] a painful injury that you get when you suddenly stretch or turn a joint too much

stab /stæb/ verb [transitive] to push a sharp object quickly into something: *She stabbed the meat with her fork.*

stakeholder /ˈsteɪkˌhəʊldə/ noun [count] someone who has an interest in the success of a project or organization

tear /teə/ verb [intransitive or transitive] to pull something so that it separates into pieces: *It's made of very thin material that tears easily.*

trigger /ˈtrɪgə/ verb [transitive] to make something happen

turn-around /ˈtɜːn əˌraʊnd/ noun [count] time needed to complete an operation

water down /ˌwɔːtə ˈdaʊn/ phrasal verb [transitive] to make something less effective or offensive by diluting it

weld /weld/ verb [intransitive or transitive] to join two pieces of metal or plastic by heating them and pressing them together

wrap /ræp/ verb [transitive] to cover something by putting something such as paper or plastic around it

wrestle /ˈresl/ verb [intransitive or transitive] to fight or struggle: **wrestle with**

3.2 Vocabulary
Specifications and features

beta test /ˈbiːtə ˌtest/ verb [transitive] to have a new product tested by customers

bird's-eye view /ˌbɜːdz aɪ ˈvjuː/ noun [singular] a good view of something from a high position

blueprint /ˈbluːˌprɪnt/ noun [count] a drawing that shows how to build something

chart /tʃɑːt/ noun [count] a map used for navigation in boats or planes

focus group /ˈfəʊkəs ˌgruːp/ noun [count] a small group of people who are interviewed together and give their opinions to help a company make decisions

fool /fuːl/ noun [count] someone who does not behave in an intelligent or sensible way

grab /græb/ verb [transitive] to succeed in getting something: *It's often the bad characters in a story who grab our attention.*

mockup /ˈmɒkʌp/ noun [count] a model of a future product that is the same size as the real thing

overlay /ˈəʊvə(r)ˌleɪ/ noun [count] a set of extra information that is added to a picture by a computer

retardant /rɪˈtɑː(r)dənt/ adjective slowing down a process

tamper with /ˈtæmpə ˌwɪð/ phrasal verb [transitive] to touch something and change it in a way that will damage it

3.3 Grammar
Articles, relative clauses and noun combinations

antenna /ænˈtenə/ noun [count] (plural antennas or antennae) an aerial used for sending and receiving radio signals

browse /braʊz/ verb [intransitive or transitive] COMPUTING to look for information, especially on the Internet

bump /bʌmp/ verb [intransitive or transitive] to hit against something solid

comply /kəmˈplaɪ/ verb [intransitive] to obey, do what you are asked or expected to do: **comply with**: *You are legally obliged to comply fully with any investigations.*

concentric /kənˈsentrɪk/ adjective having the same centre

cope /kəʊp/ verb [intransitive] to deal successfully with a difficult situation or job: **cope with**: *a seminar on 'coping with stress in the workplace'*

device /dɪˈvaɪs/ noun [count] a machine or piece of equipment: *Secure your bike with this simple locking device.*

drop /drɒp/ verb [transitive] to let something fall: **drop calls** to fail to connect incoming calls

empowerment /ɪmˈpaʊəmənt/ noun [uncount] giving control or power over something

flip cover /ˈflɪp ˌkʌvə/ noun [count] part of a mobile phone which folds over the keypad

frill /frɪl/ noun [count] a decoration that consists of a long narrow piece of cloth with many small folds in it: **no frills** used for something which is good enough but has no unnecessary extra features

get rid /get ˈrɪd əv/ phrasal verb to throw away, give away or sell a possession that you no longer want

lead-time /ˈliːdˌtaɪm/ noun [count or uncount] the time between planning something and starting to do it: *Local firms learned how to reduce lead time by 75-95% while still reducing costs.*

patent /ˈpeɪtnt/ noun [count] an official document that gives someone who has invented something the legal right to make or sell that invention, and prevents anyone else from doing so: **patented** adjective protected by a patent

rating /ˈreɪtɪŋ/ noun [count] a measurement of how good or popular someone or something is: *The guide gives restaurants a rating out of ten.*

replica /ˈreplɪkə/ noun [count] an accurate copy of something

retractable /rɪˈtræktəbl/ adjective able to be pulled backwards or inside something larger: **retractable landing gear** the equipment and wheels that a plane uses when it lands, and which are pulled inside the plane while it flies

sketch /sketʃ/ noun [count] a drawing made quickly that does not have many details

spreadsheet /ˈspredˌʃiːt/ noun [count] a computer file containing numbers and other data in table form: *spreadsheet analysis*

workhorse /ˈwɜːkˌhɔːs/ noun [count] a very useful piece of equipment that you use a lot

3.4 Speaking
Presentations – structure

anecdote /ˈænɪkˌdəʊt/ noun [count] a story about something interesting or funny that happened to you

bulky /ˈbʌlki/ adjective too big to be carried or stored easily

green light /griːn ˈlaɪt/ noun [count] a signal that gives traffic permission to move forward: **give something the green light** to give official approval for something to be done

hook /hʊk/ noun [count] a curved piece of metal for hanging things on: a method for getting people interested and attracted to something

lecture /ˈlektʃə/ noun [count] a talk to a group of people about a particular subject, especially at a college or university

overwhelmingly /ˌəʊvəˈwelmɪŋli/ adverb very strongly

ping /pɪŋ/ verb [transitive] COMPUTING to send an electronic signal requesting an answer from a device

precedent /ˈpresɪdənt/ noun [count or uncount] a decision in the past that is used as a guideline for later decisions: **without precedent** unlike anything that has gone before

rhetorical question /rɪˌtɒrɪkl ˈkwestʃ(ə)n/ noun [count] a question you ask without expecting or wanting an answer

tracking /ˈtrækɪŋ/ noun [uncount] the act of following or looking for a person, animal or thing

wrap up /ˌræp ˈʌp/ phrasal verb [intransitive or transitive] INFORMAL to finish something

3.5 Writing
A product description

alloy /ˈælɔɪ/ noun [count or uncount] a metal that is made from combining two or more metals

benefit /ˈbenɪfɪt/ noun [count or uncount] an advantage you get from a product or situation

feature /ˈfiːtʃə(r)/ noun [count] an important part or aspect of a product

intuitive /ɪnˈtjuːətɪv/ adjective an intuitive system is easy to use because the process of operating it is very natural or obvious

plug-in /ˈplʌgɪn/ noun [count] COMPUTING a software addition which allows an application to perform additional functions

quibble /ˈkwɪbl/ noun [count] a complaint or criticism about something that is not important: **no quibble guarantee** a promise to refund the customer without questioning their reasons for dissatisfaction

stand out /ˌstænd ˈaʊt/ phrasal verb [intransitive] to be easy to see because of being different

3.6 Case study
Big Jack's Pizza

BOGOF abbreviation buy one, get one free

chequered /ˈtʃekəd/ adjective a chequered pattern or design consists of squares in two or more different colours

dine-in /daɪn ˈɪn/ adjective used to describe meals taken in a restaurant

franchisee /ˈfræntʃaɪziː/ noun [count] a person or company that has the franchise to sell a particular type of goods or services

fusion cuisine /ˈfjuːʒn kwɪˈziːn/ noun [uncount] a particular style of cooking food combining Chinese and Western recipes

gourmet /ˈɡʊəmeɪ/ noun [count] someone who knows a lot about good food and wine

slide /slaɪd/ verb [intransitive] to move across a smooth surface

strengthen /ˈstreŋθ(ə)n/ verb [transitive] to make something stronger

threat /θret/ noun [count or uncount] something that could cause harm

USP /juː es ˈpiː/ noun [count] BUSINESS unique selling point / proposition: the thing that makes a product or service different from others

4 Careers

4.1 About business
Career choices

acknowledge /əkˈnɒlɪdʒ/ verb [transitive] to accept or admit that something exists, is true or is real: *He never acknowledges his mistakes.*

aptitude /ˈæptɪtjuːd/ noun [count or uncount] natural ability that makes it easy for you to do something well

attune /əˈtjuːn/ verb [transitive] to bring into harmony

calling /ˈkɔːlɪŋ/ noun [count] FORMAL a profession, especially one that you consider important

compromise /ˈkɒmprəmaɪz/ verb [intransitive] to accept that you cannot have everything you want

core /kɔː/ adjective most important or most basic: *We need to focus on our core activities.*

dicey /ˈdaɪsi/ adjective INFORMAL involving danger or risk

dig into something /ˈdɪg ɪntu ˌsʌmθɪŋ/ phrasal verb INFORMAL to try to find information about something

earth-shattering /ˈɜːθˌʃæt(ə)rɪŋ/ adjective extremely surprising and important

gel /dʒel/ verb [intransitive] to become stable

granular /ˈɡrænjʊlə/ adjective consisting of granules: here, in great detail

jump in /dʒʌmp ˈɪn/ phrasal verb [intransitive] **jump in (at) the deep end** to become involved in a difficult situation with little preparation

inertia /ɪˈnɜːʃə/ noun [uncount] a situation in which something does not change: a feeling of not wanting to change things

light /laɪt/ verb [transitive] **light your fire** MAINLY AMERICAN INFORMAL to make you feel enthusiastic

pan out /ˌpæn ˈaʊt/ phrasal verb [intransitive] INFORMAL the way a situation develops over time

pick /pɪk/ verb [transitive] **pick someone's brains** INFORMAL to ask someone questions to get advice or information: *I wanted to pick your brains about this idea I've had.*

posse /ˈpɒsi/ noun [count] INFORMAL a group of friends

sculpt /skʌlpt/ verb [transitive] to shape a substance such as wood, stone or clay

shallow /ˈʃæləʊ/ adjective with only a short distance from the top or surface to the bottom – opposite DEEP

shift /ʃɪft/ verb [intransitive or transitive] to change position

spark /spɑːk/ verb [intransitive or transitive] to make something happen

start the ball rolling to make something start happening

stay put /ˌsteɪ ˈpʊt/ verb [intransitive] to remain in one place or position

strike off /ˌstraɪk ˈɒf/ phrasal verb [intransitive] to go in a new or different direction with energy and determination

tap /tæp/ verb [transitive] if you tap into something you use it or get some benefit from it

think through /ˈθɪŋk ˈθruː/ phrasal verb [transitive] to consider the facts about something in an organized and thorough way

treadmill /ˈtredˌmɪl/ noun [count] a situation that is very tiring or boring because you do the same things continuously

vocation /vəʊˈkeɪʃn/ noun [count] a job that you do because you feel that it is your purpose in life and for which you have special skills

4.2 Vocabulary
Careers, personal skills and qualities

asset /ˈæset/ noun [count] a useful thing, person or quality: *Youth is a real asset in this job.*

assignment /əˈsaɪnmənt/ noun [count or uncount] work given as part of your studies or your job, often for a set period of time in a particular place

concern /kənˈsɜːn/ noun [count] HUMAN RESOURCES an employee that managers are worried about

controversial /ˌkɒntrəˈvɜːʃl/ adjective a controversial subject, opinion or decision is one that people disagree about or do not approve of

fast track /ˈfɑːst ˌtræk/ noun [singular] a way of achieving something more quickly than usual

fire /faɪə/ verb [transitive] INFORMAL to dismiss someone or make someone leave their job

flag / flæg / verb [transitive] to mark something so that you will be able to find it again

greedy /ˈɡriːdi/ adjective wanting more money, power or things than you need

headhunter /ˈhedˌhʌntə/ noun [count] a person or company who searches for good staff and tries to persuade them to leave their jobs and go to work for another company

high-flier /ˈhaɪˈflaɪə/ noun [count] someone who has achieved a lot and is determined to continue being successful

liaise /liˈeɪz/ verb [intransitive] if one person liaises with another or people liaise, they talk to each other and tell each other what they are doing, so that they can work together effectively

mentor /'mentɔː/ noun [count] an experienced person who helps someone who has less experience, especially in their job

multitasking /ˌmʌltiˈtɑːskɪŋ/ noun [uncount] doing several things at the same time

novel /'nɒvl/ noun [count] a long written story about imaginary or partly imaginary characters and events

on the spot /ˌɒn ðə ˈspɒt/ immediately

raise /reɪz/ noun [count] an increase in the amount you are paid for work

unconventional /ˌʌnkənˈvenʃn(ə)l/ adjective different from what most people consider to be usual or normal

wannabe /'wɒnəbi/ noun [count] INFORMAL someone who wants to be famous or successful

4.3 Grammar
Present tenses

appraisal /əˈpreɪzl/ noun [count or uncount] BRITISH BUSINESS an interview between a manager and someone who works for them to discuss how well they are doing their job

assault course /əˈsɔːlt ˌkɔːs/ noun [count] an exercise involving running, climbing and jumping, used in military training

cog /kɒg/ noun [count] someone considered as a minor part of a large organization

deposit /dɪˈpɒzɪt/ noun [count] a first payment that you make when you agree to buy something expensive such as a car or a house

divorcee /dɪˌvɔːˈsiː/ noun [count] a woman or man who is divorced

hand /hænd/ verb [transitive] to give something to someone with your hand **you have to hand it to someone** SPOKEN used for saying that you admire someone for something they have done

kid /kɪd/ verb [intransitive or transitive usually continuous] MAINLY SPOKEN to say something that is not true, especially as a joke: **you're kidding** used for saying that you do not believe what someone is saying

knock over /ˌnɒk ˈəʊvə/ verb [transitive] to hit something so that it falls

relevant /'reləv(ə)nt/ adjective directly connected to what is being discussed or considered

submit /səbˈmɪt/ verb [transitive] to formally give something to someone so that they can make a decision about it

undergraduate /ˌʌndəˈgrædʒʊət/ noun [count] a student who is studying for a first degree at a college or university

4.4 Speaking
Job interviews

achievement /əˈtʃiːvmənt/ noun [count] a particular thing that you have succeeded in doing after a lot of effort

come round /ˌkʌm ˈraʊnd/ phrasal verb BRITISH to change your opinion because someone has persuaded you

commitment /kəˈmɪtmənt/ noun [count or uncount] a promise to do something or to keep on doing something, a willingness to stay in a job, a relationship, etc.

cope /kəʊp/ verb [intransitive] to deal successfully with a difficult situation or job

rapport /ræˈpɔː/ noun [singular or uncount] a good relationship and understanding between people

regardless of /rɪˈgɑː(r)dləs əv/ without being affected by

resent /rɪˈzent/ verb [transitive] to experience angry or unhappy feelings because you think you have been treated unfairly

strength /streŋθ/ noun [count] something that someone does well: *Ron's main strength is his ability to motivate players.*

weakness /'wiːknəs/ noun [count] a fault or problem that makes someone less effective or attractive

4.5 Writing
A CV

faculty /'fæklti/ noun [count] a department or group of departments in a university

grade /greɪd/ noun [count] a letter or number that shows the quality of a student's work

IS /ˌaɪ ˈes/ noun [count] Information Systems

LAN /ˌel eɪ ˈen/ noun [count] COMPUTING local area network: a system that allows computers in the same building or group of buildings to communicate with each other

networking /'netˌwɜːkɪŋ/ noun [uncount] the activity of connecting computers in a network

wpm /ˌdʌbljuː piː ˈem/ abbreviation words per minute: measurement of how fast someone can type

4.6 Case study
Gap years and career breaks

accommodation /əˌkɒməˈdeɪʃn/ noun [uncount] a place for someone to stay, live, or work in: *The hotel provides accommodation for up to 100 people.*

eco- /iːkəʊ/ prefix relating to the environment: used with some nouns and adjectives

find your feet /ˌfaɪnd jə ˈfiːt/ to start to feel confident and familiar with something

gap year /'gæp jɪə/ noun [count] an interruption of one's studies or career in order to acquire a different experience, e.g. to travel

organic /ɔːˈgænɪk/ adjective not using chemicals: *organic apples*

sabbatical /səˈbætɪkl/ noun [count or uncount] a period away from work when people such as college or university teachers can study, rest or travel

step back /ˌstep ˈbæk/ phrasal verb [intransitive] to stop for a moment in order to consider something objectively

tangible /'tændʒəbl/ adjective important and noticeable: **tangible evidence**

underprivileged /ˌʌndəˈprɪvəlɪdʒd/ adjective not having as many advantages or opportunities as most other people

short-list or shortlist /'ʃɔːtˌlɪst/ verb [transitive] to choose a number of candidates for the next stage of selection, e.g. a second interview

together with in addition to something else

waste /weɪst/ verb [transitive] to fail to make effective use of something that is valuable: *It was a waste of time.*

5 Making deals

5.1 About business
E-tailing

barge in /ˌbɑːdʒ ˈɪn/ verb [intransitive] to enter suddenly and noisily, usually interrupting someone in a rude way

beware /bɪˈweə/ verb [intransitive or transitive usually imperative] used to warn someone of danger or difficulty

brisk /brɪsk/ adjective moving quickly **briskly** adverb

e-tailer /ˈiːteɪlə/ noun [count] COMPUTING a company that sells things on the Internet: **e-tailing** noun [uncount]

eyeball /ˈaɪbɔːl/ noun [count] the whole ball that forms the eye: here, a person browsing a website

flag /flæg/ verb [transitive] to mark something so that you will be able to find it again

intrusive /ɪnˈtruːsɪv/ adjective forcing itself on people in a way that is not welcome

publicly-traded /ˌpʌblɪkli ˈtreɪdɪd/ adjective a company whose shares you can buy on the stock exchange

pushy /ˈpʊʃi/ adjective INFORMAL extremely determined to get what you want, even if it annoys other people

smother /ˈsmʌðə/ verb [transitive] to cover something completely so it cannot breathe

tracking /ˈtrækɪŋ/ noun [uncount] the act of following or looking for a person, animal or thing

5.2 Vocabulary
Negotiating and e-tailing

bank statement /ˈbæŋk ˌsteɪtmənt/ noun [count] a document that shows all the money that went into and out of your bank account during a particular period of time

5.3 Grammar
Conditionals and recommendations

dust /dʌst/ noun [uncount] very small pieces of dirt that cover surfaces inside buildings like a powder

ISO /ˌaɪesˈəʊ/ abbreviation International Standards Organization: an organization that deals with agreements about units of measurement and quality

rpm /ˌɑːpiːˈem/ abbreviation revolutions per minute: a unit for measuring the speed at which something goes round in a circle

willing /ˈwɪlɪŋ/ adjective if you are willing to do something, you agree to do it without difficulty.

unwilling /ʌnˈwɪlɪŋ/ adjective if you are unwilling to do something you do not want to do it or you refuse to do it

5.4 Speaking
Negotiations – bargaining

auditor /ˈɔːdɪtə/ noun [count] someone whose job is to officially examine the financial records or production quality of a company

insignificant /ˌɪnsɪgˈnɪfɪkənt/ adjective not large or important enough to be worth considering

lead time /ˈliːd ˌtaɪm/ noun [count or uncount] the time between planning something and starting to do it

nitty-gritty /ˌnɪti ˈgrɪti/ noun [uncount] INFORMAL the most basic aspects of a situation or an activity that must be dealt with, even if they are unpleasant

package /ˈpækɪdʒ/ noun [count] a set of products or services that are sold together as one unit

reluctant /rɪˈlʌktənt/ adjective not willing to do something

tentative /ˈtentətɪv/ adjective not definite or certain

5.5 Writing
A proposal

breakdown /ˈbreɪkˌdaʊn/ noun [count] detailed presentation or analysis of information, particularly financial figures or statistics

contingency /kənˈtɪndʒ(ə)nsi/ noun [count] something that might happen in the future, especially something bad

fee /fiː/ noun [count] money that you pay to a professional person or institution for their work

mail order /ˌmeɪl ˈɔːdə/ noun [uncount] a way of buying goods in which you order them by post or by telephone and they are posted to you

mailshot /ˈmeɪlʃɒt/ noun [count] BRITISH a letter or advertisement sent to many people at the same time

merchant account /ˈmɜːtʃ(ə)nt əˌkaʊnt/ noun [count] a special account for performing e-business transactions

process /ˈprəʊses/ verb [transitive] to deal with information or documents so that something can happen: *28,000 applications for visas have to be processed*

prospect /ˈprɒspekt/ noun [count] a possible or likely customer

upgrade /ʌpˈgreɪd/ verb [intransitive or transitive] to make a computer or other machine more powerful or effective

5.6 Case study
St John's Beach Club

allocate /ˈæləˌkeɪt/ verb [transitive] to officially give something to someone, or decide that something can be used for a specific purpose

gourmet /ˈgʊəmeɪ/ adjective gourmet food is of a very high quality

incentive /ɪnˈsentɪv/ noun [count or uncount] something that makes you want to do something or work harder, because you know that you will gain something by doing this

squeeze /skwiːz/ verb [intransitive or transitive] to press something firmly, especially with your hands: **to squeeze something out of something or someone** to obtain something more than is normally possible

throw in /ˌθrəʊ ˈɪn/ phrasal verb [transitive] to include something extra with something that you are selling, without asking for more money

upgrade /ˈʌpgreɪd/ noun [count] an improvement of a product or service

6 Company and community

6.1 About business
Corporate social responsibility

adverse /ˈædvɜːs/ adjective negative, unpleasant or harmful: *An adverse reaction from the public.*

align /əˈlaɪn/ verb [transitive] to give your support publicly to; bring yourself into agreement with or be in agreement with

altruism /ˈæltruˌɪz(ə)m/ noun [uncount] a way of thinking and behaving that shows you care about other people and their interests more than you care about yourself

bean /biːn/ noun [count] a seed of various plants that is cooked and eaten: *coffee beans*

bear /beə/ verb [transitive] here, to pay: *A new study has confirmed that the wealthiest Americans bear the income tax burden.*

contend /kənˈtend/ verb [transitive] **contend that** FORMAL to claim that something is true

corporate social responsibility a company's duty to be accountable to all groups having an interest in its activities

credo /ˈkriːdəʊ/ noun [count] FORMAL a statement of your beliefs

dismay /dɪsˈmeɪ/ verb [transitive] to make someone very worried, disappointed, or sad

global warming /ˌɡləʊbl ˈwɔːmɪŋ/ noun [uncount] the slow increase in the temperature of the Earth caused partly by the greenhouse effect increasing the amount of carbon dioxide in the atmosphere: *Global warming is causing sea levels to rise.*

hybrid /ˈhaɪbrɪd/ noun [count] a mixture of two different things: **hybrid vehicle** a vehicle using two different kinds of energy

mindful /ˈmaɪn(d)f(ə)l/ adjective careful or conscious of something

offset /ˈɒfˌset/ verb [transitive] to balance the effect of something, with the result that there is no advantage or disadvantage: *Falling sales in Thailand were offset by strong performances in other markets.*

presumption /prɪˈzʌmpʃn/ noun [count] The expectation that something is true, which you don't question

sound /saʊnd/ adjective healthy: *a sound heart*

strive /straɪv/ verb [intransitive] to make a lot of effort to achieve something: *We strive to be accurate, but some mistakes are inevitable.*

sue /suː/, /sjuː/ verb [intransitive or transitive] to make a legal claim against someone, usually to get money from them because they have done something bad to you: *If we go public with these allegations, do you think he will sue?*

sustainable /səˈsteɪnəbl/ adjective capable of continuing for a long time at the same level

utility /juːˈtɪləti/ noun [count] a public service such as gas, water, or electricity that is used by everyone: *utility companies*

6.2 Vocabulary
Meetings, ethical behaviour and social performance

ad hoc /ˌæd ˈhɒk/ adjective done only when needed for a specific purpose, without planning or preparation

extravagant /ɪkˈstrævəɡənt/ adjective extreme, excessive or unreasonable

fellow /ˈfeləʊ/ adjective [only before noun] used for talking about people who are similar to you or in the same situation as you

fine /faɪn/ noun [count] an amount of money that you have to pay because you have broken the law: *Firms could face fines of up to £5,000.*

foodstuff /ˈfuːdˌstʌf/ noun [count or uncount] FORMAL a type of food

lawsuit /ˈlɔːˌsuːt/ noun [count] a case that a court of law is asked to decide involving a disagreement between two people or organizations: *The singer has filed a $100 million lawsuit against his record company.*

regulatory /ˈreɡjʊlət(ə)ri/, /ˈreɡjʊˌleɪt(ə)ri/ adjective a regulatory organization makes sure companies follow the rules and maintain standards of safety, health, etc.

6.3 Grammar
The passive and reported speech

industrial espionage /ˈespiəˌnɑːʒ/ noun [uncount] the practice of stealing important information or technology from a company in order to help another company

leak /liːk/ noun [count] an amount of liquid or gas that comes out of a hole or crack in something: *The explosion was caused by a gas leak.*

leakage /ˈliːkɪdʒ/ noun [uncount] the process of leaking a liquid or gas

nitrate /ˈnaɪtreɪt/ noun [count or uncount] a chemical substance containing nitrogen

outplacement /ˈaʊtˌpleɪsmənt/ noun [count or uncount] the process of finding new jobs for people who have been made redundant

protracted /prəˈtræktɪd/ adjective FORMAL continuing for a long time, especially longer than is normal or necessary

savings /ˈseɪvɪŋz/ noun [plural] money that you have saved in a bank or invested so that you can use it later: *The money for the flight came out of my savings.*

6.4 Speaking
Meetings – teamwork

civil servant /ˌsɪvl ˈsɜːv(ə)nt/ noun [count] someone who works for a government department

disabled /dɪsˈeɪbld/ adjective someone who is disabled is unable to use part of their body or brain properly because of injury or disease

ethnic minority /ˌeθnɪk maɪˈnɒrəti/ noun [count] a group of people who have a different culture and different traditions to most people living in a place

slim /slɪm/ adjective thin in an attractive way: *She had a slim, youthful figure.*

tender /ˈtendə/ noun [count or uncount] an offer to provide goods or services for a particular price

turn a blind eye (to something) to pretend you do not notice something, because you do not want to have to deal with it

6.5 Writing
Reports and minutes

commitment /kəˈmɪtmənt/ noun [uncount] determination to work hard at something: *I am delighted with the level of commitment you have all shown.*

derive /dɪˈraɪv/ verb [transitive] to get a feeling from something e.g. pleasure, satisfaction: **derive something from something:** *They derive great enjoyment from these simple games.*

paternalism /pəˈtɜːnəlɪz(ə)m/ noun [uncount] governing like a father, by looking after people but also taking away their freedom and responsibilities

positive discrimination /ˌpɒzətɪv dɪskrɪmɪˈneɪʃn/ noun [uncount] the practice of giving special benefits to people from a group that was treated in an unfair way in the past

stakeholder /ˈsteɪkˌhəʊldə/ noun [count] someone who has an interest in the success of a project or organization

6.6 Case study
Phoenix

derelict /ˈderəlɪkt/ adjective unused and in bad condition, usually of a building or a piece of land

flammable /ˈflæməbl/ adjective able to burn very easily and quickly

greenfield site /ˈɡriːnfiːld ˌsaɪt/ noun [count] a piece of land that has not previously been built on

hazardous /ˈhæzədəs/ adjective dangerous, especially to people's health or safety: *These chemicals are hazardous to human health.*

toxic /ˈtɒksɪk/ adjective poisonous and harmful to people, animals, or the environment: *highly toxic industrial chemicals*

upset /ʌpˈset/ verb [transitive] to make someone feel sad, worried or angry

worthless /ˈwɜːθləs/ adjective without value or use

7 Mergers and acquisitions

7.1 About business
Risks and opportunities in M&A

assets /ˈæsets/ noun [usually plural] money or property that a company owns: *The business has assets totalling £5.1 million.*

due diligence /ˌdjuː ˈdɪlɪdʒ(ə)ns/ noun [uncount] investigation of a company's activities and finances before investment or acquisition

external growth /ɪkˌstɜːnl ˈɡrəʊθ/ noun [uncount] increasing a company's size by buying other businesses

gene /dʒiːn/ noun [count] information in cells that determines a person's characteristics: *He believes that shyness is in the genes.*

homogenize /həˈmɒdʒənaɪz/ verb [transitive] to make things the same, often so that the result is boring

invoke /ɪnˈvəʊk/ [transitive] FORMAL to mention an idea to support an argument or explain an action.

laid-back /ˌleɪdˈbæk/ adjective INFORMAL calm and relaxed

open enrolment noun [count] a university class which anybody can join

prestigious /preˈstɪdʒəs/ adverb admired and respected

sorely /ˈsɔːli/ adjective very much

susceptible /səˈseptəbl/ adjective easily influenced or affected

synergy /ˈsɪnədʒi/ noun [count or uncount] BUSINESS the extra benefit that companies obtain when they combine their efforts

take one's eye off the ball idiom to pay less attention than usual

takeover /ˈteɪkˌəʊvə/ noun [count or uncount] a situation in which one company takes control of another by buying the majority of its shares: a takeover bid (= an offer to pay a particular amount in order to get control of a company): *Shareholders have accepted a takeover bid.*

turmoil /ˈtɜːmɔɪl/ noun [uncount] a state of excitement or uncontrolled activity

7.2 Vocabulary
Business performance

bid /bɪd/ noun [count] an offer to buy the shares in a company and take control of it: *a takeover bid*

expire /ɪkˈspaɪə/ verb [intransitive] when something expires, the time in which it is valid comes to an end: *When the patent expired, competitors copied the product.*

float /fləʊt/ verb [transitive] BUSINESS to start to sell a company's shares on the stock market

flotation /fləʊˈteɪʃn/ noun [count or uncount] BUSINESS the sale of shares in a company for the first time

FTSE 100, the /ˌfʊtsi wʌn ˈhʌndrəd/ noun [uncount] the Financial Times Stock Exchange index; an average of the prices of shares from the top 100 companies on the London stock exchange

patent /ˈpeɪtnt/, /ˈpætnt/ noun [count] a document that stops anyone other than the inventor from using an invention: *In 1878, Edison received a patent for his phonograph.*

prestigious /preˈstɪdʒəs/ adjective highly respected, with a very good reputation

rumour /ˈruːmə/ noun [count or uncount] unofficial information that may or may not be true: *He'd heard rumours about some big financial deal.*

wave /weɪv/ noun [count] a sudden increase in one type of activity, especially one that is unwelcome: *A fresh wave of selling sent technology stocks even lower.*

7.3 Grammar
Future forms and expressing likelihood

asking price /ˈɑːskɪŋ ˌpraɪs/ noun [singular] the price that someone wants for something they are selling

common ground /ˌkɒmən ˈɡraʊnd/ noun [uncount] similair to something that people can agree about, especially when they disagree about other things

copycat /ˈkɒpiˌkæt/ adjective similar to something else and considered to be a copy of it

freelance /ˈfriːlɑːns/ adjective freelance work is done by a person who is not permanently employed by a particular company but sells their services to more than one company

go ahead /ˌɡəʊ əˈhed/ phrasal verb [intransitive] to continue to do something, especially after waiting for permission

implant /ˈɪmplɑːnt/ noun [count] an object that doctors put into someone's body during a medical operation

prosecute /ˈprɒsɪˌkjuːt/ verb [intransitive or transitive] to officially accuse someone of a crime: *If the fine is not paid within ten days, we will be forced to prosecute.*

take something by storm to be very successful in a particular area

7.4 Speaking
Presentations – visuals

breakdown /ˈbreɪkˌdaʊn/ noun [count] a more detailed analysis of information

crucial /ˈkruːʃl/ adjective extremely important: **crucial to**: *Listening to customers' needs is crucial to designing good products.*

deteriorate /dɪˈtɪəriəˌreɪt/ verb [intransitive] to become worse: *The economic situation is deteriorating.*

disposable income /dɪˈspəʊzəbl ˈɪnkʌm/ noun [uncount] money that you have left to spend after you have paid your bills

figure /ˈfɪɡə/ noun [count often plural] a number that shows the value or cost of something: *This year's sales figures were excellent.*

highlight /ˈhaɪˌlaɪt/ verb [transitive] to emphasise or underline part of something: *The presenter highlighted the need for a quick decision.*

overload /ˌəʊvəˈləʊd/ verb [transitive] to put too much of something on something: here, to present people with too much information for them to understand easily

7.5 Writing
Presentation slides

bullet point /ˈbʊlɪt pɔɪnt/ noun [count] a circle printed before each item on a list

distracting /dɪˈstræktɪŋ/ adjective preventing you from concentrating on something

font /fɒnt/ noun [count] TECHNICAL the style of letters and numbers used in a document

offshore /ˌɒfˈʃɔː/ adverb in another country where costs are lower: *More and more companies are outsourcing work offshore.*

threat /θret/ noun [count or uncount] a situation that could cause harm or danger: *Competitors with better products are a major threat.*

vague /veɪɡ/ adjective not clearly explained or very detailed: *Witnesses gave only a vague description of the driver.*

7.6 Case study
Calisto

charismatic /ˌkærɪzˈmætɪk/ adjective a charismatic person has a strong personality that makes other people like them and be attracted to them

Cost of Sales /kɒst əv ˈseɪlz/ noun [uncount] the direct cost of producing goods, including materials and labour

EBIT /ˌiː biː aɪ ˈtiː/ abbreviation Earnings Before Interest and Taxes

meteoric /ˌmiːtiˈɒrɪk/ adjective becoming very successful very quickly

newcomer /ˈnjuːkʌmə/ noun [count] a person or organization that is new to a place or market

rock /rɒk/ verb [transitive] MAINLY JOURNALISM to shock, surprise or frighten someone

ruthless /ˈruːθləs/ adjective willing to make other people suffer so that you can achieve your aims: **ruthlessly** adverb

slick /slɪk/ adjective done in a very impressive way that seems to need very little effort

trumpet /ˈtrʌmpɪt/ verb [transitive] to announce something publicly in a way that is intended to make it seem very important

8 International trade
8.1 About business
Export sales and payment

chase /tʃeɪs/ verb [transitive] to try hard to get something you want: *Many companies are still chasing debts that are more than five years old.*

creditworthiness /ˈkredɪtˌwɜːðinəs/ noun [uncount] ability to repay debts

draft /drɑːft/ noun [count] **bank / banker's draft**: an order to pay someone that is sent from one bank to another bank, usually in a different country

level playing field /ˌlevl ˈpleɪɪŋ fiːld/ noun [singular] a situation that is fair for everybody involved

go down /ˌɡəʊ ˈdaʊn/ phrasal verb [intransitive] to produce a particular reaction: **go down well**

pinball /ˈpɪnbɔːl/ noun [uncount] a game played by hitting a metal ball across a board and trying to hit targets

proactive /prəʊˈæktɪv/ adjective taking action and making changes before problems develop: **proactively** adverb

take on board /ˌteɪk ɒn ˈbɔːd/ phrase to consider an idea, to accept criticism and learn from past mistakes

think outside the box /ˌθɪŋk aʊtˌsaɪd ðə ˈbɒks/ phrase to find new and unusual ways of doing things, especially solving problems

trace /treɪs/ noun [count or uncount] a slight sign that someone has been present **disappear without trace**: *She was seen last week, then disappeared without trace.*

wizard /ˈwɪzəd/ noun [count] someone who is very good at something

would-be /ˈwʊdbiː/ adjective [only before noun] hoping or trying to do something: *would-be diplomats*

file /faɪl/ verb [transitive] to take official action involving sending a document

frequent-flyer scheme /ˌfriːkwəntˈflaɪə ˌskiːm/ a system to encourage people to travel with the same airline by giving them reductions or gifts

8.3 Grammar
Prepositions

drop off /ˌdrɒp ˈɒf/ phrasal verb [transitive] to take something to a place and not stay there long: *Is it OK if I drop the documents off later?*

jet-lagged /ˈdʒetˌlægd/ adjective feeling tired and sometimes confused after a long flight

levy /ˈlevi/ verb [transitive] to officially request payment of a tax

pitch /pɪtʃ/ noun [count] an oral proposal designed to persuade someone to buy your product or support you

policy /ˈpɒləsi/ noun [count] a contract with an insurance company

preliminary /prɪˈlɪmɪn(ə)ri/ adjective [only before noun] coming before the main or most important part of something: *A preliminary discussion was held before the negotiation.*

scope /skəʊp/ noun [uncount] the things that a particular activity deals with: *I'm afraid this issue is outside the scope of this meeting, so we can't discuss it.*

8.4 Speaking
Negotiations – diplomacy

implication /ˌɪmplɪˈkeɪʃn/ noun [count usually plural] a possible effect or result: *We need to consider the financial implications.*

quit /kwɪt/ verb [intransitive or transitive] to leave a job or project: *She quit after only six months in the job.*

8.5 Writing
Requests and reminders

disregard /ˌdɪsrɪˈɡɑːd/ verb [transitive] to pay no attention to something

extend /ɪkˈstend/ verb [transitive] FORMAL to agree to lend someone money or give them credit

factoring /ˈfæktərɪŋ/ noun [uncount] selling a company's receivable invoices in order to obtain funds more quickly

outstanding /aʊtˈstændɪŋ/ adjective an amount of money that is outstanding has not yet been paid

overdue /ˌəʊvəˈdjuː/ adjective if a payment is overdue, it should have been paid before now

oversight /ˈəʊvəˌsaɪt/ noun [count] something you do not think of which causes problems later

settle /ˈsetl/ verb [transitive] to pay all the money you owe someone: *He has thirty days to settle his bill.*

we trust /wiː ˈtrʌst/ phrase FORMAL used for saying that you hope and expect something is true

8.6 Case study
Jeddah Royal Beach Resort

accommodation /əˌkɒməˈdeɪʃn/ noun [uncount] a place for someone to stay, live or work in: *The hotel provides accommodation for up to 100 people.*

armoury /ˈɑːməri/ noun [usually singular] a set of skills, equipment or powers that is available for someone if they need it.

incentive /ɪnˈsentɪv/ noun [count or uncount] something that encourages you to do something because you will benefit: *They want to stimulate growth in the region by offering incentives to foreign investors.*

loyalty /ˈlɔɪəlti/ noun [uncount] continued use of the products or services of a particular business: *a high level of brand loyalty*

resort /rɪˈzɔːt/ noun [count] a place that people go to for a holiday: *a ski / seaside / mountain resort*

uncollectible /ˌʌnkəˈlektəbl/ noun [count] a bad debt which cannot be recovered

vet /vet/ verb [transitive] to check someone's character, reputation or credit record

vulgar /ˈvʌlɡə/ adjective someone who is vulgar is rude, unpleasant, and offensive

word of mouth /ˌwɜːd əv ˈmaʊθ/ phrase information communicated by people speaking informally to each other

Macmillan Education
Between Towns Road, Oxford OX4 3PP
A division of Macmillan Publishers Limited
Companies and representatives throughout the world

ISBN 978-1-4050-8185-6

Text © John Allison 2007
Design and illustration © Macmillan Publishers Limited 2007
First published 2007

Original design by Keith Shaw, Threefold Design Ltd
Illustrated by Mark Duffin, Peter Harper, Gary Kempston, NAF and
Keith Shaw
Cover design by Keith Shaw, Threefold Design Ltd
Cover photograph by Getty / K.Steele

Author's acknowledgements
Thanks first of all to everybody at Macmillan Oxford for making the
project not only efficient, but also fun: Erika Green, for thorough market
research, essential input and skilful, supportive editing; Anna Cowper,
for inspirational management, enthusiasm, and for pushing the project
to another level; Gail Pasque, for thinking outside the box, and for final
editing and supervision; Steve Hall, for boldly going where no man has
gone before in managing the DVD-ROM, and doing a superb job; Karen
White, for discreet and efficient production management; Nick Canham,
for his work on the DVD-ROM.
Thanks also for ideas, skill and professionalism in their specialist fields to
Sebastian Hockliffe, Keith Shaw, Sally Cole, James Richardson and Mike
Raggett.
Special thanks to Roger Miller of ESDES Lyon for his invaluable input on
the syllabus.
Once again I have to thank my partners and colleagues at Infolangues for
their patience, help and encouragement, especially Tessa Wisely, Peter
Wheeler and Jeremy Townend.
Last but not least, many thanks to my wife and family for allowing me
to spend so much time in front of the computer or with my head in the
clouds.

The publishers would like to thank the following people for piloting and
commenting on material for this coursebook: Johan Strobbe, University
of Leuven, Belgium; Elena Angelova, Pharos School of Languages
and Computing, Sofia, Bulgaria; Markéta Černá, Prague University
of Economics, Czech Republic; Dagmar Ryšavá, University of West
Bohemia, Czech Republic; Kevin Gore, Helsinki Business Polytechnic,
Finland; Irene Cros, ENSEEIHT, Toulouse, France; Marc Hyde,
ENSEEIHT, Toulouse, France; Anne Britain, ENSEEIHT, Toulouse, France;
Judit Szücs, Berzsenyi College, Szombathely, Hungary; Ilona Máthé,
Tessedik Samuel College School of Business and Economics, Békéscsaba,
Hungary; Terri Bland, Università Carlo Cattaneo, Castellanza, Italy;
Anna De Angelis, Università Carlo Cattaneo, Castellanza, Italy; Elaine
Jones, Università Carlo Cattaneo, Castellanza, Italy; Danuta Korta,
Gdynia Maritime University, Poland; Delia Radulescu, ECHO, Bucharest,
Romania; Brindusa Nicolaescu, University of Bucharest, Romania;
Irina Ciobanu, Petre Andrei University, Iasi, Romania; Catalina Chiriac,
Academy of Economic Studies, Bucharest, Romania; Irene Novikova,
Moscow State University of Printing Arts, Russia; Lydia Korzheva,
Moscow Diplomatic Academy, Russia; Tatiana Baranovskaya, Higher
School of Economics, Moscow, Russia; Marina Fedotova, Plekhanov
Russian Economic Academy, Moscow, Russia; Lucia Hlubenova,
Bratislava University of Economics, Slovakia; Juan Carlos Palmer,
Universitat Jaume I, Castellón de la Plana, Spain; Thomas Lavelle,
Stockholm School of Economics, Sweden; Anette Nolan, Folkuniversitetet,
Stockholm, Sweden; Preeyanuch Chanprasert, The University of the Thai
Chamber of Commerce, Bangkok, Thailand
And to all the other teachers around the world who took the time to
complete Macmillan's tertiary business English questionnaire – a big
thank you.

The authors and publishers would like to thank the following for
permission to reproduce their material: Extracts based on entries taken
from Macmillan English Dictionary For Advanced Learners (Macmillan
Education, 2002), copyright © Bloomsbury Publishing 2002, reprinted
by permission of the publisher; Adapted extract from Unlocking Your
People's Potential by Eddie Davies (Fenman Training, 1995), copyright
© Eddie Davies 1995, reprinted by permission of the publisher; Extract
from 'At the end of the line' by Helen Taylor originally published by

UNISON, the public service union, taken from http://www.unison.org.
uk, reprinted by permission of the publisher; Extract from 'Help Desk
Call' taken from Funny.co.uk 08.02.03; Adapted extract about 'Maptech
i3' from www.maptech.com; Extract from 'Did you know?' taken from
www.didyouknow; Adapted extracts from 'OpenOffice.org 2 – Product
Description' taken from www.openoffice.org, reprinted by permission of
the publisher; Extract from 'Ten Tips for Creating a Career That Lights
Your Fire' taken from http://www.passioncatalyst.com/passioncatalyst/article1.
htm, reprinted by permission of the publisher; Extract from 'Is Your Job
Your Calling (extended interview) by Alan M Webber taken from Fast
Company Magazine Issue 13: Feb 98, reprinted by permission of Copyright
Clearance Center Inc; Extract from 'E-Tailing: It's All About Service'
by Sarah Lacy taken from www.businessweek.com 06.07.05; Extract from
'The Johnson & Johnson Credo' taken from www.jnj.com, reprinted by
permission of Johnson & Johnson Ltd; Extract from 'Interview with Mark
Gunther on Trends in Corporate Responsibility' by Steve Inskeep taken
from Morning Edition www.npr.org 04.03.05, reprinted by permission of the
publisher; Extract from 'Doing Well by Doing Good' by Rhonda Abrams
taken from www.inc.com August 2001, reprinted by permission of the
author; Extract from 'Good neighbours are good for business' by Barnaby
Briggs first published in Observer No.248 May 2005 www.oecdobserver.
org, copyright © OECD 2005, reprinted by permission of the publisher;
Extracts from 'Methods of Payment in International Trade' taken from
www.sitpro.org.uk.

Although we have tried to trace and contact copyright holders before
publication, in some cases this has not been possible. If contacted we will
be pleased to rectify any errors or omissions at the earliest opportunity.

The authors and publishers would like to thank the following for
permission to reproduce their photographs: Alamy / J.Eckersall p44,
S.Porter p55(b), B& C.Alexander p63, Mediacolor's p66, Acestock p75,
Arco Images pp80,81, TF1 p80(t), Profimedia p101; Corbis / M.Harvey
pp10,11, D.Kenyon p12, J.Craigmyle p14, D.Galante p33, I.Kato p40, Mika
p54(t), P.Schwartz p55(mt), B.Krist p68(m), D.Lehman pp68,69, Lucidio
Studio Inc p76, R.Kaufman p98, J.Feingersh p106(bl); Getty Images / J.Kirn
p9, W.Howard p13, M.Crabtree p19, S.Battensby p20, W.Packert p24(r),
D.S.Robbins p24(l), B.Vincent p28, Paxton p29 (r), Bongarts p35 (br), T.
Yamanaka p35(bl), S.Gallup p35(mr), J.Hutchens p41, D.Woolley p42(tl),
J.O.Lasthein p45, T.Flach p49, M.Malyszko p50, D.Koenigsberg p52,
G.Allison p54(b), J.Lamb p64, J.Hunter p68(l), A.Wolfe p70, A.M.Manton
p77(l), C.Renee p77(m), S.Derr p77(r), J.Raedle pp 78,79, T.MacPherson
p84, R.Lockyer p85, A.Freund p93, Hulton Archive p95, C.Elliott p97,J.
Mueller p99, B.Barkany p106(t), C.Jackson p106(br); Nature PL /
A.Shah p7, A.Shah p17; Panos Pictures / L.Taylor p55(t); Photolibrary /
U.Alvis p15, Hemmerich p32(l), L.Ellert p32(m), E.Kelly John p32(r),
R.Jeff p35(bm), B.Laurance p72; Still Pictures / M.Kolloffel p55(bm);
Cartoonstock / p73; Knight Features / Dilbert p25;

Fedex packaging on p34, published with kind permission of Fedex
Express; Maptech on p35 published with kind permission of: http://
www.maptech.com ; Portrait of Rhonda Abrams p 73, published with her
kind permission, http://www.planningshop.com/.

Commissioned photographs by J.Cole p36.

Printed in Thailand
2013 2012 2011
9   8   7   6